10.25

GW01444983

WALTER A. LOGAN
3600 - 4TH
REGINA
S4T 0H4

Theology
and
Christian Ethics

Theology
and
Christian Ethics

James M. Gustafson

A PILGRIM PRESS BOOK

from United Church Press, Philadelphia

Library of Congress Cataloging in Publication Data

Gustafson, James M
  Theology and Christian ethics.

  "A Pilgrim Press book."
  Includes bibliographical references.
  CONTENTS: The burden of the ethical.—Faith, un-
belief, and moral life.—Education for moral responsibil-
ity.—[etc.]
  1. Christian ethics—Addresses, essays, lectures.
I. Title.
BJ1251.G88   241   74-510
ISBN 0-8298-0270-3

United Church Press, 1505 Race Street,
Philadelphia, Pennsylvania 19102

To my brother
Paul,
and my brothers-in-law,
Donald E. Roos and C. Theodore Roos

Contents

Introduction

The fourteen essays collected in this volume were written by Prof. James M. Gustafson, formerly of Yale University and now university professor at the University of Chicago. Although any grouping of these articles must be to some extent arbitrary, they may be profitably viewed as falling into three major sections. The first part of this book, "Perspectives on Theological Ethics," consists of four chapters *about* the discipline of theological ethics. The five chapters that make up the second section of this book, "Some Substantiative Issues," are concerned with problems *within* the discipline of theological ethics. The third part of the book, "Ethics and the Sciences," has five chapters about the *relation* of theological ethics to other disciplines. Thus the general movement of this book should be clear. The purpose of this introduction is to draw attention to several of the recurring themes and motifs which are characteristic features of the articles collected in this volume and representative of persisting tendencies in Gustafson's thought as a whole. What follows, of course, is neither a systematic nor a comprehensive account of his thought.

One of the most prominent characteristics of Gustafson's thought is his tendency to begin theological-ethical reflection at the point of human existence. The term human existence, of course, is not a precise one, for it does not refer unequivocally to a transparent, self-disclosing, given reality. It would be more accurate to say that different readings of human existence are motivated by differing interests, that human existence is subject to various interpretations. The result is that particular features of human experience are highlighted as significant from distinct points of view. These observations are not an argument that no single entity can be denominated as human existence. The point, rather, is that human existence is typically interpreted or comprehended in at least three different although not incompatible ways in Gustafson's thought. Reflection on human existence may involve a depiction of "the Christian life," a description of moral agency, or simply an analysis of human, moral phenomena. Whatever its form, this point of departure may be contrasted with other approaches. For example, reflection could begin with a theological affirmation, with a moral principle, or with the analysis of a particular moral problem.[1] This characteristic is only a predominant tendency in Gustafson's thought and not an inflexible methodological rule. Gustafson surely would not think it a perversion of thought to begin reflection with a theological assertion or with the analysis of a specific moral problem. Indeed, readers of Gustafson's writings are well aware that he assumes that there is more than one premise to any theological-ethical argument; therefore, there can be more than one starting point for reflection. Gustafson's tendency to begin theological-ethical reflection at the point of human existence, then, does not seem to rest on a methodological claim that it is the only way to do ethics. Rather, the claim seems to be that there will be less distortion, as one moves to other premises or to other points of reference in his argument or analysis, if he begins with or at least keeps clearly in mind primary or fundamental dimensions of human existence.

This tendency to begin reflection at the point of human existence can be illustrated by reference to three of the essays collected here. For example, in the eighth chapter, "Spiritual Life and Moral Life," Gustafson argues for a particular thesis about the relation of religion and morality: the disciplines of spiritual life are a necessary condition for a sense of the transcendent; without a sense of the transcendent the distinctive quality and tone of the moral activity of the Christian community disappear. He develops this thesis by correlating three points of reference in "the Christian life." One of these points of reference is "the predisposition to view life and to act in certain ways morally." Another point of reference, a religious one, is "certain experiences of God and beliefs about God." The other point of reference, the central one, is "certain senses, sorts of awareness or qualities of spirit, which the spiritual life engenders, sustains, and renews." Thus the Christian life, and in particular "certain sorts of awareness and/or qualities of spirit," serve as the beginning point of Gustafson's exploration of the relation of piety to morality.

Again, in the third chapter, "Education for Moral Responsibility," Gustafson begins reflection at the point of human existence; on this occasion human existence is construed in terms of the categories that are appropriate for delineating moral agency. The essay deals with several problems: the role that moral education can be expected to play in the development of morally responsible persons, how it might play that role, whether religion has anything to do with this enterprise. Gustafson characteristically addresses these problems by first providing an analysis of moral action and moral agency. He does not begin, for example, with a biblical view of moral education or with the assertion that certain moral principles or virtues ought to be instilled by using such and such a method. It is, then, on the basis of the development of a view of "persons who act"—i.e., a view of human existence—that Gustafson proceeds to deal with the problems that are the subject of the essay.

Finally, chapter 5, "Moral Discernment in the Christian Life," illustrates that Gustafson begins theological-ethical reflection at the point of human existence. In this essay, an especially representative one for demonstrating how Gustafson proceeds in moral reflection, human existence amounts to an analysis of a human, moral phenomenon; in this instance, the phenomenon of moral discernment. The problem of the essay is the question, "How do persons *discern* what they are or ought to do?" Certain ways of dealing with this problem are considered and rejected as inadequate accounts because, at least in part, they simply do not account for the human phenomenon that we know as moral discernment. Gustafson then proposes what he thinks is a more adequate account by suggesting that there are at least three constant elements in all instances of discernment: a reading of circumstances, an expression of human agency, and appeals to reason and principles. He is then in a position to inquire whether or not there is or ought to be a difference in Christian moral discernment. Again, an analysis of human existence serves as the beginning for Gustafson's reflections. His assumption seems to be that if certain elemental dimensions of human existence are kept clearly in mind, one's moral-theological analyses and arguments will be less distorted than would be otherwise possible.

A second prominent characteristic of Gustafson's thought, closely related to the first, is his insistence that a description of human experience or an analysis of a human phenomenon can be given which is not antithetical to Christian faith and life even though it is not directly derived from revelation or from scripture. This is a very early theme in Gustafson's work. In the preface to his first book, *Treasure in Earthen Vessels: The Church as a Human Community,* he comments: "I have tried to understand as much of life in the Church as possible . . . within a non-doctrinal framework. The 'natural' processes that the Church has in common with other human communities provide the principles of interpretation in the bulk of the analysis." *Treasure in Earthen Vessels,* let it be said, does not affirm that theological categories are unnecessary or irrelevant. Neither does it assert that the concepts of one discipline, e.g. sociology, can be "translated without remainder" into another discipline, e.g. theology, as if a sociologist could explain what a theologian is really saying or vice versa. Indeed, this first Gustafson book, in his own words, "expresses a conversation" between naturalistic and scientific explanations, on the one hand, and theological convictions and affirmations on the other. The bulk of the analysis of *Treasure in Earthen Vessels,* however, is on "the extent to which principles from the social sciences and social philosophy can account for that which also can be accounted for in doctrinal language."[2]

Thus we have an early witness to Gustafson's continuing conviction that descriptions of human phenomena can be given which are not derived from revelation but which are not inimical to Christian life and faith. This same conviction is manifest in many of the articles collected here. "Moral Discernment in the Christian Life," to cite chapter 5 again, provides an account of moral discrimination with which Christians or non-Christians could agree or disagree. In other words, one would presumably not argue against Gustafson's account of moral discrimination because it is inimical to revelation; nor would one argue for it because it endorses a particular view of revelation. The account of moral discrimination is intended to be more or less religiously neutral. This conviction pervades a great deal of what Gustafson has written.

These first two prominent characteristics of Gustafson's thought are misconstrued if one thereby concludes that theology has no decisive role to play in Gustafson's thought. Indeed, a third prominent characteristic of Gustafson's thought is his deeply held belief that theological convictions can and ought to play a crucial and indispensable role in addressing the problems of moral existence, albeit not an absolutely unique role. This conviction is manifest in Gustafson's writings in a variety of ways, two of which we shall note here. In the first place, Gustafson's characteristic *pattern of thought,* a pattern of exploratory inquiry matched with constructive proposals, simply assumes that theological convictions may make a decisive difference in addressing the problems of moral existence. To put the matter in a fairly simple manner, Gustafson first gives a description or analysis of human existence which is more or less religiously neutral; he *then* asks how theological perspectives, concepts, beliefs, etc., might modify, qualify, or be channeled through the analysis given. The presumption is that theological convictions will affect the analysis in a significant although not unique way; the analysis of human existence may be qualified, modified, or intensified, but it will not be erased. Thus, in the essay on discrimination (chapter 5), as we have already seen, Gustafson first provides an analysis of the phenomenon of moral discernment with which, presumably, Christians and/or non-Christians could agree. It is *then* asked what differences Christian or theological convictions might make.

> The human processes of discernment are no different among Christians than they are among other men. . . . Whatever the gifts of grace are, they function in and through the human capacities of discernment that are probably fairly evenly distributed throughout all mankind. . . . All this, however, is not to say that moral discernment in the Christian life ought not to be different, cannot be different, and sometimes is not different. Just what some of these differences ought to be, can be, and are is the subject matter of the remainder of this chapter.

This pattern of thought is thoroughly Gustafsonian in character, and it can be discovered in many of his writings. The pattern is clearly present, although in somewhat different ways, in the first three chapters of this book, for example. It may also be discerned, I believe, not only in *Treasure in Earthen Vessels,* but also in Gustafson's major book to date, *Christ and the Moral Life.*[3] It is a significant pattern of thought for several reasons. Not the least of these is that the question "What differences can or ought theological convictions to make in moral existence?" is posed in such a way that it is assumed that theology may play a crucial and indispensable role in the answers given, albeit not an absolutely unique one. Again, the contribution of theology in this pattern of thought is recognized to be a limited one. To put the matter in sequence with the first two prominent characteristics mentioned in this introduction, the analysis or description of human existence with which Gustafson often begins reflection is not derived from theological affirmations nor is it antithetical to theological convictions. But neither are such descriptions identical with theological convictions which are, in turn, presumed to be able to affect the analysis or description without erasing it. Thus theological convictions are assumed to be able to make a significant but limited contribution in addressing the problems of moral existence in Gustafson's characteristic pattern of thought.

In the second place, Gustafson's belief that theological convictions can and ought to play a crucial although not a unique role in addressing the problems of moral existence is manifest in the way in which he approaches the problem of the relation of theology and ethics to the social and natural sciences. The general problem, as it presents itself to the theological ethicist, may be briefly formulated in the following way. We live in an age which construes human existence from differing points of view. There are a variety of images, categories, and data that can be brought to bear on a given moral problem. A careful consideration of the problem of abortion, for example, needs to take into account biological, legal, and psychological considerations. No one of these perspectives, however, is privileged as the only point of view that is relevant; neither is any particular point of view privileged in that it can explain the meaning or exhaust the significance of other perspectives. The problem, in brief, is how differing considerations which are the product of different disciplines of thought can be related to each other while retaining their own integrity. Gustafson's general stance toward this problem is already implicit in this brief description. He assumes that there are differing perspectives, each with its own integrity, that are and ought to be brought to bear on the moral problems of human existence. This general orientation, of course, leaves a large number of complex questions unsolved and a generous amount of room for argument about ways to proceed. It does, however, reject two extreme approaches to this problem: on the one hand, the belief that theological and ethical language have no relationship to the vocabulary of the social and natural sciences is rejected; on the other hand, the belief that the images, categories, and data of the social and natural sciences can simply be "translated without remainder" into ethical and theological language is rejected. The five chapters that make up the third section of this book exemplify Gustafson's rejection of the belief that there is no relationship between theological ethics and the sciences. The first part of chapter 11, "The Relationship of Empirical Science to Moral Thought," for example, is an outline of the ways in which the empirical sciences impinge on moral thought. The empirical sciences, it is suggested, influence the ways in which the ethicist understands persons, describes circumstances, predicts the consequences of particular choices, and develops moral norms. Thus it is recognized that the language and vocabulary of theological ethics simply do not exhaust the ways in which human existence can be significantly described and interpreted. There is also the awareness, to quote from chapter 10, that the theological ethicist cannot "divinize the natural in such a way that everything ought immediately to be related to the divine Presence and activity."

The opposite extreme, that there is no difference between the sciences and ethics, is also rejected in the last five chapters of this book. Gustafson's rejection of the position that "good medicine is good ethics" or that "the moral question can be purely a question of economics" in chapter 12 ("What Is the Normatively Human?"), for example, amounts to a rejection of the suggestion that moral and theological language can be translated into scientific language without suffering a loss of meaning.

In dealing with problems that emerge where moral and empirical science converge, Gustafson usually begins reflection by asking the question, "What do we value about human life?" The last chapter of this book, "Genetic Engineering and the

Normative View of the Human," is a specific example of this tendency. It argues that

> the question of what constitutes the normatively human [i.e., assumptions about what is valued about human life] is the most important issue that lurks in all the more specific and concrete problems that we face when ethical issues are raised about developments in the field of genetics.

Gustafson presses this question on a variety of materials in a number of interesting and instructive ways. The question itself, of course, emerges from a perspective that influences the way in which human existence is portrayed. It is, for example, a question whose answers can be informed by theological convictions. Again, it is evident that Gustafson forms his questions, orders his material, and then proceeds to constructive proposals with the presumption that theology can play a crucial although not an absolutely unique role in addressing the problems of moral existence.[4]

A fourth prominent characteristic of Gustafson's thought is the heavy stress placed on the role of analysis in theological ethics. In some ways this stress may be regarded as nothing but an item of common sense, as a point that is so much a part of implicit wisdom that it should not need to be mentioned. Nonetheless, this point is so deeply rooted in Gustafson's thought and so far-reaching in its implications for one's normative understanding of the tasks and functions of the discipline of theological ethics, that attention to this matter in some detail is justified.

To no small extent, Gustafson stresses the role of inquiry and analysis in theological ethics because of the commonsense belief that clarity in stating moral issues is an aid in discussing them and may also facilitate their resolution. Chapter 13, "Basic Ethical Issues in the Biomedical Fields," is a good example. In this article Gustafson distinguishes nine pertinent issues and addresses conflicting propositions to each. For example, one of the nine issues pertains to the moral evaluation that ought to be placed on biomedical research. Two contrasting propositions are stated: biomedical research qua research is morally neutral; or, the scientist as researcher must accept moral responsibility for his work. Gustafson then examines the reasons that support each of these contrasting positions so that what would count for or against each position is clearly stated and becomes a part of public discourse. It is not necessary to pursue in detail Gustafson's treatment of this particular issue to see that this way of proceeding is potentially fruitful for the ethicist. The outcome of the procedure may be that some disagreements are overcome, for they may be seen to rest on trivial reasons or inadequate bases. The outcome of the procedure may be that the nature and extent of the moral disagreement is located with a greater degree of specificity; in that instance, even if the disagreements cannot be resolved, the moral dispute gains some degree of objectivity by the elucidation of what exactly is at issue. Again, the outcome of the analysis may be that a new, constructive position may be advanced, or perhaps only the first steps in the direction of a constructive position may be taken. In any event, clearly stating the issues that are involved in a particular problem provides a framework for public discussion and for discourse that has some measure of objectivity.

The matter of the role of moral inquiry in Gustafson's thought may be stated in a slightly different way. One of the most important reasons that he stresses the role of analysis in theological ethics is due to the commonsense recognition that the way a moral problem is described plays an important part in the way one responds to the problem. As is noted in the eleventh chapter ("The Relationship of Empirical Science to Moral Thought"), for example, the description of the situation of a dying patient in a hospital—are the financial circumstances of the family an important part of the situation?—determines in part the way in which moral issues are conceived. The recognition that the description of a moral problem influences the way one responds to the problem has both objective and subjective bases in Gustafson's thought. Objectively, there is the awareness that no completely objective portrait of a moral situation can be given since any one portrait must be based on a selection of data.

> Every moral argument, no matter who makes it and what is the issue at hand, must limit the factors that are brought into consideration. No one can handle all possible relevant bits of data, ranges of value, sources of insight, and pertinent principles in a manageable bit of discourse. What one admits to the statement of the moral issue in turn is crucial to the solutions given to it.[5]

Subjectively, Gustafson's constant reference to the perspective or stance of the moral agent draws attention to the fact that different individuals have different experiences, find themselves in differing circumstances, and view particular moral problems from differing points of view. The simple recognition that moral problems may be described in differing ways, then, seems to demand that a heavy stress be placed on the role of analysis in theological ethics; the demand is that as fair, as accurate, and as morally meaningful a description as possible be given to any particular moral problem. Again, clarity in stating moral issues will aid in their discussion and may also facilitate their resolution.

At least two interlocking suppositions seem to underlie Gustafson's emphasis on the role of analysis in theological ethics. The first supposition is that human existence is a changing phenomenon whose character can at least in part be meaningfully grasped by means of rational inquiry; the second supposition is that human existence is a mysterious phenomenon to the extent that it is in part morally ambiguous. These two suppositions support not just an idle curiosity but a moral-ethical inquiry that is presumed to be able to make a difference in the way in which responsible men participate in human life.

In regard to the first supposition, Gustafson assumes that human existence, in whatever form one wishes to speak or write about it, is not a static, unchanging, and self-disclosing phenomenon; it is rather dynamic, open in character, and subject to inquiry from various points of view. In chapter 14 ("Genetic Engineering and the Normative View of the Human"), Gustafson argues that "the procedure for thinking ethically about human experimentation ought not to begin with a fixed image of what was, is, and always ought to be," for it seems more compatible with certain of our experiences to have a style of practical ethics which emphasizes man's freedom "to explore, develop, expand, alter, initiate, [and] intervene in the course of life in the world, including his own life." Again, in chapter 12 ("What Is the Normatively Human?"), Gustafson asserts that "finding what is human is an ongoing process of discovery." The point here is a fairly simple one although its implications for one's conception of the discipline of ethics are profound. Because human existence is not static but dynamic, the knowledge we possess about ourselves and of our situation in the world is subject to continuing modifications. Therefore, moral inquiry and analysis is both appropriate and necessary in order that we may gain as accurate a perception as possible of who we are, of our relation to the world, and particularly of those dimensions of our experience which are appropriate to moral and ethical concerns. In Gustafson's thought the role of analysis in theological ethics is not confined to the description of particular moral problems. It also includes inquiry into such substantive issues as the nature of moral agency and the role of moral principles in making decisions. This point can be made in the context of a cautionary note that needs to be sounded about the supposition that human existence is subject to change. It is certainly not the case in Gustafson's thought that human existence is viewed only as a matter of change and never as a matter of continuity. Indeed, a polemic against those who emphasize flux and change at the expense of continuity is a motif that persists throughout his writings. Chapter 9 ("The Relevance of Historical Understanding"), for example, raises this issue in reference to the use of historical analogies in moral arguments. Their use, Gustafson asserts, bespeaks of "continuities" in experience which "presuppose that man has a nature as well as a history." Thus the substantive issue of the nature of moral agency becomes a subject for inquiry. An important question for ethics becomes "How does one account for persistencies in selfhood, and how does that account affect the way in which one does ethics?" If a moral agent is radically free to choose whatever good he desires whenever he wishes, then one's proposed solutions to particular social problems will differ considerably from the proposals of one who assumes that the moral agent is wholly determined in what he does by environmental factors.

The need for striking a balance between continuity and change may also be viewed as the context in which the role of moral principles in theological ethics needs to be considered. How, for example, in the face of the particularities of historical circumstances, can the universality of moral principles be retained? Does the particularity of historical circumstance imply that moral principles should simply be dismissed? Obviously, the conception of the role of moral principles in ethics is a substantive issue. It affects the way in which particular problems are analyzed. Hence inquiry into this issue is in order. In sum, Gustafson's presumption that rational inquiry plays an important role in theological ethics applies not only to the analysis of specific moral problems, but also extends to a variety of substantive issues. The five chapters that make up the second section of this book illustrate the importance that Gustafson attaches to the analysis of substantive issues.

The second supposition that underlies Gustafson's emphasis on the role of analysis in theological ethics is his belief that human existence is a mysterious phenomenon to the extent that it is in part morally ambiguous. This supposition may be approached by noting that Gustafson seems to have a penchant for seeking out and trying to comprehend the complexities and perplexities that seem inherently to accompany proposed and actual solutions to moral problems. In part this proclivity can be attributed to a lively curiosity and a penetrating intellectual style. But what nourishes and sustains this intellectual style of moral inquiry and analysis? There are undoubtedly many sources for it; one of the strongest of these is Gustafson's perception that there are fundamental dimensions of moral ambiguity in human existence. This matter may be generalized and stated propositionally in the following way. If there were no moral ambiguities to human existence, moral curiosity would not likely be provoked. On the other hand, if human existence consisted wholly of morally ambiguous elements, one might despair of moral inquiry altogether. But if it is the case, not that the whole of human existence is a complete moral puzzle, but rather that basic dimensions of human existence are morally ambiguous, then an appropriate response to those perplexities is a response of moral inquiry and analysis. Thus the conviction that basic dimensions of human existence are morally ambiguous sustains and nourishes moral inquiry and analysis.

In certain senses, of course, the conviction that life is morally ambiguous and thus deserves moral scrutiny is common to all ethicists. The point that needs to be stressed about Gustafson's thought is that the moral inquiry appropriate to human existence is not capable of doing away with moral ambiguity; at the same time, however, moral inquiry is required so that conscientious choices can be made, choices which may be judged to be more or less moral.

This matter can be stated in several ways. Because human experience is in part morally ambiguous, it must be recognized that moral questions cannot be suspended by philosophical categories or dissolved into theological formulations. Moral problems remain moral problems in Gustafson's thought. One would be surprised to find Gustafson asserting that the moral question demands a religious answer, for example. Certainly Gustafson is aware that there are postethical levels of discourse, i.e., that the question "Why be moral?" cannot be satisfactorily answered by ethical reasoning alone, and that it is thus a question that refers to one's basic commitments.[6] But he is also aware that recourse to postethical levels of discourse, even though necessary, cannot remove or take away those features of human experience which are morally ambiguous. It would be more characteristic of Gustafson to say that moral questions require moral answers which, in turn, may be influenced by religious or postethical perspectives. In Gustafson's thought, then, there is an appeal to the experience of moral ambiguity itself. It is an experience that must be dealt with on its own terms, and in moral terms; these terms may in turn be influenced by metaphysical or theological categories. It is an experience that invites moral inquiry.

Because human experience is in part morally ambiguous, one finds a persisting refrain throughout Gustafson's writings to the effect that no one intellectual formulation—be it a unitary affirmation about the nature of the good or the locating of value in a single moral principle—can do justice to the confusion, puzzlement, and suffering that are part of the experience of moral ambiguity. This whole matter, as has been stated, comes to attention in various ways throughout Gustafson's writings. The problem of abortion as faced by one particular woman in a particular set of circumstances is one poignant example.

> To be a creature is to be limited, and the good and the right are found within the conditions of limitation. . . . Not only physical risk, but moral risk is fundamental to human action, and this risk in the life of this woman involves potential tragedy, suffering, and anguish. . . . What many men find out about the dark side of existence through novels and dramas, she has experienced. Action is required within the limits; the good or the evil that is involved will be concrete, actual. Thus there is no abstract standard of conduct that can predetermine without moral ambiguity what the right action is in this predicament. Since predicaments like this have emerged before, however, one's conscientious moral interpretation can use those generalizations that have emerged out of the past for illumination, and for direction. . . . But the choice remains in the

realm of the finite, the limited, and the potentially wrong as well as right.[7]

In brief, Gustafson's perception that there are fundamental ambiguities in human existence sustains and nourishes moral inquiry and analysis. Gustafson's stress on the role of analysis does not result in overestimating the role of reason within the discipline of theological ethics or in overintellectualizing the moral life itself, as even a cursory acquaintance with the essays collected here will demonstrate. Chapter 1, "The Burden of the Ethical," to cite one example, explores what Gustafson calls an attitudinal polarity. Is the attitude of the ethicist to be that of wholehearted devotion to moral passions and to practical involvement in moral problems? Or is the attitude of the ethicist to be that of a singular commitment to disinterested reflection about moral problems? Gustafson analyzes the significance of both disinterestedness and involvement and discusses the contributions and limitations of each attitude to moral life. The burden of the ethical, he concludes, is that each attitude requires the other. Chapter 2, "Faith, Unbelief, and Moral Life," to cite one more example, is about a related polarity. Gustafson provides an analysis of moral life as including dimensions of both moral faith (which highlights "visceral" elements in experience) and moral belief (which highlights "cerebral" elements in existence). He explores the contributions and limitations of both of these elements, arguing that both are indigenous to moral existence. It can also be noted, simply in passing, that Gustafson's stress on the role of analysis does not prohibit use of the language of obligation; indeed, the notion of obligation is an essential ingredient of his thought.[8]

This fourth prominent characteristic of Gustafson's thought can be summarized briefly. The role of moral inquiry and analysis is strongly emphasized by Gustafson, and it is an emphasis that is deeply embedded in his thought. It is nourished and sustained by his apprehension that fundamental dimensions of life are morally ambiguous. It is also supported by his perception that human existence is dynamic in character and subject to inquiry from various points of view. Gustafson recognizes the need for giving as clear and as morally meaningful a description as possible to moral problems. A wholly objective delineation is impossible since any description depends upon a selection of data and the perspective of the observer. Nonetheless, a clear statement of what the problem is and what substantive issues are involved in it, gives some measure of objectivity to the problem and places discussion of it in the public forum.

A fifth prominent characteristic of Gustafson's thought, and the last one that will be drawn to attention in this introduction, is that his writings presuppose what can be called, for lack of a better term, a "turn to the human subject." Put simply, Gustafson assumes that the ways in which persons experience and know reality is a hinge on which reflection ought to turn in theological ethics. This matter can be put in the following way. Different theological ethicists make varying sorts of claims about what ought to be done. In one way or another, these claims are influenced by the moral agent's perceptions: of the world and its structures, of the self and other selves, of God and his relation to the world, of the role of moral principles and rules in decision-making. To take a "turn to the subject" is to recognize and take into account as fully as possible that it is the human subject who has these perceptions and makes these claims. It is not to claim that the human subject is the only reality, nor is it to claim that immediate experience is the only premise in theological-ethical discourse that can be epistemologically substantiated. It does mean that attention must be focused on understanding and comprehending the nature of the human subject. Two chapters from the second section of this book can be cited to illustrate how Gustafson's understanding of the human subject affects the way in which he does theological ethics. In both, the significance of the "turn to the subject" is at least twofold. On the one hand, it sets limits to the kinds of claims that can be made in theological-ethical discourse. On the other hand, it provides a base point from which constructive proposals can be made. Hopefully, the following comments will also provide a somewhat broader perspective in which to view preceding portions of this introduction.

As has already been noted, the fifth chapter of this book, "Moral Discernment in the Christian Life," proposes that there are three common elements in all instances of moral discernment: a reading of circumstances, an expression of agency, and appeals to reason and principles. The implication is that "human processes of discernment are no different among Christians than they are among other men." This latter statement assumes a "turn to the subject," i.e., it focuses attention on the human agent as the subject of moral discernment. This latter statement also constitutes a limit on the types of claims that can be made in theological-ethical discourse.[9] If Christians do not possess better capacities or special faculties for moral discernment, then it is difficult to claim on strictly theological grounds that God's grace affects the believer by making him a better discerner than the nonbeliever; that claim would seem to rest on the assumption that faith in God alters one's capacity to discern what is good. Again, if Christians do not possess special faculties or better capacities for moral discernment, then it is difficult to claim on strictly theological grounds that that which is morally right is that which God immediately commands the believer to do at the moment of decision. Why? Because it does not adequately take into account that "human processes of discernment are no different among Christians than they are among other men."

Gustafson's "turn to the subject" not only sets limits on the claims that theological ethicists might make, it also authorizes an understanding of the self as a base point for reflection about the "differences" Christian life and faith might make in moral discernment. The constructive proposal that is the thesis of this chapter is that Christians have a "particular stance, or perspective," and that it is this stance or perspective which accounts for the differences there are and ought to be in Christian moral discernment. The reader of this book will have to read this essay to discern what exactly is involved with this claim. The point here is that the theological claims that Gustafson does make have a basis in an understanding of the human agent who is the subject of moral discrimination.

The seventh chapter, "The Relation of the Gospels to the Moral Life," also provides an illustration of how Gustafson's understanding of the human subject affects the way in which he does theological ethics. The problem of the chapter is to appropriate and make sense of the traditional claim that Christ is the pattern or example for Christian faith and life, particularly in reference to moral life. Gustafson's "turn to the subject" sets limits on the claims that theological ethicists might make. To be a human subject, Gustafson observes, is to be an agent who possesses individual capacities, attitudes, and powers; it is to live in a particular historical epoch, to be influenced by the particularities of one's culture, etc. Thus Christians cannot become duplicate copies of Christ, and the effect of Christ as pattern or example on the believer cannot be a denial of the fact that human agents are individual subjects with individual differences. Gustafson's "turn to the subject" also constitutes a base point from which theological-ethical reflection can proceed. For Gustafson the human subject has a nature as well as a history, and he assumes that a delineation of man's nature can be given which is not antithetical to Christian faith and life even though it is not derived from revelation or from scripture. In this chapter Gustafson focuses attention on the dispositions (a preferential readiness to act in a certain way) and intentions (primarily, the specification of purposes and ends under particular circumstances) of the human subject. Thus the problem is to specify how Christ as example affects the dispositions and intentions of the believer without making the believer a duplicate copy of Christ, and to indicate what sorts of dispositions and intentions are formed. Gustafson suggests that Christ, as pattern, is a "paradigm," that is, an example of a way of life "from which follow certain consistent attitudes, outlooks (or 'on-looks'), rules or norms of behavior, and specific actions." His thesis, in brief, is that Christ as paradigm "*in*-forms and flows into actions, intentions, and dispositions which are governed also by many other specific and situated realities of human experience." Again, the reader will have to read this article to discern exactly what is involved with this thesis. The point here is that Gustafson's "turn to the subject" provides limits to the claims that some theological ethicists might make about Christ as pattern or example, and it also constitutes a base point from which theological-ethical reflection proceeds.

The bibliography that appears at the end of this book was compiled by the Rev. Ms. S. Anita Stauffer who is presently pastor of the Good Shepherd Lutheran Church in Coatesville, Pennsylvania.

I am grateful to Professor Gustafson for his confidence in allowing me to select from his written materials as I have deemed appropriate and for his trust in allowing me to introduce them.

Charles M. Swezey
Nashville, Tennessee

Theology
and
Christian Ethics

I

Perspectives
on
Theological Ethics

1

The Burden of the Ethical:
Reflections on Disinterestedness
and Involvement

The American Society of Christian Ethics represents a historical development of very modest proportions in the academic study of religion and in contemporary Christianity in North America. It represents the confluence of interests and capabilities that have characterized persons who have taught or "worked in" Christian ethics and moral theology over many decades. The range of these interests and capabilities is so broad that "Christian ethics" as a field is just about what anyone who considers himself a "Christian ethicist" does. In Catholicism we are the heirs of moral theology and of Catholic social action, both of which were basically fields of applied ethics or of practical ethics. In Protestantism we are the heirs of the social gospel and its reformers in the thirties, who were at least as much social actionists as they were scholars of a body of literature that could be called "Christian ethics" or objective analysts of the moral actions of communities denominated as Christian. Even a cursory survey of the professional activities of our members and of the sort of writing that they do, suggests that there is not only a

Originally prepared for and delivered at The American Society of Christian Ethics, Annual Meeting, Jan. 22-25, 1970. Reprinted from *The Foundation* (Gammon Theological Seminary), LXVI, No. 4 (Winter 1970), 8-15. Used by permission.

wide range of interests, but also that much of the more scholarly and theoretical work done by our members continues to focus on the "theory of Christian moral practice." The history of the field is one of a practically oriented teaching program both in seminaries and colleges growing increasingly but slowly more theoretical and academic.

We are still weak in certain areas of the academic study of Christian ethics as a historical body of literature, or Christian morality as historical practice. Biblical and historical monographs are still rare, though there are noteworthy contributions in the past decade. Interest in the theological issues of Christian ethics seems to be waning as the pressing practical issues take the attention; and where theology is taking a lively interest in matters that involve the human good, it seeks to do so by moving from theology to politics by leaping over ethics. There are signs that some younger men in the field have a lively interest in moving between contemporary moral philosophy and Christian ethics, and this cannot lead to anything but improvement in the quality of work in Christian ethics by clarifying the forms of discourse, and even by opening a meaningful conversation with secular moral philosophers. An irony of the times in Christian ethics, as well as in other areas of the study of religion, is that just when scholars in the field are coming to a kind of academic maturity and rigor, when the field is being accepted in certain quarters of universities as a legitimate field of scholarship, students, churchmen, social reformers, scientists, and others are calling upon all scholars to get out of their "ivory towers" and speak to the moral conditions that pervade human society.

This is to suggest that applied or practical ethics seems to be carrying the day. But there is a difference between the prophetic utterances of the moral preacher and the practice of applied or practical ethics. There is a difference between ecclesiastical moral pronouncements on the issues of the year and substantial and persuasive Christian ethical argumentation which might support a position. There is a difference between courting the moral outrage that exists, proper as that outrage is, and substantial moral education. When we have sensed the doom that the prophets in the fields of population growth and ecology are announcing, there remain serious issues about the sorts of ethical considerations that are involved in alternative courses of action. When we read a statement by a denominational group which uses the verb affirm ("We affirm that the fetus is not a person") in place of a plausible or persuasive argument, we wonder what this committee would say to a counteraffirmation. It is both interesting and distressing to hear undergraduates vent their wrath against the war, but not be able to develop a coherent argument in favor of the position of selective conscientious objection, which most of them would apply for if it were a clear legal option.

The membership of this society, almost by definition, consists of persons who have both academic interests in Christian ethics and practical interests in moral problems. While some of us appear to be offensively preoccupied with obscure problems of the logic of Christian moral discourse, of the history of the just-war theory, of the relation of gospel and law, of the relation of religion and morality, others of us appear to assume that if one is not putting his body on the line for a worthy cause, he lacks moral authenticity. If this description is at all accurate, a number of polarities exist in the membership of this society, and some of them exist within individual members. I have isolated an attitudinal polarity for more sustained examination in this chapter: disinterestedness and involvement. Both as serious moral agents and as scholars, both as persons of deep moral passions and as intellectuals, the burden of the ethical for us lies in the dialectic between involvement and disinterestedness.

I

By disinterestedness I wish to suggest an attitude of detachment from our more passionate moral commitments, an attitude of objectivity that prizes *fairness* in the assessment of the evidences of circumstances in which moral problems emerge, in the assessment of different interests and moral values that are in conflict, in the assessment of the passions and the moral justifications that are marshalled in support of alternative judgments and decisions. I wish to suggest an objectivity that partially emancipates the ethicist from moral bias by subjecting his own commitments and passions to the same critical scrutiny to which the commitments and passions of others are subjected. I wish to suggest an objectivity that enables the ethicist to imagine and construct in his mind various configurations of what the problem that is denominated as moral really is, and to imagine and construct in his mind various courses of action that might lead to morally justifiable ends. The pejorative exaggeration of disinterestedness can be depicted in terms of the Olympian ideal-observer (with no offense to the philosophically serious proposals of an ideal-observer theory, represented in our society by students of Roderick Firth) whose only interest is his enjoyment of the game of human action that is in some sense moral, whose passion is not evoked by the human outcome of action, but only by the ways in which persons seem to be deciding what that outcome ought to be.

By involvement I wish to suggest here not only an observable engagement of the ethicist in actions which lead to social change, but also an *attitude* on his part of passionate moral commitment to the achievement of what he considers to be morally right or good in particular sets of circumstances. I wish to suggest an attitude that prizes *commitment* to certain moral values, *convictions* about the priorities of certain individual rights or about certain causes of the common good, and that frankly seeks to marshall circumstantial evidences and moral arguments in the service of a deeply felt moral cause. It is an attitude that uses moral rhetoric of various sorts, including moral argumentation, for the sake of persuasion. It is an attitude that thrives on sensibility and awareness which are gleaned from the experience of being engaged in moral actions, an attitude that finds authorization or authentication for judgments, decisions, and actions in a profound "feeling" of their rightness. It is an attitude that issues in action—expressive actions giving vent to moral indignation and approval, or moral actions directed toward the rectification of what has been deemed to be morally evil, or to preserve what has been deemed to be morally good. The pejorative exaggeration of involvement can be depicted in terms of the "visceral" actor, whose passions of outrage or of approval are the instruments upon which are registered the moral rightness and wrongness, goodness or badness, of what is going on in the world. The pejorative exaggeration can be depicted in terms of a highly selective use of information to support the ethicist's view of what the actual circumstances are, and the use of argumentation and rhetoric in such a way as to evoke emotional commitment to his own cause.

By the "burden of the ethical" I wish to suggest that as persons with both profound moral convictions and commitments on the one hand and with historical learning and critical training on the other, we are inhibited from the kind of wholeheartedness that some other persons seem to enjoy. While we might admire and learn from philosophers who appear to be whole-heartedly committed to the analysis of the logic of imperative statements, we find ourselves drawn away from that toward a concern with the practical moral "pay-off" of such a venture. While we admire and learn from theologians who seem to be persuaded that if we would get our theological categories straightened out a lot of our ethical problems would be resolved, we find that our practical concerns offer resistance to such a position. While we admire and learn from historians who can clarify the development of the moral teaching of the church during an ancient period, we look almost instinctively for the ways in which such study might illuminate a contemporary issue.

In a parallel way, while we find the moral and religious rhetoric of the Christian social reformer or prophet to be insightful and moving, there lurk in our mind the questions of logic of his proclamations and of the almost inevitable oversimplification of his analysis and his solutions. While we admire our students' commitment to a moral cause with singleness of heart, we find ourselves asking them for religious, moral, or historical justifications for their commitment—not for the sake of dissuading them, but for the sake of making sure that they have thought through the assumptions and implications of their positions. While we commit ourselves to organizations engaged in social action for various causes, we retain reservations about certain goals or certain strategies used to achieve those goals.

There are some special aspects of the burden of the ethical within Christian faith, life, and understanding. While we are involved both in attitude and action in the sorrows, the wants, the injustices, and the wars against evil in the world, we bear the burden of theological suspicion that self-deception, self-interest, and self-aggrandizement lurk in the moral intentions of even the morally best of men; yet at the same time we stand under obligation to God to act even in the limited and warped conditions of man. While we face the moral problems with an involved concern to solve them, with the employment of the best of human understanding and knowledge, with the most appropriate forms of power, and with the aspiration for the improvement of human well-being, we also know that there is a Power which limits our powers, a Judgment—and indeed we can candidly affirm, a Wrath—which presses its Word upon us when we misuse the gifts of creation, and when we disorder human life even in our efforts to order it better. When we painfully suffer the agony of the world with its denial of full humanity to individuals and peoples, with its terror in the face of destruction of life through a possible big mistake from nuclear weapons, or its accumulation of little mistakes through pollution, we nonetheless believe with some confidence and some hope that there is a redeeming power of love, a forceful power of justice, an order of man with man and with nature that in the end will prevail over the errors of mankind.

II

We belong to a Western tradition in ethics that has always assumed that practice and involvement were important for the development of moral life. Aristotle long ago suggested that one becomes a courageous person, is trained in that moral virtue, only by engaging in courageous deeds. Some of us have been formed in an ascetical training that has been based on the assumption that a man's spiritual and moral character is shaped by a schooled practice and involvement in a certain pattern of life. In our educational practices we have moved toward a "case study method" of teaching ethics in order to "involve" the students in the particularities of moral decisions, and yet we recognize that there remains something hypothetical about such an approach. There is a different kind of understanding that comes from being in the position of moral responsibility, in the position of making choices and engaging in actions that require conviction, determination of will, sensitivity, and risk of unintended consequences. We perceive that something happens in "involvement" that does not happen in disinterested objectivity. The physician who attends dying patients understands himself as perceiving the problems of euthanasia in a different way than the textbooks in moral theology discuss it. The undergraduate student undergoes a kind of conversion by putting his body on the line: "Nothing radicalizes you like being gassed," he testifies upon return from the Justice Department altercation during the November moratorium. Just as one experiences and understands the meaning of bereavement at the loss of parents in a peculiar way only by losing one's own parents, so also it seems that one understands some things about moral agents and moral actions only by involved experience.

There seems to be general recognition that these observations are commonsensically true. But they do not solve the puzzle of just *what* we learn from involvement and *how* we learn from involvement. My limited capabilities and training are not sufficient to permit me to solve the what and the how questions, at least not in the time it takes to read a presidential address. There are many disciplines to be brought to bear upon these questions—psychological learning theory, philosophy, and others. I do wish, however, to make some suggestions about what I understand persons to learn from profound involvement in moral questions and actions. I will indicate subsequently some things that I believe we do not learn from involvement, and some things that we do learn from disinterestedness, which are also important for our tasks as ethicists of Christian moral practice.

One thing that most of us learn is that we have a status of determinateness, of particular capabilities and limitations, that gives a relatively fixed character to our personal possibilities of action. It is in going through the forge of moral commitment and action that we find out the qualities of our personal metal (if I may draw upon my maternal family's several hundred years in the blacksmith's trade for a metaphor). We not only learn to live with the determinate person that we are, but we also learn both the limitations and the possibilities for growth and development as moral agents. The full range of human personhood is subject to new understanding as a result of our involvement.

Not only as isolated individuals, but in interaction with other involved persons we perceive and understand many things about ourselves and others as specific human moral agents. We find, for example, that some persons seem to be gifted with imagination more than others; they seem to have the capacity to perceive different possibilities of action, different constellations of the nature of the problem involved, different ways of interpreting the intentions and the powers of those persons toward whom actions are directed. We find that we have certain moral sensibilities, and others seem to have other moral sensibilities. It is in involvement that one's capacity to sense the aroma of injustice or of deception gets tested; it is in involvement that one's capacities to feel deeply and empathetically the human suffering that moral evil causes are refined. Certain dispositions are not only formed, but refined and understood through involvement. Courage to take risks, temperateness in assessing what actions would be fitting under the circumstances, hopefulness in circumstances that are desperate—these and others come to be understood. We learn our own limitations or weaknesses and the limitations and weaknesses of others; we learn our own strengths and the strengths of others. The powers or capabilities of action reside in the sorts of persons we are, and these are known in their determinateness through involvement.

Thus, one of the principal things we gain through involvement is self-understanding. And we perceive the importance of self-understanding and of understanding other moral agents in their determinateness for judging what moral actions are possible under what circumstances, which ones promise some effectiveness in changing the course of events and which ones would be folly. We also perceive what possibilities there are for development of our human capacities that are important in determining our moral actions; we learn what untapped personal resources exist and we learn how to exercise them.

If we learn to understand our powers and limitations of powers as persons through involvement, it is also in involvement that we come to understand the issues of power in more general terms. Through the frustration of moral attitudes and moral intentions in the face of lack of access to power which is needed to alter the course of events, we become acutely aware of the roles that various forms of power have in moral action. Political power enables certain persons to influence the course of events in accord with their moral intentions; the absence of political power prevents the actualization of changes that we know need to be made in the name of human rights, or of justice. The power of mass communications to instruct in overt and in sublimated forms the desires, the horizons of awareness, the comprehension of what the world in which we live is like, that people develop becomes clear to us when we probe behind the choices, the parochialisms, and the perceptions of social reality that exist around us. The absolute necessity of sufficient economic power to engage in programs of social change in accordance with moral ends is something we learn most cogently when our moral intentions are rendered into naught in the face of the absence of resources.

We learn through involvement the need for power; we also learn through involvement the resistance to change that the control of power often brings. The power of public opinion, cultivated by those whose eyes are on Mars and the stars, resists the reallocation of our national resources and priorities. The power to determine who has access to opportunities in education, housing, and jobs resists the efforts of those engaged in social change. The recalcitrant powers of certain states of emotion and disposition in persons seem to blind them to certain moral values and to render them hostile to moral purposes that can be justified on ethical and religious grounds. It is in involvement that the problem of power becomes vivid to our minds and to our moral efforts. It is in involvement that our heightened sensitivity to and perception of all the issues of power in the world in which we act morally grow.

Certainly, it is through involvement that we gain a needed measure of confidence as moral actors. There is a test of our capacities of moral discernment that can be made only in commitment to causes, in the risk of action, and in living with the consequences of our initiatives. We learn the virtue of *epikeia* through moral practice, the virtue which makes discriminating judgments and actions under particular circumstances. We learn to live with the occasions when we have missed the mark in our moral actions, and we learn the need to aim more precisely toward the ends that we have in view.

The presence of evil becomes more than a theological belief in our involvement. We confront the sloth and the pride of others in the forms of their resistance to our efforts at moral persuasion and to our actions. We become sensitive to the deviousness of the others toward whom our actions are directed and the deviousness in ourselves and our allies by engaging in wholeheartedness in interactions directed toward moral ends.

Involvement yields personal understanding, personal perception, personal knowledge of ourselves, of the others with whom we act, and the others who are the objects of our actions—other persons, institutions, and the fluid course of events. It is involvement that yields to us a knowledge of the concreteness and determinateness of ourselves as moral agents and of others as those toward whom our actions are directed. It requires us to understand and to know, as best we can, the specific order or reality in which we are engaged. We learn what the limits and possibilities of moral action are through our attitudes and actions; we sense them not only as data in a problem to be intellectually solved, but as capabilities and powers in an action to be done.

For the Christian, the dimensions of involvement might well have distinctive elements. Not only does he *interpret* the significance of his own moral vocation and the significance of events in the light of certain beliefs, he also *senses himself to be participating* in human existence in relation to both a cause of love and a power of love, of life, and of justice that is grounded beyond the particularities of any individual person or special social power or unique set of events. His involvement in suffering caused by the moral evil of men is involvement in the anguish of God over the disorder that man creates in a universe meant for human well-being. His involvement in loving is involvement in that power of love that seeks to restore and to redeem human life. His involvement in justice is involvement in the steadfast justice of God, which renders all human injustices offensive not only to the particular offended persons at a particular time and place, but offensive to humanity both of the present and of future generations. His caring for his neighbor and for the created world in which he and his neighbor live is a participation in the caring of the ultimate power of life that seeks the fulfillment of the creation. His struggle against moral evil is one whose cost he recognizes, and the power of evil against which he struggles is one he knows to be the power of darkness lost to the light of the presence and purpose of a living God. His vocation is not simply that of being the arbiter of how moral principles and values apply to particular circumstances, but a vocation in the cause of God's peace, of God's justice, of God's love. The horizon of his vision, both of his responsibilities and of his aspirations, extends beyond the time and space box in which he fixes his moral action for reasons of practical necessity to a power which renders new possibilities and new hopes. His involved discernment is not only in finding what is right and good in the circumstances in which he acts, but in seeking what God is requiring and making possible. His sense of obligation is not merely to his neighbor, nor merely to his people, nor merely to political peace and economic justice; it is a sense of obligation to the author and end of life, to be the worthy servant and steward of what God in his gracious goodness has given to man. His awareness of evil in himself is not merely measured by the distance between his best intentions and his actual deeds, but measured in terms of his betrayal of what God seeks for all men to be and to have as his children.

It is in involvement that the Christian community knows that the things theologians write and speak about are realities encountered in man's moral experience. He learns of the requirements and the possibilities that God is giving only by involving himself in the requirements and possibilities of conscientious participation in the moral struggles of his time and place.

III

But there are some things one does not learn by involvement, and that is why we have the burden of the ethical, the dialectic between disinterestedness and involvement. I intend to write about this only in the context of moral practice. The task is too large to develop in one chapter all the issues that involvement raises for disinterested ethical reflection, or the input it would make to a comprehensive ethical theory—a theory that could account for the characteristics of individual moral agents, the forms of power, etc., as well as matters of moral values, principles and rules, and consequences. Here I wish only to suggest some of the contributions of an attitude of disinterestedness to the practice of the moral life.

Involvement is, on the whole, a necessary limitation of attitude and of action. It is governed by commitments and convictions that are deeply held or by ends that are particular in character. It operates with reference to the concrete and the determinate, to the particular moral agents, to the particular circumstances of action. It is the attitude of *disinterestedness* that gives some freedom from the determinateness of involvement, and that is necessary in order for us to view ourselves, our actions, and the consequences of our actions in a more critical, and necessarily rational, perspective. The attitude of disinterestedness provides us with a broader view, with a stance of rigorous and more objective self-examination—examination of the justification for our actions, examination of our assessments of the circumstances in which we act. It provides us with the possibility of greater clarification of the ends we ought to seek and greater clarification of the appropriate forms of action in order to achieve those ends.

There are several components of Christian moral action in which the attitude of disinterestedness is a necessity. One of these is in the assessment of the circumstances in which we confront an issue about which we feel morally obliged to do something. The attitude of involvement tends to bring a limitation of vision as to what the important circumstances are, a closure of the interpretation of their complexity. The attitude of disinterestedness gives us the inner detachment not only to face the circumstances in their complexity, but also to sort out factors as being more and less important in those circumstances. It provides us a stance that enables us to perceive the mass of "raw data" of various sorts that embed in some way the moral claim that is being made upon us. It not only enables us to face the rawness of these data, but to evaluate the significance of them in giving rise to the moral problem. For example, in the national crisis of ecology, we are required to find out not only the statistical evidences of various dimensions of that problem, but also to assess the causal factors that seem to be most significant in creating the dilemma that we face. In the population crisis we are required to view the issues in a wider perspective, assessing not only population growth but food production, economic systems which make wheat pile high in the prairie provinces of Canada while persons hunger in other nations, and many other factors. The analysis that disinterestedness enables is essential if we are to be cogent in the expenditure of our passions and our other powers to rectify what is judged to be a moral wrong.

Disinterestedness also enables us to make a more objective evaluation of the moral values or human interests that are at stake in any moral issue that confronts us, and in any proposals for action that are taken seriously. Involvement leads us to commitment to particular values and particular interests; disinterestedness gives us the vision of a range of moral and other human values and human interests. The ground is set upon which we can weigh the competing moral claims and calculate to a limited but important degree what the costs of pursuing certain principles or values are with reference to those which cannot or will not be pursued. Disinterestedness makes possible an awareness of the necessary tragedy of commitment and involvement: the pursuit of the well-being of an unwed mother might require the extermination of the life of a fetus; the pursuit of distributive justice will require dislocations of the present structures of society and the particular forms of peace and well-being that they provide for certain groups of citizens; the pursuit of liberation from oppression in certain circumstances might require the cost of violence. These are but examples of simple and general conflicts; in particular circumstances of action they might well be more precise and multiple.

Disinterestedness permits and requires us to be cogent and reflective examiners of the choices of moral principles and moral ends that are determinative of our actions. Involvement often leads to a single-hearted dedication to certain consequences that appear to be prima facie morally good or to certain rules of conduct that appear to be unambiguously right. Disinterestedness sets the frame of mind in which our intellects go to work, testing the consistency of our moral thinking, requiring justifications of our rules of practice, pressing toward legitimation of our selections of desired states of affairs or desired courses of action. This is not the imposition of an academic interest upon the pressing moral concerns; rather, disinterestedness enables the use of intelligence and reason in providing ethical and theological substantiation and judgment of the moral choices that we make.

Disinterestedness provides the context in which we can make cooler choices of the means and programs of action that will most effectively and with least human cost bring our moral purposes to fulfillment. Involvement often shortcuts even the prudential calculation that is required to determine what actions are most effective to achieve the fulfillment of our morally justified purposes. In disinterestedness we can have the composure to assess whether economic boycott is more effective than the power of political change to achieve certain forms of distributive justice, whether one medical procedure or another causes least suffering or the greatest possibilities of recuperation in our commitment to the human value of health and inner peace. Disinterestedness enables discrimination in the determination of the forms of powers that are to be used in our involvement in moral action.

Finally, if involvement in a Christian context leads us to understand ourselves as being in interaction with the powers that transcend our personal finitude and limited capacities, disinterestedness in a Christian context opens us to the intellectual task of discerning and formulating those purposes and those principles of action that are in accord with what we believe the ultimate power of life to be. We not only sense ourselves to be participating in a power of love, of healing, of justice that wills man's good; we must also risk the delineation of those principles and purposes that are in accord with that power, so that they can give direction to the determinations of our capacities and powers toward the ends of the preservation of human life and dignity and the fulfillment of human potentialities. As persons interested in moral action as Christians, we are required to detach ourselves sufficiently from our involvement to reflect upon the consistency between what we choose to do and what we trust that the ultimate power of life is enabling and requiring us to do. There is no a priori guarantee that the depth of one's commitment to doing what God requires us to do yields apart from disinterested reflection the comprehension (limited as it necessarily is) of the principles and purposes that ought to govern our actions.

IV

The burden of the ethical is the inhibition of wholehearted and singular commitment either to the involvement of our moral passions or to the disinterestedness of our ethical reflections. It is, I believe, for many of us, a burden, for it makes us fair targets of those who believe that disinterestedness cripples the will to act, and those who believe that passionate involvement cripples the necessity of scholarly work and examination. We are, many of us, standing between the vocation to be historical, theological, social scientific, philosophical, or biblical scholars of the Christian ethical tradition on the one hand, and the vocation to be engaged in the pressing moral struggles of our time and place of life on the other. Each of us learns to bear this burden in his own way, and among us there is room for persons whose weight of interest and talent falls toward one or the other. But as scholars of ethics and as persons of profound moral commitments, our more comprehensive vocation requires each of us to exist in the dialectic of disinterestedness and involvement. This is our vocation; by now for many of us it is our fate; and also it is what makes our odd field demanding, exciting, and rewarding.

2

Faith, Unbelief, and Moral Life

A seminarian recently came into my office and with great passion said, "Mr. Gustafson, the issues are so visceral, and you're so damned cerebral!" In a sense, his comment, which I take not to be untypical of this generation that wills to be where the action is, provides a text for what follows. It is not that I accept it as an accurate description of my own view of moral life, but I shall use it as an expression of a view of moral life that pervades many of the young students whose courage and deeds I deeply admire.

This seminarian's comment seems to suggest a number of things. He trusts his moral sensitivities, his profound feelings of compassion, his sense of injustice, his activated will, his moral responses that involve his deepest emotions. He is suspicious of moral ideologies that ratify religious or moral beliefs; he is suspicious of ideologists who assume that they have done something for the well-being of man when they have refined and stated the doctrines and dogmas they believe to be true and correct. He is suspicious of preoccupation with ethical reflection that makes distinctions between teleological ethics and deontological ethics, between different approaches to the logic of moral decision-making that spins theories about the relation between intellect and will, between intention and action, between fact and value. In short, he is suspicious of *beliefs,* but is a man of profound *faith* (in the sense that he feels deeply and trusts heavily his perceptions and his sensitivities). *Belief,* in a sense of credence, in the sense of intellectual assent to and use of articulated and formed moral doctrines and dogmas, is not of great significance in his admirable moral life. *Faith,* in the sense of a deeply personal trust, in the sense of reliance upon his feelings for and perception of the needs of the neighbor and the world, is at the heart of all his words and deeds.

There is something disturbingly right about this student's protest against the preoccupation with doctrines of right and wrong, with the refinement of religious dogmas that support those doctrines, with abstract moral problem-solving. At least he and we all know institutions and men who have been so concerned to prejudge the moral correctness of certain actions that they have lost both their compassion and their will to act. We can find books on moral theology that seem to be devoid of any breath of charity and freedom that would remind the reader that his concern for persons is primary, and that his concern for right moral belief and reasoning is not an end in itself. We know philosophers and theologians who cannot be easily faulted on the outcomes of their moral syllogisms, once their premises are granted, but forget that neither divine grace and love nor the human good can be encapsuled in propositions that are then available for logical manipulation. We know that the concern for a rational justification for moral deeds often stifles the promptings of the human spirit to act with heedlessness. We know that life in which we have moral opportunities and obligations often moves faster and freer than the reformulation of doctrines and the reflective processes do. We know that the crucial opportunity to do a morally fitting thing might well pass while men are trying to get their ideological principles tidied up and authorized.

We know that something about our own moral natures is left unsatisfied if the cerebral is attended to in such a way that the affections and the will become peripheral. We have become interested in and involved in issues of civil rights not because someone made a convincing intellectual demonstration that such interest and involvement is a logical deduction from the premise that God is love or that man tends toward the good, but rather because we *feel* the profound injustice of a society that suppresses other men on the basis of an accident of birth, because we can imagine what it is to be deprived of rights and opportunities even when we have them, because we are *disturbed* in our hearts by the sight of suffering and human brokenness. We know that, in itself, no belief about the good has ever moved man to do the good, but we know too that belief about the good must be coupled with a will to do the good. We know that there are occasions when the heedless impulse to meet the neighbor's need overpowers us, and when we have acted there is a sense of well-being that comes from our well-doing. Moral life is not just something cerebral; it is visceral.

There is something admirably wholesome about this student's visceral approach to moral life. He and we know that a depth of personal involvement exists wherever there are persons who are willing to make the sacrifices necessary to change an unjust social order. We know that social and moral change takes place when a profound commitment is made to a cause, when one's moral passions are strong enough to lead to identification with a costly and unpopular cause. We know that a sense of moral integrity usually comes only when thought and action are integrated, or at least correlated, and that commitment, involvement, and action are the existential tests of moral seriousness. We know that there is a leap between the best of our moral reflection and the commitment to moral action that calls for an affirmation of freedom, a courage to risk, a willingness to bear the consequences of having affected the course of events. We know that moral action seems more authentic if it has come from a struggle of the soul, from a personal certitude that is more a certitude of the will than the mind, more authentic if it is an expression of our personal freedom rather than conformity to the rationalized expectations of others. We realize that our sense of indignation about social or international injustice is a matter of our emotions more than our convictions about abstract justice or abstract love. We realize that we are moved by a deep longing of the soul, by a profoundly inward desire, when we seek peace and freedom for all men.

We know that Christian morality has love as its primary form, and we know that love is never reducible to an idea about love. We know, with Bernard Häring, that Christian morality is a "dynamic morality of love," that love is a power as well as a principle, that love requires heedless self-sacrifice as well as the cool reflection of the virtue of prudence, that love claims and moves us sometimes to do more than, and sometimes other than the civil law requires. We are both emancipated from the past and moved toward the future by the conviction that the Christian life has as its law the dynamic presence of God's spirit working in and through us and in and through the events to which we respond. We are convinced that the law of the spirit of Christ and the empowering and authorizing principle of love bring a vitality and freshness that the stale thoughts and moral laws of men have long ago smothered.

If we can use the word belief to point to intellectual assent to moral and doctrinal ideology, to credence, and to a prizing of the activity of the intellect in explicating and refining moral and doctrinal distinctions, ours is surely a generation of *unbelief*. It is not so much that there is an aggressive antagonism against doctrines, as if a movement had to be organized to abolish some if not all of them. It is more that they have the appearance of unreality, of insignificance, of irrelevance. Indeed, for some of us, they would simply wither away from ineffectiveness and disuse like the tail withered away on the erect vertebrate called man, if there were not institutions seemingly dedicated to keeping doctrines and principles alive.

If we can use the word faith to point to a profound consent of the will, to a personal reliance of man's whole being, to involvement and commitment, to loyalty, ours is a generation of *living faith*. There is a confidence (at least on some days) that man is for the future and the future is for man. There is a "gutty" hopefulness that we sometimes feel without having to justify it with doctrines about the kingdom of God which will come, or about the Omega point that draws all things to a fulfilled and loving future. There is a reliance upon both the goodness of life and upon the capacity of free men to realize it that does not ask for explanation about why life is good or how man's freedom is to be interpreted. We *trust* in the goodness of life, we trust in freedom, we trust in love. There is no burning interest among many of our contemporaries to articulate *beliefs* about the goodness of life, beliefs about freedom, beliefs about love.

But now some questions have to be asked. What is the relation between the cerebral and the visceral? What is the relation between moral beliefs and moral actions? What is the relation between articulated religious convictions and profound religious trusts? Is there an intrinsic connection between them so that my *knowledge about* values, about the goodness of life, about the right, has some effect upon what I value, how I respond to life, and how I act? Or are we faced with a disjuncture, an unfathomable gulf between formed beliefs and living faith, so that belief does not inform and direct trust and action? This is a generation that is very sensitive to the dishonesty, insincerity, inauthenticity, and phoniness of the observable discrepancy between what men say they believe in and what they obviously really trust in and obviously really do. Is the disjuncture a necessary one? Or is it an accidental one? Or is it one that points not to the irrelevance of belief, but to the moral failure of men? Can we have trust without some conviction about that in which we trust, some belief about that in which we have faith? Are there not unexplicated beliefs, implicit beliefs in our trusting personal lives? Is it not the case that unless we articulate and examine critically the things in which we trust, that we are likely to be deceived by ourselves and others about their reliability, their validity?

Such big questions, which consume the energies of philosophers and theologians, cannot be answered here. But I would like to approach an answer by beginning with experience and practice, and working somewhat inductively from it. For instance, when someone tells me that he knows what he is doing is right because he feels that it is right, I like to have time for extended conversation with him. I cannot tell him that I am sure that what he is doing is morally wrong simply because he is relying upon his feelings to validate it. He may be more perceptive, more helpful, closer to the bull's-eye of the moral target than those who work with great deductive skill from universal moral propositions to the particular case in hand. But I would like to ask him if his assurance that his action was the right one was based *only* on his feeling of its rightness. If he says that it is, that he senses in his bones that it is right, then I have to ask another question. I have to ask how he would judge between his act and its feelings and the act of another man who does what is opposed to his act, but also is validated by feeling. This is to bring the moral discourse to a certain objectivity, to find out what things other than feeling would determine, between two judgments and actions, which was better and which was worse. Perhaps both a member of the John Birch Society and a member of the New Left would say that they feel deeply the rightness of their respective causes. But something else than their feelings would be involved in the determination of their allegiances and conduct.

My "someone" is likely to provide some reasons either for trusting in *his* feelings but not trusting the other man's feelings; or reasons why his action, because of its consequences or because of the principles which govern it, is better than the other man's. My "someone" may say that one has to go behind feelings to find out what generates and informs them, if he wills to defend his feelings against another man's. He might claim that his have a moral validity because he has had a wider experience than another man has; his are tested in the crucible of moral seriousness, of experience of injustice, of involvement in action, of suffering. To this I might respond: you not only *believe* that feelings are trustworthy, but you *believe* that moral feelings are engendered by *experience,* and that some experiences are more appropriate than others in order for proper moral feelings to be engendered. I could press for articulation and defense of these implicit, unexplicated beliefs, not for the sake of sophomoric dialectic, but for the sake of clarification of what my "someone" *trusts* in, and *why* it is trustworthy.

If my "someone" does not want to show why feelings and particularly his feelings are morally reliable on the basis of an inward introspection, he may tell me that the authentication of his feelings is *in the consequences* of the actions that expressed those feelings. We can see quite simply, however, that he now will be asked why those consequences are good. He may say they are good because injustice has been rectified, or that suffering has been relieved. What would he say if I asked him why injustice ought to be rectified, why suffering ought to be relieved? He might say different things. He might say that it is self-evident that injustice and suffering are bad, and what relieves them is good. And I might ask, "Why is it self-evident?" This could be pursued, if his patience permitted, to the point where he might have to declare that he *believes* that all men have an inclination to abhor suffering and injustice; he believes something about human nature not only to be true, but to be important in the determination of conduct.

Or he may say his actions are good because his feelings are loving feelings and because he trusts in love. Let us assume my "someone" has a traditionally Protestant turn of mind, and answers my query about *why* love is trustworthy with this: "Because the Bible says so, and because the Bible says that God is love." He is stating some things about what he trusts in (he trusts in what the words of the Bible say), and he is opening up the way for an intellectual defense of that in which he trusts. Thus, we can examine with some objectivity what it is upon which he relies, and we can compare it with other possible convictions. But what have we achieved? A scintillating conversation? Not just that. We have hopefully achieved clarity. But is clarity important, and if it is, why? It is important because it aids one in examining his conduct and moral being. It helps one to judge himself and to be judged in the community of which he is a part, not as if this earns him grace and merit, but in order to live with greater moral effectiveness and accuracy.

What generalizations about the significance of beliefs can be extrapolated from my hypothetical discourse with my "someone"? I would like to cite four interrelated points.

First, clarity, while not the exclusive value in life, is nonetheless of great importance. Self-consciousness of what one trusts in, what one relies upon, what one values, what one desires, leads to more accurate self-understanding, sharpens one's awareness of who he is. I am not talking about the formulation of an ideal self-image or about a self-image that can be marketed when the representatives of industry come to interview you for prospective employment. I am talking about accuracy in one's perception of what he is, what his words and deeds express and represent, what values and convictions give him that measure of moral wholeness, consistency, and integrity that he has. If I do what I deeply feel like doing, then it is worth knowing that I am one who trusts in his feelings, that my integrity is based upon such consistency as my sensibilities and affections have. This self-knowledge, based on articulation of what seem to be the objects of my loyalty and trust, in turn affects my further responses.

Second, bringing objects of loyalty and trust to articulation, to a stage of assertions of beliefs, enables me to examine myself.

In the light of what do I examine myself? In the light of a normative understanding of what I am or what I ought to be; a normative understanding of what ends I ought to have, what deeds I ought to be doing. Even in the best of men there is often a discrepancy between their highest and best intentions and the ruling desires and impulses that govern their actual behavior. There is an abrasiveness between a normative self-image and normative self-understanding on the one hand, and the actual portrait one might induce from critical reflection upon one's actual objects of trust, one's actual values. As Socrates taught long ago, the unexamined life may lead to self-deception, as well as to deeds that miss the mark. One can ask himself whether what he really trusts in is worthy of the trust that he has in it.

Third, the formulation of our trusts into assertions of belief enables us to engage in critical comparative scrutiny of alternative objects of trust. If, on the basis of self-examination, I find that on the whole I live according to the demands made upon me from one occasion to the other with a kind of other-directedness, I can ask myself whether I really believe in an occasionalism that takes its signals from others. I can subject an occasionalist view of life, an other-directed view of life to greater objective scrutiny. I can find from literature, philosophy, biographies, or personal acquaintances that there are options to the kind of beliefs I seem to have. These can be examined comparatively; judgments can be made about the alternatives; I can see whether my values, my beliefs can stand critical scrutiny in the light of these alternatives. No one can claim that we choose our objects of trust simply on the basis of relatively objective discourse about alternatives; there is always a deeply subjective aspect to moral life, a sense of allegiance and commitment that has the mark of a leap, a choice, a more than rational trust. But the beliefs by which we live can be subjected to comparative critical scrutiny, and within limits new choices can be made, and old allegiances revised.

Fourth, in this process of clarification both of what we really live by and what we can or ought to live by, our chances of greater moral accuracy are improved. Just as we are more likely to meet the deepest needs of a particular neighbor if we know that neighbor well, so we are more likely to do what is for his well-being if we are reasonably clear about what human well-being consists of. Just as our social action is more likely to be effective if we understand the social dynamics within which we exercise our influence and power, so it is more likely to achieve the human good if we are clear about the ends to be sought, the justice or the mutuality to be brought into being. Articulated and examined beliefs about justice help us to discern what the just act is in a particular place, just as they help us to see what the state of affairs we are seeking to bring about in that place really is.

Moral passions, visceral responses are based upon objects of trust; the cerebral can bring these to consciousness. The visceral moral man needs to examine himself; his cerebral activity can help him to see the inconsistencies and discrepancies between what he is and what he wills to be. By bringing the objects of trust to the articulation of beliefs, the cerebral can engage in the comparative examination of alternative values and beliefs. And beliefs articulated and examined by the cerebral can give direction to responses that are also deeply visceral. Moral faith without moral belief is blind; moral belief without moral faith is powerless.

What does all this have to do with Christian morality? First, it helps us to see that Christian morality is not unique and esoteric by virtue of being a morality of trust and belief. There is in each man's moral life a postethical commitment, a confidence and a trust in some values, some beliefs, some persons, some communities, some desires, some affections. The phenomenon of trust, of faith, is a human phenomenon, present in everyman. Implicit convictions, if not explicit beliefs, are present in the behavior of every serious moral being. Christian morality is not unique because it is a morality of trust; it is not unique because it is a morality of belief. What distinguishes the morality of the Christian community is its *object* of trust, its affirmations about the One in whom it trusts. What distinguishes the morality of the Christian community is the root and ground of its moral faith, its allegiance to Christ as the One who has come to disclose to all men that the Ground and Giver of life is good, that in its creation and in its newness of life God wills the well-being of his creation. Christian morality is an expression of a trust in the goodness and power of God, the creator and orderer and redeemer of life; a goodness made known in the advent, the birth, the words and deeds, the death and the new life of Jesus Christ.

Second, we can see how the moral perspective and posture of

the Christian community can and ought to be empowered, governed, and formed by the trust of its members in the goodness of God. Because of our trust in the power and goodness of God, we can and ought to act in a spirit of confidence and hopefulness, knowing that the One who has brought us to our time and place, and the One who meets us as we respond to the openness of the future is One who sustains and wills the well-being of all men. Because of our Christian trust, we ought to have the courage to risk something of ourselves and something of the past that we cherish, for the sake of finding the deeds that are fitting both to the God in whom we trust and to the needs of man in the world. Because of our Christian faith, we ought to be lovers of mankind, lovers of the life that God has given, lovers of the good. The attitude, the perspective and stance of Christians can and ought to be consistent with, congruent with the One in whom they believe.

We can see how trust and belief belong together in Christian morality. Apart from belief, apart from assertions that point to God through Jesus Christ his Son, we would not see as clearly as we do (in trust and in hope) that God is worthy of our trust, our hope, and our love. Apart from trust, we could not have that perspective and stance, that attitude toward others and the world that is the human heart of Christian morality.

Third, we can begin to see how our moral *judgments* and *actions* are formed and informed by both our trust and our beliefs. Our moral deeds are expressions of our affections and sensibilities as these are nourished by our trust in the goodness of God made known in Jesus Christ. We can and ought to be sensitive to the victims of injustice and poverty, of war and natural disaster without being reduced to globs of sentimentality. We ought to have a sense of indignation without perverting it into sheer rebelliousness. We ought to make our choices in our hope without being subject to illusions. We ought to take delight in the moral goodness of the world, and affirm it in our words and deeds without clutching it to ourselves as if it were ours to possess. We ought to be able to be humble without hating ourselves, to be joyful in our moral lives without being shallow. And yet our judgments and deeds are not just the expressions of affections and sensibilities nourished by our trust in the goodness of God.

Our judgments and deeds can and ought to be congruent with

our beliefs about the One in whom we trust. Belief in God's disclosure in Jesus Christ can form and inform the ends that we seek in our deeds. Consonance rather than dissonance with the purpose made known and fulfilled in him can and ought to be the objective of our moral acts and deeds. Not consonance with Christ as the be-all and end-all in himself, but consonance with him in order that we ourselves might be agents bringing newness of life into being, bringing moral good out of moral evil, serving the well-being of man. Our words and deeds in human relationships, in the exercise of political rights and power, in the important and unimportant things of life can and ought to have a coherence and integrity formed by our convictions about what God has done and seeks to do for man in and through Christ his Son. Beliefs give us direction, beliefs shape our ends and intentions, beliefs become norms for guidance in our judgments and deeds. Our discernment of what we ought to say and do, of what we ought to be, can and ought to be formed both by our trust and our belief in Christ, the One in whom God has made himself known. Both visceral sensitivity and rational discrimination are part of Christian morality; both are grounded in Christ. God's gracious initiative in giving and renewing life gives and renews our spirits and our minds.

Someday I shall meet my seminarian in the hall, and passionately say, "Mr. Seminarian, the issues of moral life are awesomely visceral and awesomely cerebral." I shall say, "It is worth articulating those things in which you trust, it is worth examining your profound feelings." I shall say, "Judge those beliefs, judge those feelings, and use both in your discernment of what you ought to do." I shall say, "Trust and belief are two sides of one relationship: to God and to your neighbor." I shall say, "Faith in God is faith in a God who has made himself known. We can trust him because we have beliefs that disclose him to us." I shall say, "Christ not only gives us a newness of life on which we can rely, but he is for us the pattern of our reliance and our deeds." I shall say, "Faith without belief is blind; belief without faith is powerless." I shall say, "Moral man is both visceral and cerebral; moral action requires both trust and belief."

3

Education
for
Moral Responsibility

Meno asks Socrates, "Can you tell me, Socrates, whether virtue is acquired by teaching or by practice; or if neither by teaching nor practice, then whether it comes to man by nature, or in what other way?"[1] This reminds us not only of the venerable age of the question of moral education but also of its complexity. A normative question of the highest order is involved: what virtue or virtues are to be acquired? There is a pedagogical question of how virtue is acquired which runs into questions of man's nature and even into religious questions (at the end of the *Meno*, Socrates entertains the possibility that virtue is a gift of the gods). An institutional question is involved, namely, who is responsible in the social order for the acquiring of virtue on the part of the young?

In our time the complexities are compounded. The question of moral education has become more inclusive than the question of how virtues are to be acquired. Less consensus exists on what characteristics constitute the morally commendable life, for our culture is heir not only of the Greek tradition but of the Jewish and Christian ones also. There is a radical questioning of the

Reprinted by permission of the publishers from *Moral Education: Five Lectures* (Cambridge, Mass.: Harvard University Press). Copyright, 1970, by the President and Fellows of Harvard College.

traditional values and norms, and of their religious and philosophical sources, not only because of exposure to still other historic traditions but also because of the inadequacy of much of traditional morality to cope with the possibilities and problems of modern life. Our circumstances for facing the question of moral education are very different from those of ancient Athens, of an even more ancient Sinai, and of a later Galilee.

In this essay the following procedure will be followed, even though it excludes many facets of the subject matter and simplifies many technical and complex issues. First, moral action and the moral actor will be briefly characterized in a way that functions both descriptively and normatively. Second, some salient aspects of that characterization of the moral actor will be briefly developed in order to suggest some kinds of education that might have commendable effects upon the moral life. Finally, some observations about the role of religion in moral education are made.

Moral Action and Moral Actors

Prof. F. A. Olafson correctly discerns a common strain in continental existentialist and phenomenological ethical theories, on the one hand, and contemporary Anglo-American moral philosophy on the other, in that both are progressively developing the idea of moral autonomy in contrast with the idea of absolute moral truth.[2] The idea of moral autonomy is not only prominent in academic ethical theory; it is also consistent with what contemporary persons are claiming for themselves and with the vision many ordinary people have of what normatively the moral life ought to be. In religious morality this trend is dramatically illustrated in the contemporary Roman Catholic church. Whereas in its history the Catholic church has institutionalized a certain set of moral truths, and with a juridical ecclesiastical authority has demanded obedience to these moral truths, today many Catholics are calling for a revision of this legal and magisterial model in favor of a Christian ethics of responsive and creative action for human well-being. The new Catholic ideal of the moral person is not so much one who is free from the strains of sin through scrupulous obedience to the eternal moral truths of the church's teaching as it is one who is motivated to be freely self-giving in service to others in the world. The new vision is one of greater autonomy: The person is responsible for discerning what is required in given circumstances; the church becomes more the enabler of freedom than the prescriber of conduct and judge of moral mistakes.

Human beings are moral actors; we have experiences which can loosely be called moral before we are ever formally taught anything about ethics. We respond to one another, to rules and patterns of authority, to events, to institutional powers in ways which we judge to be right and wrong and in ways which enhance or detract from human well-being. We are initiators, whose purposive words and whose use of energy, money, and other forms of power have some beneficial or harmful effects on other persons and on the course of events. We are from our earliest years deciding, commending, evaluating, and exerting influence and power about matters which involve moral values. The subject matter of moral education, whatever it might be, is not alien to the ordinary experiences of persons.

Moral life can be conceived of primarily in terms of action and interaction; persons can be conceived of as responders and as initiators. The relations and interactions between persons, or between institutionalized powers subject to human decisions, are not absolutely determined nor are they merely a matter of chance. They provide the occasions for moral action. They provide the interstices, the gaps between self and other, between present and future, which are traversed by human actions. The person who acts is not an indeterminate self: what he does and what he becomes by his doing are in part determined by what he has previously become. The other, whether it is a person, or an institution, or an event, also has done some determinate characteristics; one responds to what the other now is, or, more precisely, what one now perceives, understands, and interprets it to be. But both the self and the other have a degree of malleability, alterability; they are subject to change, to direction, and to resistance in the processes of interaction. Persons respond and initiate responses; they intervene in a course of events or a state of affairs to alter what is, or to preserve what is, and to give some direction to what is going to be. Persons act to give some determination to the future (their own and others') in accord with intentions and purposes that they have. Persons affect the course of events and give some shape to the states of affairs by their intentional behavior.

Moral actions are interventions through the exercise of some form of power in accord with intentions, rules, and ends, which are subject to qualitative judgments of good or bad, or right or wrong. Moral values and moral obligations are involved in actions; one acts for the sake of altering the state of affairs in such a way that there is a preservation of or increment in what is morally valued by the person or by the community. One judges what he should do, or what he ought to do, in the light of responsibilities to himself, to others, and in religious morality, to God. What we seek in "moral education" is to develop or influence persons in such a way that their action is morally responsible.

Responsible moral action involves at least these salient features. There is an evaluative assessment of the circumstances in which action takes place, an interpretation of what the possible courses of action are in the situation. There is reflection about what ends are to be sought, what intentions are to direct behavior, what rules are to be followed; there is, in short, a process of moral decision-making. There is reflection about the person's moral commitments, loyalties, and beliefs, and what light they shed on the circumstances, on the proper decision, and on the appropriate means of action. There is the person as an agent, his unconscious determinants, character, dispositions, attitudes, and emotions, as well as his capacities to make rational judgments. There is a "willing" determination of capacities and powers in order to achieve intentions. A more precise and detailed elaboration of this outline is not necessary for the purpose of this essay.[3]

The practical interest in moral education in this general view is to make possible the development of persons who are capable of responsible moral action. We want them to accept their autonomy and to exercise their capacities to be agents in the ongoing processes of human interaction. We want them to accept moral accountability for what they do and to accept responsibility for others: for persons to whom they are significantly related and for the course of events and states of affairs of which they are part. We want them to be agents and initiators, not merely passive reactors, in the lifestream of which they are part.[4] This sort of person is to be preferred to the excessively scrupulous keeper of a clean conscience, who seeks authoritative moral prescriptions from some person or institution by which to govern his conduct, and thus denies his autonomy, and incidentally is probably a boring and ineffectual member of the human community.

Salient Aspects of Persons Who Act

Persons, not acts, are subject to education. But certain aspects of persons which seem to be involved in moral action are more susceptible to the intentional influences of education than are others, and there are no doubt different ways of learning and teaching that are more effective for some aspects of "moral selfhood" than for others. Several aspects of what we shall loosely call "moral selfhood" are indicated in order to raise the question of which are teachable in some sense and how they might be "taught." The exploratory character of this essay makes what follows more a matter of stating an agenda for further work than a detailed and precise discussion.

1. One aspect of persons who act morally is sometimes called "unconscious motivation"; that is, those presumably "real" determinants of behavior which underlie and often are different from the reasons we give for our actions. Some say that the determination of the unconscious is final and absolute and that therefore the notion of responsibility is a mistake. Others say that the unconscious is not really involved in moral conduct per se, since it is not subject to conscious purpose and intention; for example, Paul Ricoeur suggests that all we can do is to consent to unconscious motives. At least they affect some characteristics of moral agents. A loving disposition, for example, is difficult to have if one has been unloved in childhood; or moral indignation and hostility to social evils might be sublimated forms of hostility to one's parents. Are "unconscious motives" subject to education? Does psychotherapy become part of "moral training," at least in some cases?

2. One's beliefs or convictions about certain moral values, about what is morally right and good, what is to be preferred, condition the sort of person one becomes. Beliefs or convictions can be stated at various levels of generality, and each person cannot necessarily, upon request, recite a credo of moral values. Nor is it suggested that a person's statement of moral beliefs absolutely determines what he does in each situation. There are beliefs about God, about the ultimate course of events, about persons to be emulated, about principles to be used to test one's proposed actions, about particular rules to be obeyed, and many

more.[5] Further, *believing* is not always the same; there is more or less consent, assent, passion, loyalty involved in different persons; there is more or less doubt, skepticism, and even cynicism. What moral beliefs are worthy of being "taught"? Is "believing" teachable?

3. Character, habits, disposition, and attitudes all suggest persistent "traits" of persons. A great deal of dispute exists about the use of these terms, and this is not the place to sort out all the complexities. A suitable notion of "character" for our purposes is that which marks "the sort of man" one is, the persistence of identity that makes us expect some consistency in a person's moral judgments, attitudes, and actions. A person's most persistent tendencies to judge and act in certain ways, as these are inferred from observations of his behavior, mark his character. Disposition can be used to refer to tendencies to respond and behave in certain particular ways; they are bearings toward others and toward events and affairs of the world. Thus, we can speak of loving or hopeful dispositions. Habits are routinized forms of action in which reflection is of minimal importance. Attitudes might be persistent preferences for certain ends, values, and forms of behavior. These all are formed by human experience in very complex ways; while critical reflection and judgment about them might change them, they are less subject to alteration than particular moral judgments might be, though they deeply condition both judgments and actions. What kinds of educational experience might affect these more persistent characteristics of moral selfhood?

4. Affective and emotive aspects of persons are important, for example, indignation with injustice. It is no doubt true that emotions are evoked by particular circumstances, persons, or events; a person may have a latent hostility toward tyranny, but his actual indignation is aroused only in the circumstances of actual unjust uses of power. There are differences in the emotions of different persons; some have a greater sense of indignation about injustice than others. And there are differences among persons in the extent to which they rely upon their emotions and sensibilities to determine their judgments and actions. Among moral philosophers, Max Scheler and Nicolai Hartmann both had a great deal of confidence in moral "feelings" for values. Hartmann could even write about "an astonishing infallibility" of the "order of the heart."[6] Just as affective life, as "sensibil-

ities," are involved in discriminating responses to works of art, so they are involved in responses to human moral situations. What kinds of experiences or instruction make for refinement of affections, sensibilities, and emotions?

5. Motives and intentions have always been deemed to be important. Again we are faced with terms whose usage is subject to much discussion and dispute. For our purposes, these terms can be used to refer to "backward"- and "forward"-looking reasons for action, as they are commonly used in contemporary English moral philosophy (Anscombe and others). The question can be put in terms that are quite simple, as Nowell-Smith does: "For the sake of what does a man act?" The answers to this question will be many, and they raise the normative question of which reasons for action are morally more justifiable than others. The answers will vary in the extent of the generality of their reference also; in the same circumstances one person might say that he acts for the sake of the general welfare and another that he acts for the sake of preventing physical pain. There are general intentionalities which provide a basic direction for moral action but do not determine what one should do in every particular situation. What kinds of experience and education would be involved in the formation of motives and intentions that would meet with moral approval?

6. The capacity to make judgments is obviously involved. That men make moral judgments is a fact; how they make their judgments differs. Some are governed by stipulated traditional and institutionally authorized rules of conduct; others rely more upon intuitive responses. Some are governed by the strength of their emotions; others are more prepared to give rational accounts of their judgments. Can we teach better and worse ways to make moral judgments?

If what we have called moral selfhood includes at least these aspects, what is required in moral education depends upon what is most fitting to influence various ones of them. While moral education cannot be programmed so that parts of it will be related to aspects of moral selfhood, and so that it all will add up to the creation of morally responsible persons, it is clear that moral education, no matter under whose auspices it takes place, must be conceived in such a way that it does not ignore the complexity of persons who act.

Varieties of Moral Education

Hartmann wrote that "no one becomes good through instruction."[7] The sentence in itself is loaded with ambiguities, but his general point is clear enough and indicates at least a proper warning about expectations of the efficacy of education in morality. What was stated earlier must be remembered; even small children are already making moral judgments and are engaged in moral action. How persons are becoming the moral selves they will be is subject to various kinds of empirical research such as that conducted by Piaget, Kohlberg, and others. These studies can be used for clues as to how moral education might proceed. The failures of various kinds of moral education that have been attempted in the past could be rehearsed, for example, the memorization of moral beliefs and rules which have not necessarily altered moral conduct. What is offered here are observations and suggestions of an ethician who is not a specialist in educational techniques. Some of them are pertinent to various aspects of moral selfhood that have been outlined above.

First, it is possible in public schools and elsewhere to provide the occasions in which persons become critically aware of what is involved in making moral decisions and moral judgments. Social studies, for one example, are being taught at the junior high school and high school levels in such a way that students are required to make a judgment about the justice of some historical decision and defend the judgment that they make. Those skills in critical rational discourse that often in the past were confined to the debating team are being taught across the student body, thanks to new materials and teaching procedures coming from Cambridge. Beginning with the judgments students do make about historical or contemporary situations, they can be helped to become aware not only of the factual matters needed to understand the circumstances but also of the moral values and principles by which they justify their decisions. They can be helped to analyze what they mean when they say that a decision or action is unjust, unfair, or right or good. There is no way to guarantee that they will become morally "better" persons; indeed, professors of ethics who spend their professional lives dealing with such matters are not by virtue of that necessarily morally "better" men. But opportunities for critical analysis of moral decisions and actions, and of the arguments given in their defense can be provided, and thus greater sophistication can be developed in moral judgment-making on the part of students.

Second, some of the most profound and discriminating teaching of morality takes place through the study of drama, novels, poetry, biography, and motion pictures. No doubt moral educators from Moses to the present have had, on the whole, a bias toward the highly generalized formulation of ethical principles and rules, or moral values. But moral actions are particular and concrete. Often the agenda of moral education has been set by the discrepancy between the generality of principles taught and the concreteness of particular deeds; we have had to show how general principles and rules can be applied to particular circumstances. This has been difficult for many reasons, not least of which has been the conflict that exists between certain general rules or between certain moral values. For example, persons might be taught to approve of both liberty and justice for various reasons; yet on particular occasions such as in proposed laws against racial discrimination in the rental of housing units, the conflicts between the abstractions become apparent as they are applied to the particular case. In contrast with this, drama, novels, poetry, biography, and motion pictures are often portrayals of particularities, and thus make vivid the nuances of emotion and sensibilities, of motives and intentions in moral experience.

Jesus, as a moral teacher, in continuity with a good rabbinical tradition, can be used to illustrate this point. He was arguing with a lawyer about a religious question that had a partially moral answer, "What shall I do to inherit eternal life?" They rehearsed the answers of the law, which included the requirement to love one's neighbor. Then the lawyer asked, "And who is my neighbor?" Jesus did not respond with a discourse on general principles and demonstrate how they could be applied to a concrete situation. Rather, he told a story, the widely remembered parable of the good Samaritan. The concreteness of the parabolic literary form has a cogency which more abstract discourse does not always have. It appeals to sensibilities as well as to intellect; it is nuanced and in some situations is eminently more effective for educational purposes than other modes of discourse.[8]

Certainly the morally and aesthetically sensitive teacher of the dramas of Sophocles and Shakespeare enables students to engage in moral reflection about motives and consequences, about sensibilities and emotions, about commitments and beliefs. Perhaps the aversion of a whole generation to "phoniness" and its prizing of honesty and integrity has been expressed by and informed by the widespread study of J. D. Salinger's *Catcher in the Rye*. The history teacher who is emancipated from textbooks that chronicle historical facts, and who uses case study materials or biographies and autobiographies, can enable students to think morally as well as politically, militarily, economically, and socially about crucial decisions made by statesmen and by other citizens. Martin Luther King's *Stride Towards Freedom* portrays the concreteness and ambiguities of sensibilities and emotions, motives and intentions, beliefs and loyalties, character and disposition in a way that no ethics textbook can, even when it is sprinkled with illustrations and examples.

Third, action projects, whether under extracurricular programs of public schools or under religious or other auspices, can have a profound significance in the moral development of their participants. Aristotle reminded his readers that to become a lyre player one has to practice playing the lyre; to become a courageous person (courage is a moral virtue) one has to do courageous deeds. Not only moral virtues can be developed from action projects; attitude changes, awareness of the complexities of proposed actions, determination of means appropriate to the ends sought, sensitivity to both evil and good can be nurtured by new occasions which demand decisions and actions. No doubt reflection on such experience is a required part of its use for moral nurture; here in contrast with the use of dramas and other writings the reflection can be based upon personal experience.

Those persons who have a technical understanding of how people learn and develop, and who have more imagination than I, can, no doubt, conjure up more effective ways of moral nurture. The most controversial issue for them in a pluralistic society will be the normative matter of moral beliefs, of commitments and loyalties to particular values and ends, often embodied in particular communities and persons. Which beliefs, which commitments and loyalties, which values and ends are to be preferred? And why? In free societies undergoing rapid change these questions will always be answered differently by different persons and groups, and the strains that this pluralism produces can become severe. Neither novelty nor tradition is a sufficient justification for moral beliefs. In the public forum of rational discussion, and in the events in which persons acting from radically different beliefs are in conflict, the examination of various aspects of morality necessarily goes on. It might be necessary to develop some minimal consensus out of the conflict of beliefs, even though the consensus might be justified differently by different religious or other groups. At least, critical inquiry into all moral beliefs is necessary and valuable for the community as a whole; and certainly particular communities have the right to develop moral beliefs within such consensus as is necessary for just order in society, a consensus which is usually reflected in the public law.

Who is responsible for moral nurture? Certainly the family, the religious communities, the mass media, the public schools, and a host of voluntary associations. If moral nurture is thought of not in terms of packaged moral and spiritual values to be learned and sometimes applied but in terms of a continuous development of personal moral life, the dispersal of responsibility for it can be more readily understood. If morality is thought of as a dimension of human life and action, it cannot so readily be separated from our politics and economics, our literature and uses of science. There is no ready differentiation of function in our society which places responsibility for moral nurture exclusively on one institution or community. Respect for differences in belief and respect for moral autonomy ought not to deter public education, particularly from providing occasions in which persons can develop as responsible moral actors.

Religion and Moral Education

Our interest here is not so much in analzying the division of labor between church and school as it is in stating briefly how religion *can* (not necessarily does) make some difference in a person's morality and in his attitudes, decisions, and actions. Training in religious beliefs and attitudes is clearly the responsibility of the religious communities.

First, critical reflection about morality often leads to the question, "Why be moral?" That is, men seek a justification for morality itself. Religions provide ways of justifying morality in general, as well as particular moral actions. This can be illustrated from the Bible. In the statements of the ten commandments in both Exodus 20 and Deuteronomy 5, there is a kind of "preamble" which is assumed to be the justification of the commandments themselves. "I am the Lord your God, who brought you out of the land of Egypt, out of the house of bondage (Exod. 20:2; Deut. 5:6)." Because "I am the Lord your God," therefore "Thou shalt not kill," etc. Because I have done something liberating for you, in gratitude you ought to do the following sorts of things: not commit adultery, etc. Or, in the Christian letter to the Ephesians, the author writes, "Be sure of this, that no immoral or impure man, or one who is covetous (that is, an idolator), has any inheritance in the kingdom of Christ and of God (Eph. 5:5)." The reason for being moral is here a religious one; to have an inheritance in the kingdom one must not be impure or immoral or covetous.

It is obvious that not all men who refrain from killing conform to that rule because "God is the Lord." It is just as obvious that many men in the history of the Christian community who seemed to want to inherit God's kingdom were immoral, impure, and covetous. What is suggested here is that the connections between religious reasons for being moral and moral conduct itself are neither logically nor psychologically necessary. To refrain from immorality neither logically nor psychologically required belief in the Lordship of God, or the aspiration to inherit his kingdom. Training in morality does not necessarily require training in religion.

Second, yet it is the case that believing (in a strong sense) certain things about God does, should, and ought to affect what I have called moral selfhood, and the moral actions of persons. This can be illustrated from a passage in the Bible, 1 John 4, which has love as its focus. A number of verses will be quoted, with remarks interspersed to show how religion and morality are related.

"Beloved, let us love one another." This commends a certain intention toward each other. "For love is of God." This makes God the author or source of this love; it authorizes the intention. "And he who loves is born of God and knows God." This is to claim that the person who loves is God's creature and is dependent upon him, and that by loving others he even knows or experiences God. "He who does not love does not know God; for God is love." This asserts in propositional form that God *is* love, and that therefore the person who does not act in love cannot know God. Through the congruity of the human act of love with what God is, one knows him. "In this is love, not that we loved God but that he loved us and sent his Son to be the expiation for our sins." This is to affirm that man could not love God without God first having loved man, having done something to show that he loves man. "Beloved, if God so loved us, we also ought to love one another." If God loved, then we ought to love; a moral command is inferred from the statement of what God is and what God does. Man's moral life ought to be consistent with his beliefs about what God is and does. Man is to imitate God. "No man has ever seen God; if we love one another, God abides in us and his love is perfected in us." Here the astonishing claim is made that when men are loving, God is present.

The relationships between (a) God is love, (b) God loves us, (c) love is of God, (d) where men are loving God is present, (e) human love enables us to know God, (f) human love is "born of God," and (g) we ought to love one another, cannot be sorted out here. The modest intention is to show how religious faith and belief are claimed to affect moral dispositions, attitudes, and intentions, and to indicate how a moral imperative to love is inferred from a religious belief. Consistent with, or congruent with, belief in the proposition "God is love" are loving attitudes, a disposition to be loving, a commandment to love, and even rules of conduct. But the relationship is not just one of congruence between religious propositions and moral statements. The relation of the religious man to God is one of confidence in him, of faithfulness to him; it is believing with passionate assent. This relationship, analogous to personal relationships with others, enables and requires certain moral beliefs, dispositions and attitudes, sensibilities, motives, and intentions.

What is the significance of these remarks for the conjunction between religion and moral nurture? These can be stated in brief form.

1. Moral training does not necessarily require religious training. There are other justifications for morality than religion; there are other experiences than religious ones which evoke commendable attitudes, intentions, and actions.

2. Religious training does not guarantee morally commendable conduct.

3. Religious training, trust, and belief have an intention distinct from moral education, namely, faith in, or orientation of life toward, God.

4. Religious training, trust, and belief have implications for

morality. There are dispositions and attitudes, sensibilities, motives, and intentions which can be and ought to be evoked and nourished by religious life and faith. There are moral dispositions, motives, etc., that religious men ought to have if their actions are to be consonant, congruent, or consistent with their trust and beliefs.

Finally, religious moral training is not confined to authoritative rules of conduct and to sanctions of punishment and reward in eternity. It can and ought to, like other moral nurture, aid in developing autonomous, morally responsible persons. To quote from the apostle Paul, "For you were called to freedom, brethren; only do not use your freedom as an opportunity for the flesh, but through love be servants of one another (Gal. 5:13)." And the same author wrote in a tract of religious and moral instruction, " 'All things are lawful,' but not all things are helpful. 'All things are lawful,' but not all things build up (1 Cor. 10:23)."

4

The Theologian
as Prophet, Preserver,
or Participant

The title of this chapter suggests three possible social roles for the theologian. The first is that of social critic; the theologian stands in a position which gives him distance and moral objectivity with reference to the society and the culture, and from this position he calls into question the moral and spiritual health of existing institutions. The second is that of social defender; the theologian stands within the society and the culture, offering theological warrants for the preservation of existing values and institutions. My intention is to develop the contrasts between these two social roles and a third possible one, that is, the theologian as participant. This role carries with it elements of the first two, but moves beyond them. In this role the theologian would share in the processes of public opinion formation, of decision-making, and the exercise of powers which are formative in the shaping of events in the course of social development. He would participate with others in the interactions of perspectives, technical knowledge, and moral beliefs, out of which come the convictions and actions that shape the future.

These three roles are ideal-typical; that is, they are constructs

From *Christian Action and Openness to the World,* ed. Joseph Papin (Villanova: Villanova University Press, 1970). Used by permission.

rather than empirical generalizations. No good theologian would find his activities confined to either of the first two. In his criticism of the culture the prophet is likely to be defending at least certain ideal values that are historically available, if not institutions that give social embodiment to these ideals. In his defense of culture the preserver is likely to select certain values or institutions for his theological and moral justifications, and be critical of other trends in the society. As a participant in social and cultural development, the theologian is likely to be the critic of some and the defender of other values and institutions that are present in his time of history.

Each of the three ideal-typical social roles has certain attitudinal, institutional, theological, and moral correlates. A judgment about the proper social role of the theologian is likely to be correlated with judgments about, for examples, the relation of Christ and culture, the interpretation of the significance of history, and the role of the church in society. Thus, one would evaluate the conception of the social role in the light of the adequacy or inadequacy of these other correlates, and not merely on the basis of some subjective preference for one type or the other. The procedure of the chapter will be to take each of the types in turn and develop some of the significant correlates. In the development of the second and third types, I shall draw contrasts with previous exposition. It will be clear that the third type is the one which I would wish to defend as normative for our time in history.

I. The Theologian as Prophet

The title of the chapter indicates that the principal division to be examined is in the first instance a social one, not a theological or moral one. Prophet and preserver suggest relationships to the culture in which the theologian lives; they suggest the kinds of activities in which the theologian will be engaged with reference to institutions, cultural values, historical developments, and mores. Prophet, more than preserver, is a term with a long historical tradition in Western religion, and for certain purposes it ought to be conceived in terms of its biblical foundations, in terms of the critical interpretations of the nature of prophecy as one finds it in the Bible. This major and proper task is not engaged in here; rather, we are seeking to develop an ideal-type of the prophet for the purpose of contrast and insight into various options available to the theologian and the church.

As I have indicated, the term prophet is used to designate the role of the theologian as a social critic. In this role he stands with and for God over against the existing society and culture, over against the spiritual and moral ethos of his time and place. He has a theological position from which he makes independent judgments about the spiritual and moral health of the society and he calls men to return to the ways and will of God. He sees himself as God's appointed man in a society and culture estranged from God and corrupted by its failure to obey God's commands, to be conformed to God's will.

The *attitude* of the prophet is likely to be a combination of sorrow and indignation. He observes the injustice of the world, the corruptions of human ends and purposes, the presence of moral evil in many and varied forms, and is likely to weep over Jerusalem, to mourn for the state of life in the community of which he is a part. He and the people know a better way, a higher way, to live, but they have not followed it. They suffer as a result of their own turning away from the path in which they ought to go. The prophet feels deeply both their suffering and its causes: lack of faith and obedience. But the prophet is not only a man of sorrows; he is also a man of moral indignation. He burns with passion in the presence of moral evil in the world. He hates the corruption of communal and personal life; he is angered by the gulf between what men know they ought to do and what they actually do, between what the possibilities for a just and fulfilling way of life are and the state of affairs that actually exists. He can lash out in word and deed, pointing to evil and its causes, blaming men for their failures, cursing them for their sins. He is likely to be impatient in his indignation; impatient with sloth, with the slow pace of change, with the technical requirements of new developments. He knows an order of righteousness and sees an order of corruption; he is sorrowful and he is indignant.

The prophet is likely to speak of *God* in terms of his righteous wrath and judgment. The impatience and indignation of the prophet are themselves expressions of the impatience and indignation of God. The sorrow of the prophet is the sorrow of God. God stands in perfect righteousness, in perfect justice, aware of the hiatus between what men have established and achieved and what they ought to be as his children. Men must suffer the consequences of their disordered lives; men must bear the burden of their failures truly to obey the way and will of God, truly to develop the way of life that God enables man to know and to fulfill. Men are responsible for the condition of their communities; they are actually guilty before God for the ills which they endure. Indeed, God's wrath and judgment are at least in part made known in the sufferings that befall men and societies that do not conform to the way of life, the way of peace, the way of justice.

In terms of H. Richard Niebuhr's typology of theological positions on *the question of Christ and culture*, the prophet is likely to take the stance of Christ against culture.[1] Christ, both in his deeds and his teachings, represents a "higher way," a way of life in contrast with a way of death. He demands obedience to him, and this obedience rules out compromises with the established orders of culture and society. The institutions of society, the mores of the community, the powers of the state are all things that have not yet been claimed by Christ, that are not in allegiance with his way and his life. They are to be brought under the judgment of Christ, and those who are faithful to him will at least be wary of these established powers and perhaps also isolate themselves from their corrupting influences. Christ is not an ally of military movements, of imperial powers, of successful economic institutions, of middle-class mores, of entrenched politial power, of white Anglo-Saxon Protestants, of ecclesiastical pomp and authority, of entrenched cultural values. Rather, Christ stands over against all these things, calling them into judgment, and calling his followers to live a different and higher way, an exemplary way that will by its own witness shame the world around it. The prophet speaks with and for the Christ who calls men to faithful discipleship to him, to take up their crosses and follow him, to be despised and rejected by the sophisticated and the successful compromisers and achievers in the established order, to witness to his perfect love in a spiteful and conniving society.

The correlative of these positions with reference to the status of *history and society* is that they are realms dominated by sin and its consequences of moral corruption and evil. The prophet is seldom, if ever, an optimist about the state of the world in which he lives or about its future developments, short of some divine interventions. Whether he spells it out or not, he seems to believe that the fall of man has profoundly affected his capacities to be what God created him to be, and that the course of history is the story of sin rather than salvation, disorder rather than order, despair rather than hope, injustice rather than justice. He has no illusions about the achievement of an earthly utopia; he is not the purveyor of the message that human problems are relatively superficial and susceptible to ready manipulation to bring about improvement. With the emergence of each new good quality of life, new level of justice, new mark of love, he readily sees the possibilities for new perversions and even the intensification of human evil and destruction. He knows that technical achievements do not alter the level of moral purposes, nor do they resolve the profound spiritual difficulties of the human condition. The prophet, though indignant in response to moral evil, is not surprised that it exists. History and society are realms of sin.

The prophet's view of the *kingdom of God* is likely to be futuristic, and its coming apocalyptic. His trust and belief in God is not often shaken by the absurdities of moral experience and historical events; he believes in and expects God's decisive reign to come. But it is not now present in a historically effective form. Indeed, given the rebelliousness of men and communities against God, the rule of God will not be like the growth of a seed of moral renewal and spiritual regeneration. Rather, it will come through the devastation of the perverted old order. The more cataclysmic events in history become, the more likely some event will lead to the birth of the kingdom, the new society and new man. We are living, in the prophet's view, between the times; in the hope of the coming future kingdom we can struggle with the present historical evils, or at least abide their annoying existence.

The prophet sees the vocation of man to be faithfully *responsible to ultimate values*.[2] Max Weber describes the person who holds to the ethics of ultimate values in somewhat pejorative terms.

> The believer in an ethic of ultimate ends feels "responsible" only for seeing to it that the flame of pure intentions is not quenched, for example, the flame of protesting against the injustice of the social order. To rekindle the flame ever anew is the purpose of his

quite irrational deeds, judged in view of their possible success. They are acts that can and shall have only exemplary value.[3]

The prophet is more concerned to be faithful to the absolute claims of an absolute justice, an absolute righteousness, an absolute peace, an absolute will of God, than he is with calculating the kinds of compromises that will be required to achieve a slight moral gain in the complexities and vicissitudes of the social order. His words and his deeds express his sense of responsibility to the truth of ultimate values, even though they appear to be historically unrealizable in the eyes of realistic and sophisticated men of the world.

What is the prophet's position on *social change?* It is likely to be one of two. He might despair of history and its possibilities to the extent that he seeks merely to be the exemplary man, visibly manifesting a higher way, with an aspiration to be a forceful conscience among the masses of expediently oriented persons. Indeed, he might gather around himself an exemplary community which, while not taking a significant part in the development of the social and political affairs of men, demonstrates through the rectitude of its own life and structure the possibilities of another way of life. The prophet might, thus, withdraw from the human fray to announce its futility and to witness to his ultimate values.

He might, however, be moved to instigate revolution in the oppressive, corrupt society to which he ministers. The contrast between the "ought" and the "is" is so vast, the historical evils so horrendous, the institutions of the world so oppressive, that in the name of obedience to God it is the duty of men to engage in revolution, to bring in the day of hope in the midst of despair, the day of peace in the midst of war, the day of freedom in the midst of oppression, the day of justice in the midst of inequality.

The *role of the church* either might be an exemplary island in the sea of corruption, or the vanguard of God's army of righteousness, overthrowing the embedded Philistinism of established social orders.[4] If the prophet moves toward the first, he is likely to identify himself with a community of people who are, like him, rigorously faithful to their ultimate values, and seek to provide in their own isolated conditions a bodying forth of a true community of justice, love, and peace. The community would seek to avoid contamination by its contemporary Canaanites and their seductive Baals; it would be a true Israel for others to see. If the prophet sees the church as the vanguard in the struggles for a new order and a new life, he is likely to seek to bring the existing church into both a new internal moral and spiritual purity that matches its true norms, and a new zeal for radical change in the conditions of the world of which it is a part. In both views of the role of the church, a monastic- or sect-like discipline is the vocation of God's people. In the first its fruit is to be an example for emulation; in the second it is to be an agent involved in bringing in the kingdom of righteousness.

Theologians who take the social role of the prophet do so for reasons expressed by these several points. If one chooses to repudiate the social role of the prophet in the ideal-typical sense I have formulated, he would have to attack the validity of any, several, or all of the theological, institutional, and moral correlates of the role. He might bring scriptural and theological arguments to bear on certain of them, ethical arguments on others, arguments about actual social conditions on others. If one chooses to defend the prophet, he would similarly have to defend him for this variety of reasons.

II. The Theologian as Preserver

Our formation of an ideal-type of the preserver will be even more an essay in exaggeration than was the type of the prophet. It would be difficult to find any significant theologian, historically, who was the absolute defender of the status quo. But there have been, and are, theologians who call for the preservation of existing values and institutions. In this role the theologian stands with God against the forces which threaten the order of society, the established moral values, the practices and procedures of social institutions. He interprets the threatening events around him as onslaughts against the ways and will of God that are already embodied in the mores and structures of his time and place. He sees himself as God's appointed man resisting the forces that would alienate the society from God, that would corrupt it by turning to new gods, that would conform it to a will that he sees to be estranged from the human good now bodied forth in the social order. We shall examine the correlates of this type in the same order we did those of the prophet.

The *attitude* of the preserver is likely to be both defensive and combative. He may have indignation like the prophet, but rather than being directed at the present injustice, it is directed toward the forces, movements, and persons who seriously question and threaten the established order. He sees the forces of change as the forces of dissolution, breaking up and destroying the achievements so difficultly gained in the past history of man. He sees no promise of a higher and better way that would improve the human lot, and even the cost of attempting significant alterations in modes of life, structures of social organization, and mores seem too high to risk. He is stability-, rather than change-oriented. Like the prophet, he might also burn with passion, but it is a defensive combative passion, flaying at new ideas which threaten established patterns of thought, at new modes of participation by the many that threaten the autocracy of the elite few, at the radical questioning of the young and the disinherited. He appears to an outsider, to be a person of closed mind; to him the outsider appears to be a person of no firm convictions or commitments. The established order of righteousness is imperiled by the proposed order of corruption; he is defensive and combative. He stands as the preserver of the tradition.

The preserver is likely to speak of *God* in terms of the creator and ruler of an order of life, established in the foundations of the world, known to men, and embodied to a high degree in the mores, the institutions, and the ways of life that now exist. The order that he defends is God's order, the laws that he seeks to preserve are God's laws, the values he wishes to continue to inculcate are the divine values. God stands for order against chaos, for truth against all thought that is not captive to traditional ways of thinking, for known virtues against all changes in moral development. God's people and the institutions they have founded are bulwarks against the powers of evil that threaten society in the forces of change that run amuck in the world. Life is to be conformed to the order of creation, the rule of God that is immutable, and that has already penetrated and informed the structure and customs of life that we know.

Perhaps the preserver adheres to a form of the *Christ of culture* position in Niebuhr's typology. He sees a present reconciliation of Christianity with culture. Christ himself is interpreted in terms of the preserver's own ideals or the prevalent ideals of his own time. Christ represents the virtues of thrift and hard work, of scrupulous honesty and sexual virtue, of spiritual love for the poor and the oppressed. Christ has, through the impregnation of culture and society, informed what the preserver judges to be the best in human culture. He represents philanthropic love, as contrasted with power that seeks to bring justice into the world. He provides the forgiveness of man's sins more than the empowering of a new way of life. Any effort to change the values of the society is viewed as an attack on Christ and on Christianity. To be sure, there is a higher way that stands as the ideal toward which men ought to move, but the direction of social and intellectual development is slowly and inevitably moving toward that goal. The preserver identifies faithfulness to Christ with faithfulness to the things he approves of in the world in which he lives.

History and society, while struggling with manifestations of sin and evil, are already bearing the fruits of the redemption and creative purposes of God. Their orders are established in the goodness of their creation by God and in the ruling purposes which he exercises through the institutions that nurture and preserve human society. The preserver believes in the goodness of what exists in history, especially when he sees it against the ideas, aspirations, and forces that would dissolve what he knows to provide a medium of justice, of order, of law, and of peace. Each slight improvement of justice bears testimony to the trustworthiness of God's work in and through the contemporary forms of social organization. Rather than seeing history as the story of sin, he sees it as the story of God's rule and power. The increments of forms of value are testimonies to the truth that God is still on his throne, and that he has not left his people without the aid of his spirit. Human problems are manageable within established channels and procedures; the destruction of these is a threat to the reliable forces of history that have brought us the successes we now enjoy. The preserver reads the moral significance of history in a different light than does the prophet.

The preserver might articulate his view of the *kingdom of God* in terms of the signs of its historical presence, and its gradual development and fulfillment. God's reign is not that which will come out of the Armageddons of history, the holocausts of revolution, the aspirations for a more perfect future. Rather, God's kingdom is at work like the mustard seed, growing and penetrating in its own good time the laws, the institutional structures, the mores of the people. The kingdom comes not through devastation of the old order, but through the preservation and improvement of the existing order. The preserver's devil, the force that threatens the kingdom, is not in the society he lives in, but in the events that threaten it. He is the preserver and defender of the marks of the kingdom that exist—in the church, in society.

The preserver sees the vocation of man to be faithfully *responsible to traditional, practical, and proved values.* He does not kindle the flame of protest against the injustices of the present social order so much as he calls attention to the achieved levels of justice that are present in both law and informal social relationships. The claims of absolute justice, absolute righteousness, absolute peace, appear to him to be utopian and unrealistic. He will opt for what has come into being as a result of historical compromises; he will preserve the things that have proved their rewarding significance in the real world that he knows. The preserver will cite the good consequences that have emerged from what persons have believed in and lived by in the past as evidence for his point of view. He is the social realist, who understands how visionary are the dreams of the young, the aspirations of the poor, the expectations of the oppressed. He will not give up the established values if he judges the cost of the risk to be unpredictable, not to mention high. His words and deeds express his responsibility to the forming and stabilizing power of the tradition.

Social change is profoundly disturbing to the preserver. He is likely to be the defender of the status quo. Or perhaps he will concede that change must come, but slowly and gradually in order to absorb the social and moral costs that he perceives it to entail. His sense of obligation to the society and the culture as a whole does not permit him to develop such exemplary enclaves of a higher way that some prophets choose. Rather, he sees much at stake for mankind as a whole in keeping the brakes on revolutionary forces, in keeping control of radical movements, in controlling the pace and the direction of social change. The passionate and anxious traditionalistic preserver might join the vanguard of opposition against the prophets and their movements. He can be won by the forces of reaction, by the militants of the right, by the rhetoric of law and order, the purveyors of *Christian Economics* with their identification of Christian liberty with the freedom of the market. The moderate conservative preserver might avoid such extremes but be what men call "prudent," weighing carefully and exactly what society is going to have to give up in order to effect something new. What is horrendous is the thought of revolution and radical change, not the embedded evils in the historical past. The preserver has a psychological, moral, and theological stake in keeping the forces of social change in control of those who appreciate the values that are practical and traditional.

The *role of the church* for the preserver is neither that of an exemplary community witnessing to a higher way, nor that of the vanguard of God in the struggle for new forms of life. Rather, it is the conserver of the religious and cultural tradition. The church ought to be the defender of that which abides, rather than that which mutates. Even in the face of radical new problems emerging for humanity, it calls attention to the eternal verities, to the losses that will be sustained through innovation, to the values of authority and order. The church has a stake in the culture, in the preserver's view, not only for the sake of its self-preservation, but for the sake of the preservation of the qualities of life that it once imbued in society, the regulations it once imposed upon society. If the preserver should give up his aspiration to have the church effectively engage in the defense of the old, he might well cling to it as a source of spiritual and ideational inspiration for his personal sense of righteousness in the midst of a world destroying itself.

Just as the prophet has several kinds of reasons in defense of his stance, so does the preserver. One could properly repudiate his position only by arguing against the different kinds of reasons, correlated as they are, that he gives for his adherence to it. Is scripture in his favor? Does he understand properly the significance of God's creative and ordering work? the meaning of Christ? Does he read history properly? Are the values he defends justifiable ethically and theologically? To defend the preserver would require attention to these points as well.[5]

III. The Theologian as Participant

The theologian as participant is not only an ideal-type in the sense of being a mental construct. It is ideal in two other senses as well. First, whereas one can find a number of historical examples of the prophet from which to build an exaggerated typical portrait, and one can find some examples of the preserver from which to do the same, there are few, if any, historical examples from which to construct the type of the participant. More than the other two, this type is a construct from almost no historical data. Second, it is a normative ideal; it is an ideal that I would wish to endorse as fitting for the theologian in our time for theological, historical, and ethical reasons.

In one sense the participant stands between the types of prophet and preserver; in another sense it draws elements of each and moves beyond them. The participant is wedded neither to the condemnation of the existing state of affairs, nor to whole-hearted support to them. He is, however, not a passive spectator of events and institutions, judging some to be worthy of endorsement and others to be worthy of reorientation and reform. Rather, he is actively involved in the shaping of events and in the development and reordering of institutions. The participant shares in the processes of public opinion formation through his articulations of the ends and means that the human community ought to follow. He is involved in decision-making through his participation in political, educational, and other processes that have an impact on the course of human development. He seeks to influence the exercise of the powers that are formative in shaping the present and the future.

This theologian is not simply the sage generalist with great moral sensitivity and critical ethical acumen, though these are necessary gifts and talents. He also has a specialized knowledge and discipline of thought to bring to bear in the interactions of perspectives, technical knowledge, moral beliefs and opinions, out of which come the convictions and actions that shape the future. He represents a point of view about what the primary purposes of human existence in community and history are, about what the qualities of life ought to be, about what values are in accord with God's activity and intention for his creation. The participant is no less the theologian in conceiving of his social role in this way. He brings to bear the insight and wisdom of the Christian community's long historical reflection about the chief ends of man. The imagination, critical reflection, and historical awareness that have always been involved in the best of theological discipline continue to be relevant in this new role.

The participant is one partner among many in the human conversation that will give some determination to the ways in which men use their technical and political powers, their resources and talents in the development of history and society toward humane ends. The capacity to listen to and understand other points of view, to comprehend the basic options thrust up by political, technological, and scientific developments, and to speak meaningfully and clearly from his perspective is at a premium in the theologian's function. While he thinks and speaks from a perspective that is theologically informed and shaped, he does not announce it as the truth. Rather, he recognizes its limitations with reference to things that need to be known and done and its relativity and partiality that need to be corrected by others. He neither stands with and for God announcing the failings of man, nor stands with and for God defending the achievements of society and culture. Rather, he is oriented toward policy and toward actions—those of persons and of centers of power, established and nascent—that give direction through purpose as men move toward God's future.

The *attitude* of the theologian as participant has been well described by Karl Rahner in an essay in which he reflects on the developments in the life sciences. "The Christian need not march forward as toward a hell on earth, nor salute the future as a this-worldly version of the Kingdom of God. Neither inordinate enthusiasm nor lamentation is consonant with the balance that should characterize the Christian."[6] This suggests that the theologian ought to have a sufficient measure of dispassion and objectivity to see clearly and to think carefully about the world in which he is active. Perhaps other terms can be used to point to the attitude. The participant is confident without being unrealistic; his poise is not sustained by rosy illusions about man's goodness or some view of the inexorable progressive development of life that will bring utopia without suffering and evil. He is realistic without being defensive; his awareness of the actuality and possibility of costly human mistakes leads him neither to hide behind the fortress of the past, nor to fear about venturing into the future. He is hopeful without suffering illusions; he affirms the creative possibilities for man's historical achievement in both technical and moral realms without denying the treacherous character of the way toward human fulfillment. He is open without being uncritical; his willingness to listen and to learn from others does not lead to the surrender of his own worth and perspective, nor to a passivity that lets the thought of others simply carry the day.

Both the prophet and the preserver have a certitude about God's will and God's way that the participant finds excessive; both have a dogmatism which seems to foreclose the recognition of significant present values to be cultivated and developed in the case of the prophet, and significant emerging values to be explored in the case of the preserver. The participant, like the others, is a man of confidence, but his confidence is the kind that leads to creativity in his responses to events, persons, and institutions, rather than to sorrowful moral indignation or to defensive combativeness. He is not a man of fear or despair.

God, for the participant, is neither as much the wrathful judge that he is for the prophet, nor the establisher of an immutable order that he is for the preserver. Perhaps he can best be spoken of as the active presence in the events to which men respond and which in turn they seek to direct. Several current modes of theological reflection lend support to this general view of God as active presence.

Karl Rahner provides one way in which theological foundations are established for the role of participant.

> We mean first that God is not only above us, as Lord and horizon of history, but also that he is ahead of us as our own future, that future which carries history forward. For Christianity proclaims that the absolute, eternal, transcendent God who is radical, infinite mystery gives himself to the world in absolute mystery and free grace as its innermost ground and ultimate future. He guides history as something truly his own, not as a process that he merely created.[7]

God is the innermost ground and the ultimate future of the world, and he guides history, but not as an inexorable process. The theologian becomes a participant in the creativity that leads to the future that is open with many possibilities for man.

Rahner's is not the only theological and ontological option present in contemporary theology that supports the view of the theologian as participant. Daniel Day Williams, in the latest contribution from the "process theology" school to contemporary discussion, argues from a phenomenological account of the human experience of love by analogy to a conception of God's being as love. This account is built upon a critique of Augustine's view of the "absolute changelessness" of God. Williams' general point is that "process philosophy opens up for Christian theology a way of conceiving the being of God in historical temporal terms."[8] In this view God's function is not to make the future as certain as the past, but it is to give an ordered pattern to the creative life of the world, and "to bring new possibilities into existence in a real future." The work of God is a continual process of divine self-communication which presents men with the sustaining power of an involved and loving ultimate reality and creates new possibilities of love.

Although a careful drawing of inferences from Williams' theology with reference to the vocation of the theologian and the Christian would lead to a somewhat different picture than one gets by drawing inferences from Rahner, Williams and the other process theologians would support a view of the theologian as participant. He is involved, as God is involved, in the temporal and historical existence of the human community, bringing it toward a more universal and loving communion of man with man. The theologian is to embody the spirit of love, searching for new forms of community in the life of men.

A recent exposition of biblical ethics suggests that the fundamental structure of biblical faith and morality would support our view of the theologian as participant. Freeman Sleeper states that "the structure of Biblical ethics deals with God's action in creating the conditions and possibilities for human community and with human action to fulfill those conditions and possibilities through an appropriate response." He argues that the meaning of the *imago Dei* is that men, "like God . . . are able to pursue the task of creating historical order."[9] Sleeper is in accord with both biblical scholars and with theologians such as H. R. Niebuhr in seeing the vocation of man (including the theologian) to be the discernment of the appropriate human actions in society and history that are a fitting response to God's action in historical events. Here again there are grounds for the view that the theologian is the participant in response to the active and living presence of God. God is neither the uninvolved ideal-observer making judgments, nor is he the changeless ground of the established order, but the power that makes possible human creative and responsible action in directing the course of events.

Other modes of contemporary theological thinking could also be pointed to in this regard. Perhaps they indicate a rough consensus that the events in which man participates are ultimately made possible by the presence and activity of God in the historical order. In response to God's reality and to man's understanding and comprehension of his reality, the participant seeks to be an agent among other agents in giving direction to the future. In the light of God's purposes for the redemption and fulfillment of men and history, the theologian makes his contribution to the society and culture in which he lives. God is seen to be bidding men to new responsibilities under new technical and historical circumstances, offering new possibilities for human development, ambiguous though they may be. The theologian is an interpreter of what God's active presence may be calling forth in the juncture in social and historical experience where men can intervene to restrain or redirect the course of events. God is not so much static being as he is active presence; he is not so much law as he is ordering and redeeming activity; he is not so much wrathful judge as he is the opener of new possibilities and the provider of the direction in which men ought to go. He wills neither the destruction of the old for the sake of its imperfections nor the defense of the old for the sake of its values, but rather, he wills the development of human communities in which the qualities of life are present that lead to man's well-being.

Christ, to turn again to H. R. Niebuhr's typology, is the transformer of culture, rather than its radical critic or its defender. Christ seeks neither the defense nor the abolition of the historical orders; rather, he seeks their renewal and redirection, their conversion toward their proper end and their proper qualities. In Christ, man is acutely sensitive to the perversions of human society and personal life, to the ambiguities of human achievements. He knows and feels the pain and suffering of the world in which the hungry remain unfed, the oppressed remain shackled in the chains of indifferent and tyrannical social orders. He knows the potentialities for a fairer and more loving pattern of human relationships that remain unrealized because of the defensiveness and greed of those in control. But Christ seeks not the destruction of the perverse and the ambiguous, but their redemption and wholeness. He calls men not to flee from the world to form their exemplary sects and enclaves, but to be the agents of creative and redemptive action in the events in which they are engaged. He creates in men a vision of God's loving purposes, and he moves the wills of men to seek their fulfillment. He calls men to be as forgiving as they are condemning; he calls not so much for destructive action as he does for compassion and for positive participation oriented toward obedience to the claims of God's perfect reign, his kingdom.

In Christ, man is conscious of the benefits of God's providence as he experiences them in all the realms of natural and social life. He acknowledges the forms of goodness and value that are his to be the gifts of God's love and grace in his creation and governing of the world, and is thankful. He is ready to support the achievements of justice and love in the human community against the encroachments of those who would undermine them; he is willing to protect actual spiritual and social freedoms against new oppressions and tyrannies. But Christ seeks not so much the defense of these qualities of life and community as he does their renewal and development, their extension and their intensification.

Christ provides the theologian his fundamental perspective or posture toward the world of persons, institutions, and events in which he is living. He is the ground of confidence that the theologian has in the goodness of the ultimate power, source, and end of life. He enables him to see, be sensitive to, and affirm the reality and the power of the goodness of life wherever it exists and whereever it strives to come into existence. He is both the source and the symbol of the theologian's affirmation of the actual and intended goodness of human history and community. Christ provides the theologian with those dispositions of love and trust and hope that are so important in his participation in the life of the human community. He saves him from hate even in the presence of demonic forces in the world, from fear and distrust even in the presence of deception, coercion, and injustice, from despair even in the presence of intransigency and failure. He is the ground of the theologian's freedom from the dead weight of the past and from anxiety about the unknowability of the future. Christ provides the theologian his basic intentionality and direction. He orients him toward those ends that are in accord with God's purposes for human well-being and fulfillment in all the dimensions of existence. He shows the theologian positive norms of life that are the requisites of faithfulness both to God and to man, that are to be brought to bear upon the possibilities that emerge in the development of human life.[10]

History and society for the participant, in Rahner's words, will always remain both created and fallen, and the objects of both judgment and blessing.[11] There are two aspects of the view of history and society that need to be emphasized. First, they are the field of human action and human possibility. History for the participant is not the outcome of fated, inexorably determinative processes that are impersonal and absolutely beyond the powers of men to affect. Rather, there are interstices between institutions and events, between persons, which provide the occasions for the meaningful exercises of human and other powers to give direction to the world. The participant certainly does not move from this to some absurd view that each event is created out of nothing, that man's freedom is absolute in his capacities to alter the present and shape the future. He recognizes that the present possibilities for action are deeply conditioned by the past, and are limited to some extent by the present state of affairs. Not all options that his imagination might conjure are within the realm of the possible. But he does believe in a significant openness in the present and the future that enables human decisions and actions to conserve, alter, or overturn the course of social development according to human purposes. He has no illusions that human powers are great enough to determine all the effects or consequences of human innovations; he recognizes that his intended consequences interact with other factors to bring into being other effects not in accord with his normative purposes. But it is in accord with his understanding of persons as actors or agents, and history as a field of possibilities, to envision the role of the theologian as the participant.

Second, the participant understands the world to be the object of both judgment and blessing. It is not fated to human destruction by man's sinfulness and perversion. Institutions are not predetermined by man's disobedience to be repressive and authoritarian; morality exists not only as a provision of dikes against chaos. Man's knowledge is not only confined to his heritage from the past, to those beliefs that seem to have kept events and persons from sliding into the demonic. Nor is history predestined to a glorious fulfillment in the time of any one generation. The blessings of reformed political orders and of technological advances bear within themselves new possibilities of ill effects and subtler forms of coercive repression, as Reinhold Niebuhr taught a "liberal" Protestantism forty years ago. History and society will always be arenas both of achieved human good and of new possibilities for human evil.

They do, in the participant's view, offer the possibilities for significant human action, using various capacities and powers available to human agency in accordance with moral intentions and purposes. This action can be directed not only toward piece-meal change in the immediate and concrete circumstances, but also toward the development of juster, freer, and more loving orders of human community. Man can participate in the proc-esses of life in a truly human and genuinely creative and effective way.

The perfect reign of God, his *kingdom,* is a point of focus for the direction of human activities. The participant is oriented toward the fulfillment of God's creative and redemptive purposes, toward the development of a community of love and openness, toward an Omega which gives guidance and criteria for all his deeds. Man is not the defender of a kingdom that already exists. He is not to identify the perfect reign of God's purposes with the actual achievements of the institutions and orders of society in which he exists, whether these be civil or ecclesiastical orders. In-deed, the outright identification of any historical order with the realization of the kingdom of God is the utmost in idolatry, and can only lead to the myopic defensiveness that is characteristic of the preserver. Nor is man the proclaimer of a kingdom that will apocalyptically break into being through the catastrophic events of history understood to be the action of God. He does not deny that revolutions might be necessary, that a painful wrenching from the established views might be in the offing. But the suc-cesses of no revolution will be equivalent to the arrival of the kingdom of God as long as history retains its essential character-istic of possibilities and man retains his essential characteristics as a finite, sinful agent.

Rather, the participant is a member of a kingdom whose full reality is not perfectly manifest, yet whose power is at work in the actions of men that are in accord with its reality. The kingdom is the orientation point that gives both the disposition of hope and the vision of human fulfillment. It provides the participant with the fundamental direction toward which he believes God's pur-poses are moving, and consequently toward which man's purposes ought also to be moving. The participant will run the risks of drawing inferences from his understanding of God's kingdom for the direction in which society ought to move. Like the American theologians of the Social Gospel, he will hazard the opinion that social ethical correlates of the coming kingdom can be determined. Thus, the kingdom toward which he is oriented suggests that op-pression must give way to human freedom, concentration of wealth to distributive economic justice, concentrations of power to the participation of the powerless in the determination of their lives, the ways of war to the insurance of peace, deprivation of opportunities to the availability of education, health benefits, and other blessings of abundance. The participant is a creative agent in the formation of social and personal life in the direction of what man can become as a citizen in God's realm.

The participant is open to and attracted by emerging social and moral *values* as he shares in the development of man. In his freedom he is not compelled to deny the validity of existing values as the prophet might be, nor is he compelled to defend them as the preserver might be. He can appreciate the moral order that exists while he seeks a moral order that is to come into being. Perhaps it is not so much new "values" that he is sensitive to as it is the necessity and possibility of finding new embodiments of the values men have always been attracted to under new social and historical conditions. It is not that men's definitions of justice have fundamentally altered so much as it is the case that the claims for the extension of justice for more persons and over a wider range of things, come to the fore and must be responded to positively. Scientific and technical developments extend the range of opportunity for human creativity, just as new awarenesses in the media of the traditional arts do. The participant is willing to experiment and to risk in his interest in finding new forms and patterns of all sorts of values. With his orientation toward the future, while not ignoring the past, he is aware of the necessity to compromise certain traditional principles and values for the sake of achieving those that are required under a new set of conditions.

He can be trained on the lodestar of such ultimates as love and perfect justice while setting his course through the murkiness of social and historical actualities. He is not overcome by nostalgia when he sees old patterns of life fading and falling away. Rather, he sees the development of new possibilities: in the patterns of political and economic ordering of urban life; in the responsible moral ordering of relations between the sexes and of family life under vastly altered social and technical conditions; in the organization of political units, cities, states, and nations, in relation to each other; in the development of medical technology. His openness to the new is not uncritical; he can warn about the losses of rights and values that will take place if various courses of action are pursued. The participant can alter his priorities of concerns and values that have existential and historical import under specific technological and social conditions. Traditional patterns of social order might have to bend in favor of the growth of freedom from oppression, as in situations where radical social reform and revolution appear on the horizons of the society. Individual freedom might have to bend in favor of ordered justice, as in the case of fair housing and fair employment laws. Restraints might be required on the actions of individuals for the sake of the common good, as in antipollution laws and perhaps in the future in the case of family size. Cherished notions of proper means of human relations might have to be given up for the sake of certain ends, as in the case of traditional anticontraceptive morality in relation to population growth and to the personal fulfillment in marriage. The participant is sensitive and open to the kinds of responses that are required of human values as new possibilities and new threats emerge in the passage from past and present toward the future.

The theologian of our third type accepts *social change* as normal and necessary, even though its accelerated rate creates opportunities and problems in an order of magnitude not previously experienced in human history. He does not dread the ruptures that it brings, as change reverberates from one center of innovations across others and through the whole sea of human experience. Nor does he thrive on change for its own sake or for the delight in seeing the old pass away. Rather, he seeks to make as clear as possible the purposes that social change can most beneficially fulfill, and he seeks to judge those purposes in the light of his reflections on the divine and human potentialities and demands that he knows.

The participant is under an obligation to know as best he can the nature of the processes of social change. For him the social and behavioral sciences are of great importance, as are the hard sciences with their technological effects on the social life of man. This obligation is a complex and often frustrating one, partially because of the vast growth in information about men and societies that we have been accumulating in the past decades. Like all persons concerned with policy and action, the theologian has to sort out the important from the unimportant information, that which is pertinent to the issues of human well-being which he addresses from that which is trivial. But this is not his only problem; there are the inevitable differences of opinion about which information is accurate and what its proper interpretation is, even among the social and behavioral scientists who gather it. Like others, the participant is tempted to find and use the information that is congenial with his moral predispositions and ignore that which might question them. But he must keep the measure of detachment and disinterestedness that enables him to make the fairest possible judgments. He will necessarily find himself at least temporarily allied with others who interpret the practical significance of information in roughly the same way he does, but who work from different basic convictions and for different ultimate ends.

Since so many issues of social change abound, it is important that theologians find a division of labor among themselves. Not all will be equipped to engage in the conversation about economic development or about international relations, about public school problems in large cities or about changes in health care, about the population problems of the world or about race relations. Participants need to become at least lay experts in the arenas in which they concentrate their attention. This is necessary initially to gain access to the discussions being carried on among the experts in social change in particular areas, for they will not have patience to listen to uninformed judgments or to vague moral platitudes.

The participant is not so oriented toward the achievement of beneficial consequences that might come from change that he loses sight of the problem of the rightness and wrongness of the means. But he does not expect change to come without disruption, health without the pain of surgery, gain without the loss of cherished achievements, success without the possibility of costly failure. He will make his case for the illumination that can be gained from the past and for the reckoning of potential losses, even while he seeks to be an agent among others in directing the course toward the future. He is not so fast in his commitments, however, that he rules out in principle the necessity for revolution. He is not dedicated in principle to the piecemeal social change that experts sometimes find themselves endorsing. And, under certain circumstances, he might be willing to endorse the exercise of violence.

The *role of the church* for the theologian as participant is that of (to use a tired term) involvement. The people of God are not the isolated portrayers of an exemplary life in communities ghettoized from the frustrations and possibilities of events and institutions around them. Nor are they the last bastions against the hordes of change. Rather, the people of God who acknowledge his lordship are part of the whole family of man, all of whom are God's children. They work and live together with others, sharing aspirations and expectations, anxieties and suffering, striving toward the order of life that brings a greater measure of justice and love, peace and reconciliation, health and welfare. They share in the labors of the economic and political orders, the medical and scientific orders. They seek, through their participation, to bring these things to the glory of God and the fulfillment of human life. The vocation of Christians is in the places where they do and can function in the framework of life, being agents of purposive action and manifestations of spiritual resources for humane ends.

One function of the theologian in this community is to be the leader of the moral discourse that is required if Christians are to be more effective actors. The congregations and assemblies of the churches become communities of moral discourse, where moral beliefs and consciences are formed and where the ends and means of human action are clarified and discussed. The theologian recognizes that the lay members of the Christian community, by virtue of their jobs and professions, are generally in positions to influence policy and decisions in a way that he is not. Thus, internally within the community, he is both learner and teacher as the congregated Christians seek to discern what God's will might be for the particular occasions in which they are engaged. He is not the authoritative pronouncer of the obligations of all Christians under all circumstances, but rather a contributor from the point of view of his special knowledge toward the shaping of the collective and individual consciences of the church. He recognizes that the church has passed from a stage of moral teaching in conformity to highly specific and ill-understood rules of conduct to that of the moral educator who seeks to bring the consciences of its members to a sensitivity and knowledge that enables them to act as Christian participants in their societies.[12] They, like the theologian who hopefully gives them leadership, are creatively and redemptively present in the crises, struggles, and transformations of human existence.

This outline of the task of the theologian as participant needs more substantial justification and development than it has received here; indeed, it stands in need of critical examination and correction. Nor would I wish to suggest that every person technically trained in theology ought to be conformed to this type; the theological community, like other communities, benefits from pluralism of expert knowledge and divergent points of view. We can ask, as we did with the types of the prophet and the preserver, whether this type is warranted—scripturally, theologically, ethically, and socially. To some extent it is a depiction of a conventional consensus present in Christian thinking today. Be that as it may, it is also a call to a more demanding task than either the roles of prophet or preserver require.

It demands greater rather than less self-examination and self-criticism, for it lacks the simple certitude of the other types. It demands clearer and harder thinking, since its vocabulary and thought forms must communicate with and embrace the vocabulary and thought forms of other men, working from other perspectives, directed by other motives, and often seeking other ends. It demands at least as much courage and confidence as do the prophet and the preserver, for it requires that the theologian know what he is doing as he moves into alien territories and strange seas. It demands the capacity to hear as well as to speak, to be receptive as well as to be active. Its sense of responsibility is more difficult, for it cannot rest on the traditional absolutes of the preserver or on the pure ultimates of the prophet, but must be accountable to the living God and to human communities. It requires imagination: the practical access to participation is not readily available, nor is much of the world breathlessly waiting to hear what the theologian has to say. It demands competence, for the theologian will not be attended to unless his words and deeds have the persuasiveness of excellence. But not all the world has prejudged that the theologian is without significance; he and his community must be prepared to grasp the opportunities that are being made available to them, modest as they may be.

II

Some
Substantiative
Issues

5

Moral Discernment
in
the Christian Life

I. The Notion of Discernment

The practical moral question is asked in various ways. Sometimes it is, "What ought we to do?" Or, if one chooses to relax the imperative and accentuate the indicative, it is, "What are we to do?" When such ways of asking the question are scrutinized, it becomes clear that the words "ought" and "are" carry a heavy load of freight. There is not only the relative moral weight or authority implied by each, the degree of obligation that each suggests, but also an unexplored process of moral judgment-making. Indeed, the polemics out of which this essay emerges have attended primarily to those processes. Most of the polemics in Christian ethics have been about *how Christians ought to make judgments.* They ought to use rules in a highly rational way, or they ought to exercise their graced imaginations, or they ought to obey the tradition of the church, or they ought to respond to the situation of which they are a part. Not enough work has yet been done by either philosophers or theologians on just how people actually do make moral judgments, though the variously propagated "oughts" claim some validation on the basis that each is correlated with what people actually do.

From *Norm and Context in Christian Ethics,* ed. Gene Outka and Paul Ramsey (New York: Charles Scribner's Sons, 1968), pp. 17-36. Copyright © 1968 Charles Scribner's Sons. Used by permission.

In this chapter I wish to suggest that the practical moral question of what we ought or are *to do* be held in abeyance in its strongest existential moral sense; and that it would be fruitful to look more carefully at how we *discern* what we ought to do, or are to do. Moral agents exercise some discrimination in making judgments, and it is this exercise of discrimination that I wish to explore. Such exploration is not done on the basis of a sampling of opinion; I have not approached a cross section of men, not even a cross section of Christians, with a schedule of questions to find out how they actually discern what to do. Nor does this exploration lead to a full-blown theory of the relations of motives, affections, rationality, and other aspects of moral selfhood as these have engaged the attention of moral philosophers in the past. I am not proposing that what seems to me to be involved in moral discernment is something that can be packaged, delivered, and taught to people who wish to become more moral. Nor am I suggesting the absence of wide variations in the ways in which people discern what they are to do; obviously some men are more emotive in their responses, some more intuitive, some more rational.

The intention of this chapter is more limited. It is based on the following rudimentary observations. Persons of moral seriousness do exercise discrimination in making judgments. They discern what they are or ought to do. Discrimination, or discernment, takes place not only in moral experiences but in other areas of human experience as well, such as aesthetic experience. Common speech uses the adjective discerning with reference to persons who seem to be more perceptive, wiser, more discriminating than others are in judging, whether the object judged is a performance of a symphony, a person and his behavior, a political situation, or a novel. Thus, by exploring the uses of the word discern, we might be able to see what goes into moral judgments, and particularly into moral judgments that seem to have a quality of excellence.

In one usage, to discern something is simply to see that it is there; indeed, this kind of visual use of the word is the least qualitative, or value-laden. When I am driving in a fog, I might say to my companion, "I dimly discern the white line that divides the lanes." I do not see it with unusual accuracy; I am not making a qualitative judgment about what I see; I am using the word simply to indicate that I can see the line. Perhaps more commonly we use the verb discern to indicate a particular accuracy in perception or observation. Often we use it when we can locate a detail that misses the perception of others. Often we use it when some subtle shading or coloring registers on us. In accord with such use, we might call a person "discerning" who has an unusual capacity to isolate significant detail, to perceive subtleties, to be penetrating and accurate in his observations. While in one sense to discern something is simply to notice it, to see it, in another sense we reserve the word for a quality of perception, of discrimination, of observation and judgment.

It is this quality of perception, discrimination, observation, and judgment that is involved when we speak of a "discerning person" or of "discerning comments" in various realms of discourse. As one who has to read hundreds of letters of recommendations for admission to graduate school, and who has to live with admissions based upon such letters, I have come to regard certain persons who write letters regularly as being "discerning." I do not mean that they give the most detailed descriptions of the candidates, nor that they simply notice the most obvious things about them. I mean that they seem to be able to get at salient characteristics of the students that have great importance in assisting me to make my judgment about them. There is an accuracy to their descriptions and their judgments that is borne out over time; they have an eye for pertinent characteristics (pertinent to what it takes, for example, to be a good graduate student). They enable me to have some understanding of the student; I can begin to draw my own "portrait" of him. This is more than a picture of a man of twenty-four who achieved a high academic record at Princeton University, and is interested in further study of ethics. By the letter writer's discernment of the qualities of mind, spirit, and character of the man, I can grasp some of his significant features, what his strengths and weaknesses are. I rely on the discerning letters of discerning men to help me make my judgment of what I ought to do with reference to the admission of a student to graduate school.

The same sort of process occurs in other areas of experience. Good literary critics are the most "discerning" ones. The difference between the good schoolboy type of writer on literature, who does all his homework (research) and writes up accurate summaries of what he has read, and the writer who moves the discussion to another stage is one of a quality of discernment. The discerning critic helps the reader to "see" things in the literature that he might not see on his own; he helps the reader to perceive some of the subtlety of the writer's words, characters, or plots; he helps him to understand what the writer's intention is in the way in which he concretely organizes his details. The same would be involved in distinctions between types of people who go to art museums. There are the clods who pace through the rooms with nothing registering upon their consciousnesses other than the fact that at the museum they saw works by Rembrandt and Picasso, about whom everyone who reads the newspapers knows something. At the other extreme are the discerning students, who not only are open to the impressions that painting makes upon them, but sense the significance of detail, of the arrangement of color patterns, of lines, and all other aspects of the work. The discerning observer cannot only say, "I don't like that one," but he can give some reasons for his judgment that express more than his feelings, that have some objectivity to him.

By reading the works of discerning critics of art and literature my own capacities for making judgments are deepened and broadened. I begin to "see" what is involved in accurate observation so that my own perceptions of the text or the painting are altered. I learn to be more discriminating in my own judgments. Presumably my judgments will be "better," at least to the extent of being more informed. I will be less likely to miss salient points I had missed before; I will become more "sensitive" to nuances, to details and their suggestive meanings, to the structure and wholeness of the piece at hand.

What seems to be involved in the quality of discernment toward which the foregoing paragraphs point? This question might best be answered by indicating what seems not to be involved, indeed, what is excluded. First, a person who has a scheme for analysis that he woodenly and mechanically imposes on whatever he observes would probably not be called a "discerning" person. The tourist who visits art museums with one checklist of things that he ought to look at, and another of the things he ought to look for in what he looks at, would hardly at that stage of his life receive the appellation "discerning." Checklists and wooden schemes of analysis cannot attend to the subtle nuances that are involved in refined discriminations; they seem to stress the more universal elements found in all objects of a given class, rather than the particularities to be appreciated in a single representative of what might be a class. Although they may help the novice to avoid gross errors, such schemes seem to be "external," that is, imposed from the outside on both the observer and that which he observes. They do not in themselves have or require the qualities of empathy, appreciation, imagination, and sensitivity that seem to be involved in discerning perception and judgment.

Thus, also, in moral experience, someone might suggest that in making a judgment the agent ought to keep in mind a scheme that includes the following six things: the potential consequences, the variety of his motives, the moral maxims accepted by his community, the empirical data about the situation as he defines it, the love of God, and the moral order of the universe as understood by reason. A person who has to make a moral judgment might run his dilemma through such a scheme with several possible results. He might be more confused after than before. He might try to "add up" all these considerations and find that their sum is far from a judgment. Or he might find that the scheme usefully points him in a direction, and then simply follow the direction. But the critic would probably say that each of these ways of making a judgment is wooden, mechanical, external, and certainly not discerning.

Second, the person who has formulated a set of first principles, has refined his understanding of deductive logic so that he can move from the universal to the particular, and has consequently determined on a rational basis what conduct is right and good, might not be viewed as a man of moral discernment. He might be called a man of intellectual discernment on the grounds of his virtuosity in formulating the universal principles and by the authority of his deductive logic. But since moral judgments involve more than the arrangement of ideas to each other in a logical and orderly way, in actual practice such a person might not demonstrate the perceptiveness that helps one to be aware of the complexity of the details of a particular instance. Indeed, if he assumes that his intellectual virtuosity is sufficient for making a moral judgment, he has to classify the case at hand, that is, attend less to its unique elements and accentuate those it has in common with others, in order to proceed. Intellectual clarity and the use of critical reflection are involved in moral discernment, just as they are involved in discerning criticisms or discerning descriptions in response to works of art, but in themselves they are not sufficient to exhaust what we normally include in the notion of discernment.

Third, the person who is skilled in accumulating the relevant information pertaining to a subject is not necessarily a discerning judge. All teachers know instances of students who are admirably exhaustive in their bibliographical preparation, are assiduous in reading with comprehension the important treatises on the subject, and are even orderly in arranging this material and reasonably clear in writing it up, but who are not really discerning students of the subject. "Discernment" seems to be appropriate for pointing to the ability to distinguish the important from the unimportant information and the insightful interpretations from the uninsightful. It refers to the ability to perceive relationships between aspects of the information that enable one to see how it all fits together, or how it cannot fit together. It refers to the ability to suggest inferences that can be drawn from the information, and thus to an imaginative capacity. One can find sociological studies, for example, that seem to be exhaustive in the accumulation of the data pertinent to the topic under research but are of limited value because the researcher lacked discriminating judgment and imagination. So it is in the sphere of moral judgments. Accurate accumulation of relevant information about a matter that is the object of moral judgment is indispensable, but such accumulation in itself does not constitute a discerning moral decision. The raw data for making judgments might be gathered, but the act of judgment itself involves more capacities than are required simply to pull relevant information together. Or, one can find biographies that are encyclopedic accumulations of objective data about the man involved, but do not enable the reader to penetrate in any way into the "character" of the subject, that do not give a coherent "picture" of the man so that he can be understood and not just known about.

Fourth, one might find persons who are articulate in giving their emotive and expressive reactions to a subject. By feeling deeply about something they are able to give an immediate reaction to its presence. But the reaction may be much more the expression of their indignation or their inordinate admiration than a discerning account of what was worthy of approval or disapproval, what was good or bad in the subject. The first hearing of music from India, for example, might evoke a judgment that it is unbearable, or that it is fascinating. Neither would be considered a discerning judgment, for neither would give reasons for the reaction. Whether it is the rhythm that either fascinates or repels, or the tonal qualities of the sitar, or the absence of Western style of harmony, would be matters that would be developed in a discerning judgment. Similarly, in moral matters, the expressive ejaculation of approval or disapproval in itself is not a discerning moral judgment. Nor would response in action that was based only on the depth of one's sense of indignation or love necessarily be a discerning response. Some disinterestedness, some accuracy of knowledge, some reflective awareness of what the situation entailed beyond what is immediately present would be ingredients of a more discerning response. Some thoughtful discrimination between the values that compete for actualization, between the possible consequences of possible courses of action, would be likely to occur if the judgment were to be called "discerning."

Fifth, stubborn allegiance to a given basis for making a judgment hardly makes for discerning judgment. Moralistic critics of literature provide interesting examples here. All literature that uses profanity, that talks about sexual relations in four-letter words, or that details the accounts of homosexual or heterosexual relations has often been condemned as "bad." And the use of the word bad has seemed indiscriminately to include both moral and nonmoral (e.g., literary) values. The critic who makes such judgments may have a palpable consistency that gives him the appearance of integrity, of being a man who is clear about his principles of judgment. But such stubborn allegiance to such principles hardly enables him to have an appreciation for the varieties of values that might be present in a book, for the significance of the concrete and the detailed, for the cumulative effect of the character portrayals or the plot development. Discernment seems to require some sensitivity and flexibility, some pluralism of consideration that is a priori ruled out by dedicated allegiance to single principles of interpretation or criticism. Similarly, in moral experience, the person who has a highly visible integrity based upon stubborn dedication to one or two principles, values, or rules, is not likely to be discriminating in a complicated situation. His responses may be predictable, but they are not thereby discerning.

These remarks about what seems not to be part of "discerning" judgments all pertain to a quality of excellence in discrimination. By indicating what the discerning person (in a qualitative sense) may not be and do, perhaps we can get at the elements of a discernment both in a more descriptive sense of Everyman as a moral discerner, and in a more normative sense of what excellence in discernment is. Some of the same elements are involved in the discernment of the morally flat-footed clod and the moral virtuoso. When these can be enumerated, perhaps one can see what combinations and accents among them make for excellence.

Discernment of what one ought to do, even among the clods, no doubt involves a perception of what is morally fitting in the place and time of action. What is fitting is decided differently by different people: some attack a problem in a disinterested manner, with great objectivity involved in their collection of appropriate information, their use of generalized prescriptive principles or articulated values, and their careful assessments of possible consequences of alternative courses of action. Others are more passionate; they feel deeply about what the actual situation is, they trust their built-in compasses to guide them, and they express their courage and initiative in taking the risks involved in action. What is fitting is discerned with reference to some of the same things and some different things, and different valences are existentially placed on different things by different people. Some are more determined by emotions and value their moral sensitivities highly; others distrust emotions and value their moral reflection highly. But perhaps some of the same things are present in both flat-footed and virtuoso performances in each style.

What are the common elements in all moral discernment? Perhaps several. There is a "reading" of what actually is the case at hand. Sometimes this reading is simply a visual image of an event that evokes decision and action. Sometimes it is a highly researched reading. Sometimes it is checked against other readings; sometimes it is idiosyncratic. Sometimes there is a depth of interpretation: some will want to know how the case got to be what it is, what are the relations of various elements to each other, who among the participants is most important or has more at stake, what the pliable factors are, what patterns and structures are there, and how it differs from similar cases. Sometimes there is no desire to interpret in a sophisticated way; sometimes there is no time to do so. The reading is from a perspective; this is important. Because the perspectives of moral participants differ, some see certain aspects to which others are blind; different persons accent the importance of different aspects; and in some persons there is simply suppression of factual matters that are abrasive to the moral predispositions. We have seen the importance of perspectives in "factual" judgments in the arguments about what really is the case in Vietnam. Sometimes the case is read more complexly because the moral discerner understands the situation and its participants to be part of an extensive pattern of relationships to other situations and other persons; sometimes it is read more simply because the time and space box in which it is seen is limited. Even different "situationists" differ on what the situation is. But for clod and virtuoso alike moral discernment involves such a reading of the case, an assessment of pertinent facts.

It is persons who discern; and persons have histories that affect their discernment. Some have never been seriously challenged to examine the bases of their judgments; others are highly self-critical and introspective. Some have developed characters on the basis of critical evaluations of past experiences and of the exercise of their initiative in becoming what they are throughout their personal moral histories. Others have more or less bounced morally through life, accumulating the effects of one occasion or episode after the other without a sense of self-direction. Some have acute senses of justice and injustice by virtue of having been the victims of oppression, or by virtue of being members of groups that have histories of being oppressed. Others are blithely confident about the goodness of men and the world because the world and men have been blithely supportive to them. Some are committed to getting all that they can out of life for themselves, and will discern what they ought to do in the light of that commitment; others are committed to loving the neighbor and meeting his needs because they have a religious loyalty that makes them believe this is how life ought to be lived. Several things have thus been suggested about the persons who discern: they are persons of persistent moral dispositions, or the absence thereof, and some have different persistent dispositions from others. They are persons of certain moral sensitivities or sensibilities, or the absence thereof, and some have different "feelings" from others. They are persons of certain commitments or the absence thereof, and some have different commitments from others. Moral discernment in a particular occasion is determined in part by these aspects of the self. These other-than-rational aspects of selfhood partially determine perspective, partially determine what is seen and accented, partially determine what is judged to be right and wrong, and thus what one will do.

Most persons who make moral judgments live by some beliefs,

rules, and moral principles that enter into their discernment. They are members of communities that have rules of conduct and some power of sanction in enforcing them. Thus, most people decide not to steal something from a store when they go shopping, for there are rules against this, and potential disruptive consequences if they should be caught stealing. Most people discern that they ought to assist someone who is suffering not merely because the observation of the suffering of others makes them feel bad, but because the "golden rule" or the principle of meeting the neighbor's need readily applies. There are not only principles, rules, and values to which men are committed that partially determine their moral discernment; there is also usually some rational reflection about how these function at least in the instances where the normal habituated responses seem not to apply readily. Both the moral clod and the virtuoso are likely to be able to give some principles that will justify their judgments, and are likely to be willing to show that they arrived at the judgment on the basis of some rational discrimination. Some men will give intellectually sophisticated justifications, indicating their reasons for selecting some principles and not others as applicable to the case at hand, and defending the principles that are applicable. Others might simply appeal to the generalized expectations of a given society of which they are a part, or appeal to the authority of an institution, such as the church, which has taught them the principles by which they live, and supports them in their use of those principles.

Many other elements could be adumbrated either as extensions of those described or in addition to them. At the minimum, however, discernment involves a reading of the case at hand, an expression of what constitutes the character and perspective of the person, and some appeals to reason and principles both to help one discern and to defend what one discerns. Excellence in moral discernment perhaps involves various combinations of these. There is a discriminating and accurate reading of the situation, and an understanding of the relations of elements of the situation to each other, and of its relations to other situations. There is a stipulation of the more and less important factors, and empathy for its "inner" character as well as a description of its external character. There is a refined moral sensitivity that registers subtle nuances not only of fact but of value, that is not just emotion or sentiment, but appears to contribute to the perception of what one ought to do. Moral sensitivity seems to contribute in the "discerning" moral man an intuitive element that leads to accuracy in moral aim, judiciousness in evaluation, and compelling authenticity in deed. Just as discerning critics of art know much about art, so the discerning moral man often knows much about morality. He can think clearly about potential consequences and applicable principles; he knows something of the range of values that might compete with or support each other, and he can discriminate between alternative courses of action. He is likely to have a clear head, to be able to argue with himself and others before a judgment is made, and give good reasons for it afterward.

The discerning act of moral discernment is impossible to program and difficult to describe. It involves perceptivity, discrimination, subtlety, sensitivity, clarity, rationality, and accuracy. And while some men seem to have it as a "gift of the gods," others achieve it by experience and training, by learning and acting. It is probably more akin to the combination of elements that go into good literary criticism and good literary creativity than it is to the combination of elements that make a good mathematician or logician; it is both rational and affective. How we discern what we ought to do, whether we be morally flat-footed clods or moral virtuosos, is a complex process indeed.

II. Moral Discernment in the Christian Life

The human processes of discernment are no different among Christians than they are among other men. There are the moral clods and the moral virtuosos among Christians; nothing can guarantee that because a man has faith in God whom he believes to have been disclosed in Jesus Christ he will be a man of excellence in moral discernment. Nor does the morally discerning Christian have different faculties or capacities that other men are deprived of because they happen not to be Christians. No special affective capacities, logic, or rational clarity can be claimed by Christians as possessions they have by virtue of their faith. Whatever the gifts of grace are, they function in and through the human capacities of discernment that are probably fairly evenly distributed throughout all mankind. Whatever "newness" there is in the Christian life is not a replacement of insufficient moral sensitivity with more sufficient, insufficient rational clarity with more sufficient. All this, however, is not to say that moral discernment in the Christian life ought not to be different, cannot be different, and sometimes is not different. Just what some of these differences ought to be, can be, and are is the subject matter of the remainder of this chapter.

There is a text from Paul's letter to the Romans that makes a good starting point for discussion of this subject.

> I implore you by God's mercy to offer your very selves to him: a living sacrifice, dedicated and fit for his acceptance, the worship offered by mind and heart. Adapt yourselves no longer to the pattern of this present world, but let your minds be remade and your whole nature thus transformed. Then you will be able to discern the will of God, and to know what is good, acceptable, and perfect.
>
> —Romans 12:1–2, NEB

Although this passage will not be exegeted in detail, it is suggestive not only of substantive themes of morality in the Christian life, but also of what changes might be registered in moral discernment. I shall use it at least as a starting point for further discussion.

We might characterize the Christian's obligation to answer the practical moral question, "What ought or are we to do?" in the following way. *Man is to discern what God enables and requires him to do.* Full explication of this sentence would require a book-length exposition of Christian ethics; here I merely suggest various lines that such exposition would take.

What is said about discerning what God enables and requires man to do is not presumed to be a description of how any one Christian does this, or how some "mean" or average Christian constructed out of a sample of all Christians does it. It is clearly said in a mode that suggests that something like it is appropriate normatively and possible actually.

Christians have a particular stance or perspective. They stand in a particular relationship which in turn affects their self-understandings, their perceptions and interpretations of the world, and they have certain norms by which they discriminate what is right and good. In Paul's language they are a people who have offered themselves up to God; they are living sacrifices dedicated and fit for his acceptance; mind and heart are offered to God in devotion and in praise. This language suggests that something more is involved than the claim that Christians are people who hold certain ideas or propositions to be meaningful or true. It suggests that Christians are not people who are distinguished from others simply by their belief in a set of propositions about God, and by inferences they draw from those propositions about what man is and what his relationship to God and other men also is. Mind and heart are offered to God; their "very selves" are given to him. A particular relationship of man's personal existence to God is implored by the apostle. It is not only belief that certain things are worthy of acceptance intellectually, but conviction and trust that it is appropriate to rely upon God and to give oneself in this reliance and its consequent service. Christians are, by virtue of this faith, in a particular position; they have by virtue of this faith a particular perspective. Just as my sons are different from my neighbor's sons partly because of their filial relations to me that are different from the filial relations other sons have to their own fathers, so Christians are different because of the relationship in which they exist to God in whom they believe and trust. Just as the understandings which my sons have of themselves are partially determined by the relationship in which they exist to me, so Christians' understandings of themselves are partially determined by the relationship in which they exist to God. Just as the perspectives my sons have on the world of which they are a part is partially determined by their relationship to me, so also are the Christians' by their relationship to God. Just as my sons "see" and interpret life around them partially under this perspective determined by their relation to me, so Christians interpret the world around them from the perspective of their faith in God.

Thus, one impact of Christian faith as it affects moral discernment involves the self-understanding that it evokes and directs. If I dedicate myself to be fit for the acceptance of God in whom I believe, I will consciously intend to live in such a way that my words and deeds are worthy of him. If I frequently offer my mind and heart to him worshipfully, I will be renewed in this self-understanding as one who depends upon him, who is grateful to him, who seeks to be consistent with what he gives and requires of me. The situation is parallel in structure to the self-understandings of others who have offered themselves, so to speak, to other objects of commitment. The devotee of the *Playboy* way of life has a self-understanding that is determined in part by his devotion to the symbols of that way of life, to the values that are pointed to by these symbols. He will see himself to be "sophisticated" and "cool"; he will value highly the gratification of his desires for a maximum of pleasure; he will intend to live in a way that is consistent with his self-understanding, which in turn is evoked and directed by *Playboy*. To put it simply, Christians will answer the question, "Who am I?" differently by virtue of their faith.

Just as one's interpretation of oneself is altered by Christian faith, so one's interpretation of the world around him is altered. Interpretations are informed by perspectives; indeed what one discerns to be important in his perception of the world around him is informed by his perspective. As I have indicated elsewhere,[1] the notion of perspective in matters of moral assessment is analogous to its use in matters of visual experience. Some things are seen clearly and some are shadowed by the perspective of the observer. Some are accented and others are diminished in the impressions that they register. Perspective and self-understanding both make one more sensitive to some things and less sensitive to others. The national leader whose obligation is clearly and primarily to the self-interest of his nation is likely to "read the situation" of Vietnam, or some other one, differently from the person who views his obligation to be primarily to a universal God of love who wills the well-being of all men. The former understands himself to be one who exercises power for the sake of the interests of the nation; the latter understands himself to be one who is the servant of Jesus Christ. (I shall not deal here with the nest of issues that are involved in such a case as one who in a position of political judgment seeks to exercise his power as both a member of a nation and a Christian. The two "selves" are not necessarily either in irresolvable conflict or in perfect harmony.) Certain "facts" have greater importance from one perspective than from the other. Both might observe the same human suffering, but interpret its significance differently because one is viewing things from the perspective of national interest and the other from the perspective of redeeming love. The significance of what is going on is determined by the perspectives of those who see it and participate in it.

Surely H. Richard Niebuhr was getting at this when he suggested that "interpretation" is part of "responsibility." Interpretation is "in the light of" some things that are particular and thus partially constitute the perspective of the interpreter. Thus, Christians interpret what is going on in the light of their beliefs about God, and what men and the world are and are to be before him. Differences of opinion among Christians in their moral discernment are not only affected by differences in the data they might have available, but also by differences in their understanding of what the "light" of the gospel is, and what it illuminates about the world and the self. (It is not our task in this chapter to enter into that technical theological realm where these differences of the latter sort are to be adjudicated.) In spite of differences, there are certain common elements. Christian affirmations about the goodness of God and the goodness of the world he created, the reign of God in the preservation of that which he created, the willful unfaith and disobedience of men, the redemptive purpose of God to reconcile the world to himself, the hope of a consummation of all things in the coming kingdom of God, the judgment of God on human disorder, and other affirmations, are part of the "light" that Christians bring to bear upon their interpretation of the world. At another level there are things believed about man: men are created to live together in order and in love, they are to seek each other's good, their lives are to be sustained and not oppressed or destroyed, they are to live in gratitude to God and to others for life and loving care, they are to respect each other, etc. Such assertions are related both to the gospel and to normal human experience; they become "lights" that help Christians understand both what is to be affirmed in the world and what is to be sought for the world.

The perspective of the Christian affects what he values; it gives direction to the moral ends that he seeks, to the longings and desires that he has, to the preferences that he articulates in word and deed. Valuations and preferences are by no means always the result of a conscious reflective process in which certain "values" are defined, judged, and determined to be worthy of acceptance, then in turn applied in rational discrimination to the interpretation of the world in which men live. Christians do not always first engage in a process of defining "love," which by tradition and experience they value highly, and then use this definition to engage in a rational process of interpretation of events in the world in the light of love. (It is clearly the task of the person whose vocation is theological and ethical thinking in the Christian community to engage in such deliberate, careful thinking, more than it is the task of every Christian.) Rather, Christians may have perspectives that are formed in their faith and belief in a God of love, who has demonstrated his love for man in creation, and in his forgiveness and renewal of life, who enables men to love one another as they have been loved, and who wills that men should love each other. This "loving" perspective is likely to color the things that Christians value and approve of in their perception, interpretation, and choices in the world. That which restores and brings life and joy is to be preferred to that which destroys and brings death and suffering and pain, for example. Not only in his rational discriminations, but in his moral sensitivities, the Christian is likely to be sensitive to oppression and injustice, to physical and mental suffering. Christians are likely to interpret not only what is the case, but what ought to be the case in the light of valuations that are determined by the perspective or posture of their faith.

The process of interpretation that is part of discernment is, as I have suggested, an expression of fundamental dispositions that are shaped in part by the faith and trust Christians have as they offer themselves up to God. Their sensibilities are colored by their faith and its perspective. But it is also, as has been suggested, a matter of using articulated and expressed beliefs. Both are part of the moral discernment of Christians. If Christians are to discern what God enables and requires them to do, they are involved in rational discrimination as well as sensible response. Just as I am more likely to do what is acceptable to my sons if I *know* what their needs and desires are, so I am more likely to do what is acceptable to God if I have some knowledge about what God seems to require and enable. Part of my response to my sons' needs is a matter of understanding based upon the human relationship that has been formed between us, with all the nuances of feeling and affection, of intuitive insight and perception. Part of it is a matter of thinking clearly and rationally about what they need in the light of who they are, the resources available to meet their needs, the ways in which they may not understand their needs any more clearly than I do, and the kind of order of life it takes for us to live together with some harmony and joy.

It is under this latter aspect of stipulated convictions and rational reflection that moral discernment in the Christian life uses dogma, moral principles formed in scripture and the tradition, moral rules of the Christian community, and refined moral argumentation. If I am to discern what God enables and requires, I must be able to say some things about God. Thus, the understanding and formed convictions that Christians have about God are important for the way in which they discern things morally, and what they actually discern to be morally appropriate. Variations are many, and changes both within the tradition and in the beliefs of an individual man occur through time. Some aspects of Christian belief are stressed on one occasion, others on another, and elements of belief are combined and recombined in particular times and places so that different themes are accented and muted. Sometimes we recall more cogently God as the awesome judge of human evil, sometimes God the redeemer of the world, sometimes God the restrainer of men who wills that order persist, sometimes God the just and merciful who wills a disruption of an unjust order.

Moral discernment, then, has reference to belief. It is the moral agent who discerns with reference to belief what he judges God to be enabling and requiring. This statement is important, for it precludes saying that Christians are "immediately sensitive" to what God is doing in the world (Lehmann), or that they hear in a clear and direct way what the command of God is to them (Barth). Discernment is a human act made with reference to human statements about God as these statements are forged from scripture and from the theological tradition. Theologically, it might be said that God is enabling men to discern what God is enabling men to do; but the locus for the discernment is in the self as it relates beliefs about the God in whom it trusts to the situations in which it acts.

Moral rules and principles also play a part in the rational reflection that is part of discerning what one ought to do. Not all of them are rooted particularly in the Christian tradition, but certainly there are some that have historical origins in the Christian faith, and particular authority for Christians. Rules can be understood as having a social function and generally a social sanction in morality. They are determinations of what is definitely required and what is definitely prohibited in the community. As such they are ready and authoritative references for the man who is to discern what he ought to do in normal instances. He discerns clearly and quickly that the situation in which he is to act is one in which his behavior ought to be conformed to those rules that regulate the life of the community. Others before him have faced situations comparable to his own, and have interpreted them in such a way that it is clear that Christians ought to do very specific things on such occasions. There need be no ambiguity in discernment. Just as one need not engage in a unique process of discernment to judge that he ought to obey the traffic signals, so one need not engage in a unique process to judge that as a Christian he has the duty to respect another person as a human being. Elaborate reasons can be given for traffic rules and for the obligations that drivers and pedestrians have to obey them, but members of the civil community do not require that such reasons be given on each occasion. Elaborate theological and ethical reasons can be given for the rule that Christians must treat other persons with respect as human beings, but both because such a rule can be readily internalized and because its authority is clear and unambiguous, they can discern readily prohibited limits and required actions that are enabled and demanded of them. This is not to say that there are not situations in which reflection and interpretation is not required pertaining to how the rules apply. But it is to say that often rules have immediate applicability, and even when they do not seem to apply readily, the agent can begin with the rule (and not a series of arguments for its validity) in his discerning. For example, in the realm of sexual behavior, there has been a commonly accepted rule. "Thou shalt not commit adultery." Reasons can be given for the authority of that rule, but the rule has relative autonomy by virtue of its long usage within the Christian community so that its members do not have to face every human relationship with a man or woman who is not their marriage partner as one that offers the moral possibility of adultery. Indeed, if for various reasons a relationship suggests that adultery might be committed, Christians begin with the rule. The weight of evidence and reflection clearly has to be such as to invalidate the application of the rule in that particular instance. Exceptions to such rules are not made lightly, and the existence of exceptions is hardly evidence for the invalidity of the rule.

Moral principles function in a similar way, though perhaps they can be distinguished in some instances from rules by the absence of social sanction. Nor are they so determined by what sociologists and anthropologists have called one's status and roles in the community. In different human situations moral principles function differently. Certainly such a principle as the commandment to love the neighbor as the self would be part of the "light" that Christians would bring to bear upon their interpretation of the general situation and also be part of their intention in acting within it. It would function to set the direction of their activity: what they do ought to be in accord with what love requires. To discern what the principle seems to enable and require places an obligation on Christians to interpret what love seems to mean, and how this meaning is applicable in the particular occasion. Moral reflection on such a general principle requires a great degree of sophistication on some occasions; on others its requirements seem to be self-evident. When sophistication is required, the Christian is involved in the process in which the situation must be defined (its proper time and space limits determined, its complex of relationships delineated, its data formulated and organized); in which other principles bearing on the case that might not be easily harmonized with the love commandment have to be stipulated and recalled, other theological reference-points than love remembered, other values than love designated, and the use of "love" itself carefully delineated so that it has some particularity and does not cover everything. He is involved in a process in which analogies from scripture or from the moral experience of the community are rehearsed and brought to bear; in which moral sensibilities are recognized, judged, and affirmed or qualified by reflection; and in which finally a judgment is made about what God is enabling and requiring. This reflection will illumine the discernment of God's will; it will never have clear and unambiguous authority so that the reflecting man will equate his serious judgment with God's will itself. Indeed, careful reflection is necessary in discernment because of the partialities of men, and the tendency to discern what is fit and acceptable for one's own gratification or the gratification of one's own group rather than fit and acceptable to God. Reflection is necessary because Christians, like others, tend to be conformed to the expectations of their own desires and to the ethos of the time in which they live, rather than remembering that they are not to be conformed to this world.

Moral discernment always takes place within communities; the moral discernment of Christians takes place within the Christian community. The community is in part the present gathering of Christians, in a congregation or some other group, that engages in the moral discourse that informs the conscientiousness of its members through participation in moral deliberation.[2] Through moral discourse in the Christian community, both the minds and hearts of men can be trained to discernment; their capacities to make discerning moral judgments can be deepened, broadened, and extended. Such training is not an automatic accrual from hearing sermons or receiving the sacraments; if the Holy Spirit is at work in the community to make men better discerners of God's will he is present in and through the moral deliberations that occur, as well as the preached word and the bread and wine.

But the community is not only the present gathering at this time and place. Those presently gathered are part of a historical community that has lived the moral life as Christians in the past, that has reflected upon situations comparable to the present ones with references to the same gospel, and the same intention to discern God's will. This does not mean that an answer from the fourth century is the answer to the twentieth century, but it does mean that in present reflection the community does not have to begin de novo as if God's will for present and future had no consistency with God's will for the past. Certain values, or principles, or points for consideration that were arranged in one combination with reference to a past situation might be rearranged and added to with reference to a present situation to the illumination and accuracy of the present community. John Noonan's *Contraception*,[3] the greatest book yet published on the history of an issue in Christian ethics, makes this point clear. Moral discernment is in continuity with the past, not discontinuity; it learns from, and is thus informed and directed without being determined by, the past. (The current celebration of the openness toward the future is proper insofar as it recognizes that the God whose will one seeks to discern for the future is the God who has willed in the past. Much of this celebration refers primarily to human *attitude* in any case, and as such is insufficient to determine what men ought to be doing in particular instances. Attitude alone does not determine act. To be open to the future is not to discern what one ought to do in it.)

Perhaps all that has been said about moral discernment in this chapter is only another way of talking about the virtue of prudence. Prudence is the virtue that is both intellectual and moral; it involves reason, sensibilities, and the will. It is a virtue: it is a lasting disposition of the self that comes into being not in the moment by some inspiration of the spirit or by some visceral response to a narrowly defined situation, but by experience, training, reflection, and action. It does not exist independent from law, although it is the capacity to perceive what law might require in a particular case, and to perceive what might be required that is more than the law demands. It is open to the concrete situation, but not in such a way that the past is ignored, as if similar situations have never occurred before. It is an exercise of character that has been formed; the formation of character is important in the whole of the moral life of which a particular discernment is but a moment in time. It is formed and informed by love, trust, hope, and other gifts of the spirit. But it is never simply an attitude; it is a capacity to discern that uses reason and intellectual discrimination.

Prudence in the Christian life refers to the fitting judgment, response, and act. But the fitting in turn refers to what God is enabling and requiring, not just what seems to be pleasing to men. Thus, the exercise of prudence, of discernment, in the Christian life is intricate and complex; it can never be programed for all men, for some are gifted in different ways from others, and some have different roles from others. Its exercise is not only in moral discrimination; it is itself offered to God in praise and devotion, in reliance upon the grace of God to empower and inform it. But it is human; man is the exerciser of prudence in reliance upon God, and in discernment of God's will.

At best, however, the Christian who is morally discerning, who has the capacity to be perceptive, discriminating, accurate, and sensitive, probably has to modify his acceptance of the words of Paul. He said with assurance, "Then you *will* be able to discern the will of God." I suspect that more modest claims would be more precise. By offering oneself up to God, and by formation in prudence informed by love and faith and hope, "Then you *might* discern the will of God."

6

The Place of Scripture in Christian Ethics: A Methodological Study

The facets of the project indicated by this title are many and complex. Indeed, this chapter can only seek to provide some order, while doing some justice to the complexity. Certain markings can be fixed which will set both limits and direction for the present discussion; these ought to enable the reader to avoid some possible confusions.

First, the title indicates that this study does not concentrate primarily on what might properly be called "biblical ethics." Biblical ethics would be the study of the ethics in the scriptures. In itself this is a complex task for which few are well prepared; those who are specialists in ethics generally lack the intensive and proper training in biblical studies, and those who are specialists in biblical studies often lack sophistication in ethical thought. A comprehensive study of biblical ethics would, of course, render an effort to develop the place of scripture in Christian ethics easier, for one important question is the relation of biblical ethics to constructive Christian ethics. The problem here is parallel to the relation of the theology found in the Bible to constructive Christian theology.

Reprinted from *Interpretation*, XXIV, No. 4 (Oct. 1970), 430-55. Used by permission.

A study of biblical ethics would include various concerns. One is the concrete moral teachings of the scriptures—what content they give to right conduct and to ends and purposes that are good. Biblical notions of justice, of peace, of the good life, of love, would be developed. Another concern would be the forms of moral discourse in scripture: moral commands, laws, the examples of persons, narratives of actions that are judged to be faithful or unfaithful to God's moral will, parables and allegories, paraenetic instructions, and others. Such a study could be done without reference to uses the findings would have for constructive purposes.

The study of biblical ethics requires focus on yet another concern, namely, the theology in the scriptures which both validates and provides content to the moral teachings. For the people of the Bible, morality was not separated from religion in the way that it has been both in theory and in practice in later developments; ethics was not separated from theology. God and his relations to men and the world were conceived in moral terms, as well as in other terms, and this makes theology an integral part of biblical ethics. Since there are theolog*ies* in scripture, this analytical task is in itself complex; its use as a basis for constructive Christian ethics is even more so.

In the present study we are alert to the problems raised by the absence of a full development of what are the biblical ethics, and this absence indicates where certain assumptions and warrants that are not fully justified can be found in our proceedings.

A second marking is that our primary attention is not a critical analysis of writings in Christian ethics in order to see how scriptures are used by various theologians and ethicists. Rather, the present modest constructive effort makes proposals that are subject to the critical scalpels of others. Two helpful articles have been published. Edward LeRoy Long has provided one framework for interpretation in his article "The Use of the Bible in Christian Ethics." David H. Kelsey's article "Appeals to Scripture in Theology" provides a pattern that is also suggestive for the study of Christian ethics.[1] Intensive critical analysis of the ways in which scripture is used in the literature of Christian ethics would yield the range of options from the past and provide a sturdier framework for positive proposals than that given in the present chapter. Some analysis of this sort is done here, but its function is subservient to other aims.

A third marking is more difficult to shape with precision. It calls attention to the fact that how an author uses scripture is determined to a considerable extent by how he defines the task of Christian ethics. Indeed, how one defines the field and methods of ethics, whether specifically Christian or more general, will make a difference in his uses of scripture. For example, if the study of ethics is focused on the structure of moral arguments about particular acts, the question of this article would be, "How is scripture used in particular moral arguments?" Kelsey's development of Toulmin's distinctions between data, warrant, and backing would be immediately applicable. If, however, one includes in ethics a concern for the formation of the moral agent, then scripture will be used in quite a different way.[2] Or, if one attends to a vision of the future good, or to the ontological structure of morality, his uses of scripture will be governed accordingly. While I would argue that the scope of Christian ethics is rather inclusive, many aspects will be left relatively unattended in the present chapter.[3]

In this chapter I intend to develop the significance and the limitations of the uses of scripture in Christian ethics. I shall also indicate some of the various points or levels in Christian ethical reflection where scripture is used. To keep at least a backdrop of concreteness in view, I shall draw attention to a complex event which has exercised the moral passions of the American people, namely, the invasion of Cambodia by American troops from South Vietnam in the last days of April 1970. Many articulate Christians have judged this to be morally wrong and have participated in various forms of action to express their indignation about it. Our major and long-range question is this: Why do Christians judge this to be morally wrong? How does scripture enter into their judgment? To keep the chapter manageable it is confined to moral judgments about actions and does not extend to the positive determination of what alternative courses of action are morally better, or what means and ends ought to be used. Before an attempt is made to answer directly this last question, however, it is necessary to isolate the points in the decision-making and action processes where moral assessments are pertinent. These are in the assessment of the meaning of the history in which the events take place, the motives and intentions of the decision-makers, the circumstances in which it is deemed proper to act, and the consequences of the action. It is also necessary to sort out some of the more general issues in the uses of scripture in ethics before we come to address the major question more directly. Finally, in addressing the question, it will be clear that other Christian ethicists might well wish to claim more or less than I do for the place of scripture, but it is hoped that at least the points at which the arguments can be made will be clear.

The Cambodian Invasion

Not all who believe the invasion of Cambodia to be a mistake would necessarily judge it to be morally wrong; even fewer would judge it to be wrong for "Christian ethical" reasons. The adjectives that would qualify the "wrong" suggest the various frameworks of interpretation that can be used in evaluating the action.

1. The argument is made that it is legally wrong. Persons who have defended the right of American military forces to be in Vietnam on legal grounds, in compliance with commitments, and at the invitation of a legally constituted government, draw a distinction between Vietnam and Cambodia precisely on those two points. There is a violation of the delicate fabric of international law when a power moves into the territory of another nation without invitation of its government and without treaty commitments that require it. The observation that the move is illegal could contribute to two different sorts of arguments about its immorality. First, it is immoral for a nation to violate international law. Second, it is not possible to universalize the principle used to justify the breaking of the law. To do so would seem to legitimate the invasion of any nation by any other nation in circumstances judged to be similar to those existing in Cambodia.

2. The argument is made that it is a military mistake. Here the appeal is not to a legal standard, but to previous military experience of a similar sort that has not led to the intended or desired consequences. To many persons the script used to justify this expansion of the war sounds strikingly similar to those scripts used to justify previous escalations, and the evidence suggests that mutatis mutandis this will fail as well. The justifications for the judgment are made largely on factual grounds: Under similar circumstances escalations have been justified, but have not led to peace. To dispute the argument, then, one would have to appeal to factual evidences which would indicate that the circumstances are different at this time and place, and therefore the desired end is more likely to be achieved. There is a moral appeal in the argument in favor of the invasion, namely, that in the long run

the action will save more lives, and particularly American lives. As in all moral arguments from potential consequences, so in this one it is difficult to adduce the compelling evidence. Perhaps if saving lives is the moral imperative, it would be better simply to withdraw; this is clearly the case if the concern is primarily of American lives. And even the latter concern is subject to critical scrutiny: Does it assume that American lives have greater worth—intrinsically or even instrumentally—than Indo-Chinese lives?

3. The argument is made that it is politically wrong. Military actions have to be seen in their political contexts and have always to be justified by the political purposes that they serve. The judgment about the political purposes involved in the Cambodian venture is made on two counts. First, it does not appear that this action is the correct means to achieve the desired political end, namely, peace in Southeast Asia. Second, even if it were the correct means, those who chose to engage in this action did not take fully into account the consequences for other political ends, such as the political responses of the Soviet Union, China, and Western European allies, and the announced intention of the administration to bring the American people back together again. Indeed, the political consequences, intended and unintended, appear to be much more complex than anything a brief paragraph suggests. The relations between a judgment that an action is politically wrong and that it is morally wrong are complex. One can seek a moral justification of the political ends themselves: For example, is there a persuasive if not definitive moral justification for the purpose of restraining the spread of Communism in Southeast Asia? This is itself a many-faceted question. Is Communism morally evil? Or are its presumed evil consequences sufficient to warrant the evils of protracted war to restrain it? Indeed, is revolution not morally right in much of the "third world" that has been dominated by Western political and economic interests? The question of the morality of means is asked. Are the means used proportionate to the end that is sought? If what is sought is the "well-being" of the people of the region, are there not better means than war to fulfill that end? Or perhaps one does not expect such lofty moral ends from nation-states. Perhaps they are governed in their moral codes and actions by their own national interest. If that is the case, the question can still be raised as to whether the national interest of the United States is in any crucial way threatened by events in Southeast Asia.

4. An argument is made that it is economically wrong. This argument pertains to the whole military operation of which the Cambodian invasion is a part. Just as one moves quickly from what are politically correct objectives to some moral concerns, so also one moves from economic aspects. Here one confronts the arguments about the moral justifications for allocating priorities in the American economy and about the involvement of American business in the economies of the third world. Is the multibillion-dollar expenditure for the military involvement in Southeast Asia justifiable in the light of the many needs and purposes that would make for human well-being in the United States and in other parts of the world?

In each of these arguments there is an evaluative assessment of the circumstances in which action is occurring; there is no simple description of incontrovertible facts. In each there are different sorts of evaluation: Certain data are given higher valence in some arguments than they are in others; preferential evaluations of the significance of various causal factors are also involved. And, as we have shown, moral evaluations are either embedded in the other evaluations or are operating just behind the political, military, or other arguments.

Where the Ethical Issues Lie

Before we can turn to the place of scripture in relation to the discussion of Cambodia, it is necessary to sort out the ways in which moral evaluations themselves apply to any historical event.

One application is to *the structure and meaning of the historical process* or wider context in which particular events take place. This can be illustrated with reference to the differences that various views of history make in the interpretation of the course of particular events. A progressive view of history, such as was in vogue sixty years ago in many circles, might interpret the events in Southeast Asia as part of the ongoing evolution of the human race, painfully breaking from the shackles of the past, but confidently moving toward a more nearly perfect future state of affairs. An alternative to this would be a Marxist view, adopted also by important Christians, that the struggle is part of a historical process of conflict between those who seek to retain their powers and exercise them in the repression of the weak and those who seek release from the bondage of oppression in their efforts to liberate themselves from colonial or other dominating powers.

A third might be more radically eschatological; the future is drawing the present and the past toward itself in such a way that wars of the sort being fought are really revolutions of hope that a new day for mankind is dawning. In contrast to these three would be a view that sees the events as part of the ongoing struggle between the forces of disruption and disorder that always threaten the delicate fiber which restrains chaos and the forces that preserve the modicum of order that makes existence tolerable among men. Perspective on the more comprehensive meaning of historical events affects the evaluation of particular historical events; events are charged with different meanings from different perspectives; as a result of one's "view of history," certain features of events appear to be more salient and morally more significant than do other features. Biblical themes enter into the Christian's view of history and thus affect his judgments, as we shall subsequently see.

Moral evaluations are also applied to the *motives and intentions* of those whose access to power enables them to determine the direction of events more than most persons can. If we take the common philosophical distinction between motives as "backward-looking reasons" for action, and intentions as "forward-looking reasons" for action, we can see how moral evaluations enter into the assessment of each. To assess motives we can look at the commitment of the American nation to certain moral and social values, not only for its own people, but for others as well, which would provide justifying reasons for the action. These motives can be approached by asking on what grounds the United States is involved in Southeast Asia in the first place. Some lofty motives can be given in answer to this query: The nation is concerned with the preservation of freedom, with the rights of self-determination of peoples, with adherence to commitments made to other governments, with the credibility of the United States as a power that does not let its friends down in time of trouble. Such motives are subject to moral judgment in several respects. The consistency between national actions and the motives professed for them can be judged. One can also judge the moral worth of these motives in terms of whether those that appear to be dominant are worthy of their position, and whether other morally justifiable motives, such as social justice, are not left out. One can also judge whether the consequences of the actions that are justified by these motives do not create greater harm, suffering, and destruction than are worthy of the commitments which give them warrant. For example, while it is prima facie laudable to keep one's commitments, the question can be raised as to whether or not the destructive consequences of keeping those promises morally outweigh the obligation involved in them.

In a similar way, we can engage in a moral evaluation of America's intentions, its forward-looking reasons for being in Cambodia and, indeed, in Vietnam. Some of those that are professed reasons are incontrovertible in their most general form: We are seeking peace. (I paraphrase the comment of an undergraduate: "Killing for the sake of peace is like fornicating for the sake of virginity.") Other intentions of a political, moral sort are more arguable: We are seeking stability in the region. One can raise questions about the moral value of stability in relation to other moral values that are embedded in the political order, for example, justice—in terms of more nearly equitable distribution of rights, powers, economic resources.

Whenever motives and intentions are assessed, that difficult question arises as to whether the professed reasons are the real reasons for action. This points to the issue of the moral integrity of those persons who determine the exercise of powers—but further elaboration of this issue here is not possible.

Judging both the motives and the intentions of the nation involves also evaluating the *circumstances* in which these motives and intentions are acted out. The question is whether or not the actual situation warrants the actions based on the given reasons. In Southeast Asia this becomes the question of whether, for example, freedom is so threatened that it warrants the exercise of American military power to preserve it. It involves the question of whether the government to which the American commitments are made is a duly constituted, popularly elected one. In short, are the conditions that America presumably seeks to rectify sufficiently threatening to the values it wishes to adhere to that there is warrant for the use being made of military, political, and economic power?

The *consequences* of the extension of the war are also subject to moral evaluation. As critics of utilitarian and "consequentialist" ethics have long pointed out, it is not easy to judge consequences of actions in moral terms in an incontrovertible way. A moral judgment about a factual state of affairs is involved, and this requires a complex process. For example, most persons would agree that it is wrong to take human lives except under extreme conditions. Does the "benefit" gained by taking lives outweigh the cost of the moral value of the lives that are taken? If the balance of the consequences is not on the beneficial side, then it is judged morally wrong to take the lives. The consequences of massive military action are many and very complex. They extend through time; this makes it difficult to say precisely when one cuts off the calculation. Lives are not only physically destroyed, but human spirits are painfully warped; property is wasted, cultures are disrupted, repercussions in the realm of politics and economics are almost incalculable. In order to make a moral assessment of various consequences, clear notions of what constitutes the "good" and the "bad" have to be developed; and the factual aspects have to be judged in relation to these notions.

Even though these points are not exhaustive, they are perhaps the most salient in our experience. Our stated task is to interpret the place of scripture in Christian ethics. That can now be made more precise. How is scripture used in the interpretation of the structure and meaning of the historical process of which the Cambodian events are a part? How is scripture used in the assessments of the motives and the intentions of those persons who determine what forms of power are to be used in Southeast Asia and how these powers are to be used? How is scripture used in the assessment of the consequences of the extension of the war?

Ways of Using Scripture

The existence of a variety of materials in scripture necessitates some general principles for clarifying a more coherent and simpler view of the message of scripture. The use of scripture in Christian ethics first involves the determination of the theological and ethical principles which will be used to bring coherence to the "meaning" of scripture's witness. In a previous publication I distinguished a view of scripture as the revelation of a morality that is authoritative for the judgments of Christians from a view of it as a revelation of theological principles that are used to interpret what "God is doing," and thus, in turn, can give clues to what man as a moral agent is to do in particular historical circumstances.[4] If scripture is the revelation of a morality, its application to the Cambodian invasion would require that one judge that event in accordance with moral laws, precepts, and commands given in scripture. If scripture is the revelation of the action of

God, one applies it to the Cambodian invasion by interpreting that event in the light of an answer to the question, "What is God doing in our contemporary history, and particularly in Cambodia?" Here I would like to refine these types before proceeding to suggest a more constructive statement.

The most stringent use of scripture as revealed morality can be stated in the following way. Those actions of persons and groups which violate the moral law revealed in scripture are to be judged morally wrong. The idea of moral law becomes the principle for ethical interpretation. Two issues immediately emerge. One is the content of the moral law, and the other is the mode of its application. For Jewish religion these can be answered more simply than they can for Christians, although even in Judaism the answers are complex. The law would be the Torah, and *halachah* would provide the tradition for application. The parts of Torah that would be applicable, and the procedures for its application through Mishna, Talmud, the Codes, the Responsa, all involve judgments on the part of the learned rabbi who might come to a decision. But there would be clear biblical authority in the tradition for using biblical law, and the tradition provides a continuity of historical judgments and general procedures by which a new judgment might be made.

For Christian religion this use of scripture is even more difficult. What is the moral law that is revealed in the Bible? Torah would be an insufficient answer. There is also the "new law," and just what that is has to be determined. If the teachings of Jesus as recorded in the Gospels are the new law, then something like the method of *halachah* might be appropriate; but on the whole the Christian theologians have not worked in this way. Further, if the new law is the "grace of the Holy Spirit written in the heart," as it has been judged to be by both the Catholic and Protestant traditions, it can no longer be limited in its references to the moral teachings of the scriptures interpreted to be law. It is "the life-giving law of the Spirit," to quote Romans 8:2 (NEB), a text that is persistently cited in the history of Christian ethical thought.

Christians have no codifications of the moral law of scripture and its interpretations comparable to the *Shulhan Arukh* and the Code of Maimonides; even the codifications of law in the canon law tradition of the Catholic Church appeal heavily to the natural law tradition developed in the West, rather than to scripture.

Even Fundamentalists have highly selective[5] ways of using biblical evidence. There are clearly ethical principles at work that govern their choices of texts to be applied to particular moral situations and that provide ways of explaining texts which prima facie would contravene the positions they would take.

Perhaps agreement on the primacy, if not the exclusiveness, of the "law of love" could be asserted about the Christian scriptures, recognizing their continuity with Jewish scriptures. "For the whole law can be summed up in a single commandment: 'Love your neighbor as yourself,' " writes Paul (Gal. 5:14, NEB), a claim also found in other parts of the scripture. If this were judged to be the material content of the new moral law, the modes of its application to situations like the Cambodian venture would vary markedly. For some persons it might have a pacifist application; one does not love himself by taking his own life; surely one does not love his neighbor by taking his. For others it becomes a high-level general principle which is applied to the complexities of a war through the mediation of the structure and principles of just-war thinking.

A second use of scripture as revealed morality could be stated as follows: Those actions of persons and groups which fall short of *the moral ideals* given in scripture are to be judged morally wrong, or at least morally deficient. The notion of moral ideals becomes the principle of ethical interpretation. Three issues emerge here. The first is whether the language of moral ideals is itself warranted by scripture. Is the language of ideals as intrinsic to the scriptures as is the language of law? How these questions would be answered depends to some extent upon how one interprets "ideals." If a moral notion has to refer to some timeless entity, a metaphysical value, in order to be an ideal, it is safe to say that the language of ideals is more at home in Greek ethics than in biblical ethics. If, however, it refers to a vision of the future in which "The wolf shall live with the sheep, and the leopard lie down with the kid; the calf and the young lion shall grow up together (Isa. 11:6, NEB)," the promised fulfillment might well function as a vision of the ideal future. The New Testament idea of the kingdom of God has functioned this way in Christian ethics from time to time in Christian history, most prominently in the social gospel writers.

The theological doctrine that qualifies the use of the language of ideals is eschatology. Whether an ethician uses the vision of an ideal future is governed by his eschatological views. If he finds a warrant for the language of ideals within those views, then *how* that vision is used is also determined to a considerable degree by his eschatology. The double problem of the use of scripture which we pointed out previously confronts us again: One part of the problem is the significance of the eschatological context within the scriptures for understanding properly the biblical visions of ideal futures; the other is the authority that the biblical eschatological context has for the use of those visions in constructive Christian theological ethics.

The second issue that emerges in the use of the language of ideals is that of their material content. The biblical imagery in Isaiah, as well as elsewhere, suggests harmony between natural enemies, the resolution of struggles in idyllic peace—a theme often portrayed in Christian art. The social gospel writers did not hesitate to find consistent with the biblical vision of the coming kingdom of God almost all values that were judged to promote human welfare: peace, love, justice, harmony. They courageously developed these in terms of ideals and goals for the society of their own time. Clearly, there is a deep and broad gulf between the ideal of universal peace as part of the biblical vision of the fulfillment and any war, including the Cambodian venture.

The third issue is the mode of application of a moral ideal to the Cambodian or any other historical situation. If the basis for using an ideal is that reality ought to be conformed to the ideal in all human actions and states of affairs, a condemnatory verdict on the Cambodian venture is clear. If, however, the use of the ideal leads to the reckoning of *compromises* that men can live with, or *approximations* with which they can be satisfied, then a sliding scale of judgment has been introduced. The adoption of a more realistic view of the possibilities of political and moral achievement under the conditions of historical finitude and corruption leads to such applications. How much compromise with the ideal do the conditions of history, the particular circumstances, require? What degree of approximation of the vision of the ideal future ought one to strive for under the political, social, and military conditions of our time? To give warrant for a judgment against the Cambodian venture one has to indicate, in this mode of thought, that the compromises are too great, that the present approximations are insufficient to merit moral approval of the policies of the government.

A third use of scripture as a revealed morality would be stated as follows: Those actions of persons and groups are to be judged morally wrong which are similar to actions that are judged to be wrong or against God's will under similar circumstances in scripture, or are discordant with actions judged to be right or in accord with God's will in scripture. Here the method is roughly one of analogy, and it has its share of difficulties. One is the problem of providing persuasive evidence that the circumstances of, for example, a political and military situation in our time are similar in any significant respects to the circumstances in biblical times. A second is the problem of determining which biblical events will be used for purposes of an analogical elucidation of the moral significance of present events. Some prior ethical commitment is likely to determine this choice. For example, one might choose the account of the "liberation" of the Hebrew people from bondage in Egypt as the biblical narrative most applicable to present history. This choice might be made on either one of two separate grounds or on a combination of them. First, it might be judged that the Vietnamese and Cambodian people are like the Hebrew people of old and that American power is like the power of Egypt. With more refined intervening steps provided, we might conclude that intervention in Cambodia is morally wrong just as repression of the Hebrews in Egypt was morally wrong. Second, we might judge that the crucial moral issue of our time, and of biblical times, is that of liberation from oppression and repression. A general moral and biblical theme, namely, liberation, is judged on theological and ethical grounds to be central to Christian ethics. On the basis of this judgment one could turn to scripture to find the historical events which reveal and elucidate this theme, and in turn use these events as analogies for events of the present time which seem to elucidate the same theme.

The primary question in the use of scripture for moral analogies is that of control. If present events are in control, then one first responds to these events and then on the basis of that response seeks biblical events that are similar to the present ones. The predisposition is to seek those events which will confirm one's present judgments. Thus, the choice of the exodus would be more congenial for a negative judgment on present repression of a small power by a great power than would some of the prophetic interpretations of the role of a great power in chastising a lesser power for its violation of God's ways for the nations. The biblical materials would be chosen on the basis of their affinity for a present moral judgment arrived at perhaps independently of biblical considerations. Biblical support could be found for the opinions one has formed on independent ethical bases.

If scripture is in control, then one is faced with the persistent question of which events are most nearly consistent with certain central tendencies of the biblical, theological, and moral witness. One would have to decide whether the Hebrew wars of conquest of Canaan were "truer" to the central themes of biblical morality than was the liberation accomplished by the exodus. (I have been told that the Calvinists in South Africa used the analogy of the chosen people's right to the land of Canaan to justify their expansion into the territory of the Africans in the nineteenth century.) Some theological and ethical principle would have to be judged as normative for the whole of scriptural witness; this would in turn determine which events would be used as analogies normatively proper to current events, and thus as the basis for judging the moral rightness of present actions.

A fourth use of scripture is looser than the first three. It could be stated as follows: Scripture witnesses to a great variety of moral values, moral norms and principles through many different kinds of biblical literature: moral law, visions of the future, historical events, moral precepts, paraenetic instruction, parables, dialogues, wisdom sayings, allegories. They are not in a simple way reducible to a single theme; rather, they are directed to particular historical contexts. The Christian community judges the actions of persons and groups to be morally wrong, or at least deficient, on the basis of reflective discourse about present events *in the light of* appeals to this variety of material as well as to other principles and experiences. Scripture is one of the informing sources for moral judgments, but it is not sufficient in itself to make any particular judgment authoritative.

The obvious problem with this use is its looseness. The questions that were raised about what is in control are also pertinent here. It would be very easy to make a judgment on the basis of feelings or prevailing cultural values and then find *some support for it* in the variety of scripture's texts. The maintenance of any objective authority for the moral witness of the scriptures is difficult if one recognizes the variety of norms and values present there and also the historical character of the occasions in which these emerge. Thus, some efforts at generalization are necessary in order to bring some priorities of biblical morality into focus. The generalizations that are most nearly consistent with certain theological, ethical statements that appear to be more at the heart of the matter in the development of biblical religion would be used. Informed in a general way by biblical faith and morality, as well as by other relevant beliefs and moral commitments, one might judge the Cambodian venture to be wrong and proceed to cite biblical norms and values as corroborative evidence for one's judgment. We admittedly have less than absolute certitude that the judgment is biblically authorized, both because of the variety of material contents in the scriptures and because of the looseness of the way in which it is used. The necessity for appeals to the continuing tradition of Christian morality beyond the closing of the canon is taken for granted, and the fact that biblical morality is in many ways inapplicable, and in other ways wrong, is accepted.

Each of the ways in which the morality in the scripture is used can be given theological justification. Thus, no sharp line can be drawn between primarily moral and primarily theological uses of scripture in Christian ethics. But attention to some of the basically theological uses of scripture in Christian ethics, which subordinate its ethical content to its theological importance, helps us to see the range of opinion. I have argued elsewhere that the most significant alterations in Christian ethics in midtwentieth century took place not as a result of the reassessment of the liberal and optimistic interpretation of human nature, but as a result of the introduction into ethical thinking of the idea of a "God who acts," or a "God who speaks" in particular historical circumstances. Without further elaboration of that, it should be clear that biblical theology provided a framework for the interpretation of the historical events in which men and nations were involved; and out of this interpretation came certain assessments of the moral significance of events, certain clues about how they were to be judged, and what persons ought to do in them. The primary question became not "How ought we to judge this event?" nor even "What ought we to do in this event?" but "What is God doing in this event? What is he saying to us in this event?" Three articles published by H. Richard Niebuhr during World War II have titles which illustrate this: "War as the Judgment of God," "Is God in the War?" and "War as Crucifixion."[6]

The inspiration of a biblical understanding of an active God has to be specified by asking two sorts of questions. First, who is this God who acts? What do we know about him as "subject" or "person" or about his "nature" which will give a clue to the sorts of things he might be doing and saying? Second, what sorts of things has he said and has he done? What does he wish to accomplish by his acting? What do we know about his actions?

Insofar as scripture provides "data" for answering these questions, we are again faced with the task of formulating generalizations based upon a variety of materials.[7] Here we shall only indicate some of the themes that have been used in theological ethics. The theme of liberation currently finds wide usage with reference to the struggle both of black people in the United States and of colonial peoples of the world. "Jesus' work is essentially one of liberation," writes the articulate and influential James H. Cone, in his *Black Theology and Black Power*.[8] This becomes a warrant for both an evaluative description of the situation of black people in America and a normative direction for the activity in which Christians ought to be engaged. The themes of crucifixion and resurrection are used by another influential contemporary theologian, Richard Shaull, of Princeton. These terms provide a theologically warranted framework for interpreting the present course of events in a world of revolutions; the old orders must die in order for new life to be born, a life of hope and justice for all who are oppressed.[9] As does the liberation theme, so the crucifixion and resurrection theme provides a way of describing and evaluating the events of our times, and a normative thrust for the actions of Christians. They ought to be involved in the destruction of oppressive forms of life in order for new life to come into being. Jürgen Moltmann's highlighting of the theme of hope as central to biblical theology, Paul Lehmann's development of God's doing humanizing work, H. Richard Niebuhr's more complex view of God's creative, governing, judging, and redeeming work: each provides a theological ground upon which is constructed both an interpretation of the significance of events and a positive normative thrust with reference to what Christians ought to be doing. James Sellers, in his very suggestive *Theological Ethics,* takes the theme of promise and fulfillment to be central to the biblical witness. Traditional Lutheran theologians have used gospel and law, and orders of creation; Barth offers an interpretation of the God of grace who is yet the commander as a biblical theological foundation.

The use of biblical theological concepts to provide an evaluative description of historical events requires that further moves be made to determine how a particular event is to be judged and what ought to be done in those circumstances. These moves can be made in two ways or in a combination of them. One such move is from the built-in, normative content of the evaluative-descriptive terms to the basis both for moral judgment on the events and for prescriptions or guidelines for action in them. If, in Lehmann's ethics, one discerns what God is doing to make and keep human life human, whatever is not in accord with the human is judged to be wrong, and the prescriptions or guidelines for further action would be whatever is in accord with the human. The second move is a methodological one. In Lehmann's case, for example, the method for discerning both what is morally wrong and what one ought to do is akin in crucial respects to what philosophers designate as moral intuitionism; the judge and actor is sensitive to what God is doing, and in his theonomous conscience he perceives what is wrong and what he ought to do. In the case of others, however, the move from the evaluative-descriptive enterprise to the moral judgment and the prescription for action might involve a more elaborate and rational process of practical moral reasoning. The normative elements in the concepts used for the evaluative description are lifted out in statements of moral principles and values, and their application both to the judgment and to subsequent action is developed according to methods of rational moral argumentation.[10]

How the various biblical theologies of ethics use the morality or ethical teachings found in scripture is contingent upon methodological choices that can be given both theological and philosophical justification. For example, within Barth's theological ethics, it is the command of God, heard by the moral agent, that determines whether something is right or wrong. But this command is not a capricious one; it is likely to be in accord with the moral teachings of the decalogue and of Jesus. These moral teachings provide "prominent lines"; they are not unexceptionable rules or laws of conduct, nor are they moral ideals. They are coherent with the revelation of God in the scriptures; and thus, if one's judgment is not in accord with these prominent lines, it is doubtful whether one is really hearing God's command. More intensive analysis of this issue is not in order here.

The Place of Scripture in Judging the Cambodian Invasion

In the light of the previous analyses, both of the points at which one makes moral judgments and of the ways in which scripture has been used to make them, brief constructive proposals can now proceed. Certain possibilities are ruled out, at least for simple application. For example, use of proof-texts, either as the sole basis for making the judgment or in literalistic support of arguments made on other grounds, is not defensible. To cite the command "Thou shalt not kill" is not sufficient to defend the judgment that the invasion of Cambodia is morally wrong. Indeed, it is better to begin, not with the application of a particular text to a particular problem, but rather with a look at scripture's more pervasive significance.

First, in the largest dimensions, scripture has informed the moral ethos of Western culture, and particularly that of the Christian community. Even when the actual determinative moral ethos is not in accord with the more objectively normative elements of the wider ethos, the latter remains as a point of critical judgment on the former and on particular events. This affirmation involves not only a historical appeal, that scripture has informed the approvable moral values of our culture and religious community, but also a theologically normative appeal. The biblical witnesses testify to religious communities' developing understanding of what God's purposes for man and the world are; with a significant measure of confidence in the scriptures as a developing revelation of God's purposes, the Bible ought to inform the moral ethos of the culture and the church. The moral ethos of church and culture is always in a process of development or change in the light of new historical events and of unfolding awareness of the meaning of biblically informed morality for new issues. Indeed, the contributions of biblical tradition are not only unfolded, but often revised and judged wrong in the light of historical developments; for example, the inferior status of women, the acceptance of slavery, and the support of capital punishment. In this large dimension, then, one's appeal is not directly to scripture as a verbal basis for supporting a judgment that the Cambodian invasion is morally wrong, but rather to the moral values of the culture and the church which have been and ought to be informed by scripture.

Second, scripture provides data and concepts for understanding the human situation, both in terms of its limits and its possibilities. The biblically informed moral judge is not taken aback at the presence of moral evil in the world; he is not surprised that the technical and other achievements of a nation tempt it to pride, that its accumulation of many forms of power tempt it to arrogance, that its activities which are destructive of human well-being are rationalized by appeals to unexceptionable moral values and ends such as freedom and peace for men. Nor is he surprised by his own faulty moral judgments, past and present, for they are in part a result of his finitude: his limitations of time, place, knowledge, insight, sensitivity, and imagination all prohibit him from achieving that position of the "ideal observer" who can judge events as God himself could judge them. They are also a result of his sin: his bondage to nationalistic loyalties, his pride in the achievements of himself and his nation, his failure to consider the purposes of God, his longing to make secure what sustains his good life even at heavy cost to others, all keep him from hitting the moral mark.

Scripture also provides a vision of human possibilities. It gives clues to what God is enabling, as well as requiring, man to be and to do. It not only becomes a basis of confidence in the community of faith that the unknown future is in the care of a Being who is ultimately benevolently disposed toward his creation, but also provides a vision of what the human future ought to be and can be in the care of the God of love, of justice, of peace, of hope. Biblically informed vision sees in the longings for peace and justice that are found in protests against the Cambodian invasion and in the aspirations of oppressed people in the world, a thrust toward the future, not with the illusion that the kingdom is coming, but with the confident hope that present moral and social evils will no longer be tolerated. This scriptural faith disposes the Christian community toward moral seriousness, toward profound dissatisfaction with those events that are destructive of human life and value, toward aspirations for a future which is more fulfilling for all God's creation; and thus toward negative judgment on events which are not consistent with the possibilities that God is creating for man.

Third, and perhaps this is simply a specification of the second, scripture provides an account of the sorts of human actions and events which the morally and religiously serious communities of the past have seen to be in accord and out of accord with the purposes of God for man. Certain generalizations about God's prevailing aspirations and purposes for human life can be formulated on the basis of the scriptural witness. In the light of these generalizations present events can be judged to be more or less in or out of accord with those purposes. One need not appeal to strict analogies between events recorded and interpreted in scripture and events of the present, but rather one can appeal to theological affirmations that are informed and governed by the biblical witness. The purposes of God, as gleaned from the scriptures, provide not only a reason for being morally concerned about the Cambodian invasion but also the basis for moral values and principles in the light of which the events in Cambodia can be judged.

Fourth, the scriptures provide a variety of types of discourse which express the purposes of God as these were understood by the religious communities, and passages can be used as corroborating evidence (but not proof-texts) for the judgments made in the light of the more general theological and ethical principles that are used. Certain moral laws or precepts given in both Testaments can be used as concise specifications of the more general intent derived from scripture and can be brought to bear upon the judgment of particular events. One would not judge the Cambodian invasion to be morally wrong simply because it violates the love commandment; the love commandment is a specification of a moral precept consistent with the biblical understanding of God's will for men, and thus it has a theological backing which is also biblically based. Similarly, one might find that certain narratives of events in which writers understood the judgment of God to be present are applicable to the present historical occasion by way of a rough analogy. But the use of such narratives would be governed by their consistency with the generalizations about God's purposes that are gleaned from the whole of the scriptures. Other forms of discourse could function in a similar manner— parables, wisdom sayings. The appeal to these would not be on the basis of their absolute authority, but both as informing sources of judgment and as corroborations of judgments informed by a variety of appeals.

The procedures I am proposing are not *sola Scriptura* in character. In judging the Cambodian invasion to be morally wrong one is informed by and appeals to many other bases than scripture: to the accounts of what is happening; to an assessment of the motives, intentions, and consequences of what goes on there; to general ethical principles upon which most persons might agree without recourse to biblical backing for them. Indeed, the scriptures are not used as the exclusive source of backing, warrants, and data (to use Kelsey's pattern of analysis) for the moral judgments of the Christian community on the Cambodian invasion. Ultimately for Christian ethics, a biblically informed theology provides the bases for the final test of the validity of particular judgments: For Christians these judgments ought to be consistent, consonant, coherent with the themes that are generalized to be most pervasive or primary to the biblical witness. But this is not to suggest that the judgments are solely derived from the scriptures; rather, there is a dialectic between more intuitive moral judgments and both scriptural and nonscriptural principles and values (recognizing that these latter two are not mutually exclusive); there is a dialectic between principles of judgment which have purely rational justification and which also appeal to the tradition expressed in scripture and developed in the Christian community.

This dialectical process is necessary for several reasons. First, there is a variety of theological and ethical themes in the scriptures themselves; and thus, while theological and ethical themes can be formulated to provide the dominant principles of interpretation for the whole of scripture, the variety itself must not be lost sight of. Biblical theology and ethics, for example, are not exclusively a theology and an ethic of love; thus love cannot become the single principle used to judge events and actions even within scripture.

Second, on theological grounds, themselves backed by scripture, it can be affirmed that the moral responsibility of men, and particularly of men who acknowledge God as lord, is to judge what God is enabling and requiring men to do under the natural, historical, and social conditions in which they live, not simply to apply biblical morality from an ancient time in a casuistic way. Thus, there is awareness of novelty both in the forms of moral evil that exist and in the opportunities for rectifying them. These aspects of novelty have to be taken into account in making a judgment. While the American invasion of Cambodia is not unlike many previous invasions in the history of the world, it is not the same as any other previous invasion in its character.

Third, the process of making a moral judgment about an event is undertaken with reference to principles and values that are widely shared with others outside the Christian community. These principles and values have their own status with practical, if not ultimate theoretical, independence from theological grounds and are properly appealed to in support of a judgment against the Cambodian invasion. The inferences drawn from these principles—the sorts of principles that a rough use of "natural law" has always acknowledged in the Christian tradition (and probably in scripture itself)—are usually consistent with those drawn from scripture. There might be, however, very special claims made upon those who seek to judge events within the framework of biblically informed Christian ethics: In the ethics of discipleship to Jesus Christ, for example, there is a weight of obligation to be willing to suffer and to die for the sake of the needs of the neighbor, or for the sake of the cause of witnessing to the requirements of peace, justice, and love in the world. There is a heavy pull toward the pacifist position, not only because of the primacy of love, but also because of many sayings, actions, and implications from varieties of literature in the New Testament.

In arriving at a moral judgment about the Cambodian invasion, scripture, informing one's particular analysis of that event, would be used at the various points, indicated earlier in the chapter, that moral judgments are made. A brief rehearsal of these points in relation to subsequent developments in the chapter will provide at least the outlines of a fuller account.

First, scripture informs the terms, concepts, or categories that one uses to give an account of the structure and meaning of the historical process of which the Cambodian invasion is a part. How this is done depends upon what theological principles are used (a) to provide generalizations about what the biblical meaning of human history is (or what those meanings are—to suggest pluralism in scripture), and (b) to decide which biblical accounts (precepts, narratives) are pertinent to the particular historical situation in which we now live. Choices made about the meaning of biblical theology are crucial for the interpretation of history. For example, if the theology is one of a struggle between God and the devil in history, and if God is judged to be on the side of Americans, and if the devil is identified with revolutionary forces in the world, then one gets a different account of the meaning of present history from what is derived if God is identified with the revolutionary forces in history, and the devil, or the powers of sin, are identified with American action. Or, if the crucial biblical theme is crucifixion and resurrection, and American action is identified with the powers of recalcitrance and oppression that are being crucified, a particular interpretation of the meaning of our present history is forthcoming.

Second, scripture informs the principles by which one judges the motives given for the justification of the American invasion. If, for example, one judges that the desire to protect American lives is morally insufficient to justify the extension of the war, various appeals that are biblically supported or derived might be cited. The special concern for American lives might be judged immoral because it violates a pressure toward the equal valuation of all human beings in the sight of their Creator and Redeemer, or it violates the principle of love of enemy (with the implication that one cannot easily justify killing persons who are the objects of one's love).

Third, scripture informs the principles and values used to judge the intentions and goals of the invasion in a process similar to the way it informs judgments of motives.

Fourth, scripture informs the principles used to assess the particular circumstances for which reasons are given as sufficient justification for the invasion. If the circumstances at the time of the invasion were judged to be a threat to the freedom of the Vietnamese and Cambodian people, an interesting and complex issue is opened. Part of the argument about it would be more or less factual—is their freedom really being more threatened by the presence of North Vietnamese and Viet Cong military forces than it is by the presence of American and South Vietnamese ones? But other issues which bear more directly on moral concerns are also raised. What sort of freedom are the Americans seeking to defend? What is the place of that sort of freedom in a scale of values that are pertinent to Southeast Asian culture as well as to a scale of values that might be more valid in the West? Should there be assessment not only of threats to freedom, but also of the destruction of life and property, of Cambodian village culture, and of self-determination? Or another line might be taken: Were the circumstances desperate enough to warrant the illegality and immorality of invasion? Scripture could not be used to provide texts which would "prove" that the invasion was wrong, but it could provide (to use Kelsey's terms) data, warrants, and backing for the principles and values that could counter the assessment of those circumstances that were used to justify the actions.

Finally, with reference to the judgment of consequences, one would ask whether the consequences are consistent with the understanding of the fulfillment of human life that a scripturally informed theology would support as being in accord with God's purposes for men. Scripture alone is clearly insufficient as a ground for assessing the consequences, for many historical developments have intervened since biblical times to enlarge the scope of the Christian community's understanding of what human life is meant to be, and particularly under the circumstances of the times in which we live. But one could give biblical data, warrants, and backing for the position that the consequences occurring are not in accord with those ends of man which scripture and the general moral values of mankind both support.

Conclusion

The suggested constructive procedure is more in accord with what I stated earlier to be a looser use of scripture than its use as moral law, moral ideals, or the source of moral analogies. Indeed, it can incorporate elements of each of these within it. It has the problems of the looser use; these ought to be fully acknowledged. The principal problem is to determine how decisive the authority of scripture is for one's moral judgment. Only the two extremes are absolutely precluded: It does not have the authority of verbal inspiration that the religiously conservative defenders of a "revealed morality" would give to it, nor is it totally without relevance to present moral judgments. Within the broad spectrum between the excluded extremes, a number of other judgments are crucial in determining both its authority and how it should be used. Some of these judgments are theological in character; they depend upon choices about what theological themes are central to scripture's understanding of God's work, God's purposes for man, and the human condition. Other judgments determine what moral principles and values are most consistent with the theological framework developed in relation to scripture. Still others are philosophical in character; how we use scripture is determined to some extent by our framework for interpreting the tasks of ethics as a discipline of thought. If it is focused on the assessment of consequences, scripture will be used differently from the way it will be used if its function is to provide unexceptionable rules of conduct. Another question of the authority can be approached by asking whether there is a "method of ethics" in the scripture, and if there is, whether the Christian ethician in the present is bound to its use. The answer I have suggested to the first is that there are several methods of ethics in the Bible; how they will be used is determined by what methods are judged to be consistent with one's theological principles as well as by judgments made on philosophical grounds.

The outcome of this essay on the question of authority of scripture can thus be stated succinctly, but indefinitely. Scripture *alone* is never the final court of appeal for Christian ethics. Its understanding of God and his purposes, of man's condition and needs, of precepts, events, human relationships, however, do provide the basic *orientation* toward particular judgments. Within that orientation many complex procedures and appeals are exercised, and there is room for a great deal of argumentation. The most decisive justification for this looser use of scripture can be stated as follows: The vocation of the Christian community is to discern what God is enabling and requiring man to be and to do in particular natural, historical, and social circumstances. Its moral judgments are made in the light of that fundamental ought, or demand. Thus, scripture deeply informs these judgments in ways I have outlined, but it does not by itself determine what they ought to be. That determination is done by persons and communities as finite moral agents responsible to God.

7

The Relation
of
the Gospels to the Moral Life

The Gospels can be related to morality in three important ways. First, they can be interpreted to provide a theological justification for the moral life. For example, the Farewell Discourses in the fourth Gospel can be interpreted to provide a Christological justification for a morality of love and self-sacrificial service. This can be seen in the author's understanding of the relationship of the love of the Father for the Son, the love of the Son for the disciples, and the Son's commandment that the disciples should love one another.[1] One finds in the fourth Gospel a reason for being moral that is present throughout the scriptures, namely, that in response to the love of God for his creation and redemption, the people ought to be grateful and ought to walk in his way, follow him, and, indeed, imitate his loving deeds in their actions toward one another. The ultimate reason for being moral is that God has shown his love toward man, and thus man, both out of joyous

Reprinted with permission from *Jesus and Man's Hope*, Vol. II., ed. Donald G. Miller and Dikran Y. Hadidian (A Perspective Book; Pittsburgh: Pittsburgh Theological Seminary, 1971), pp. 103-17. Copyright © 1971 Pittsburgh Theological Seminary. This chapter was originally delivered as a lecture at the Pittsburgh Festival on the Gospels held on the 175th anniversary of the Pittsburgh Theological Seminary.

gratitude and out of obligation to God, is to be concerned for the well-being of others.

The second way in which the Gospels can be related to moral life is by interpreting them to provide moral commands, rules, and principles to be applied to particular moral acts. Here I wish to accent not the theological justifications for these commands, rules, and principles, but their function in the determination of particular acts of the members of the community. Theologians, biblical scholars, and others continue to have interminable arguments about how the moral contents of the percepts in the Q materials, for one example, are to be understood, both from the point of view of the intention of the author and from that of the community which responds to them. Are they to be read as a new Torah? Or are they "prominent lines" which give some guidance to the Christian in his choices? Is one to read them as proposing an important but impossible ideal?[2] The authority of these teachings has been defined by scholars in various ways; the Christian community has responded to them in different ways. With all the divergence, however, there has remained a persistent history of receiving them seriously as in some sense important (if not decisive) in the determination of the conduct of the community and its members.

A third way in which the Gospels can be related to the moral life is by interpreting them to influence the development of the "sort of persons" members of the community become. Here I wish to accent not the impact that moral precepts have on the determination of particular acts, but the impact that the Gospels have on the formation of the agent, the person, who acts. The question to be explored is "In what ways do, can, and should the Gospels qualify or accent the persisting characteristics of the person as a moral agent? In what ways do they affect his attitudes, his dispositions, his basic orientation of intentionality toward the world and other persons?"

It is this third way of looking at the relation of the Gospels to moral life that I shall discuss in this chapter. By concentrating on it, I do not intend to suggest that it is either more important than the other two ways, or that in itself it is sufficient to exhaust the moral significance of the Gospels. I am also very much aware of the philosophical and theological difficulties, not to mention those that range into psychology, that inhere in dealing with this subject.

I. A New Testament Warrant for the Task

I believe that there is warrant in the New Testament itself for engaging in this sort of exploration. Two passages in Philippians, each of which poses difficulties in English renderings, have struck me as worth attending to in finding a warrant for the work of this chapter. They are Philippians 1:27 and 2:5.

Writing to the Christians in Philippi, with the intention of encouraging them to maintain unity and strength in the face of opposition, Paul says in 1:27: "Only let your manner of life be worthy of the gospel of Christ." The textual difficulty for my purposes lies in the translation of *politeuesthé*. The Revised Standard Version fixes on "manner of life," which is, for my intentions, convenient, for it suggests not simply individual instances of conduct, but persisting characteristics of life. The King James Version uses "conversation" and *The New English Bible* uses "conduct," both of which are more action-oriented than agent-oriented references, and thus are less useful. Marvin Vincent, in the International Critical Commentary, suggests alternative renderings, "be citizens" or "exercise your citizenship"; the former is agent-oriented, the latter action-oriented. In his translation of the whole passage, however, Vincent says, "I exhort you to bear yourselves as becomes members of the Christian community," which appears to be more agent-oriented.[3] Ernst Lohmeyer uses the German *wandelt*, which is clearly action-oriented.[4] Joachim Gnilka, in the Herder commentary, uses *"Führt euer Gemeindeleben."*[5] This makes clear that it is a corporate manner of life. Karl Barth, in his 1926-27 lectures on the epistle, uses the word state, which is expounded in the following way. "Their state, their 'form,' their bearings must therefore here and now already be under the invisible discipline of that kingdom, must in fact be in accordance with *the* 'state' which is to be reflected in their conduct, 'worthy' of the Gospel."[6] Thus, he also supports an agent-oriented interpretation.

For purposes of this chapter, the point is best made in the Revised Standard Version rendition: the apostle is stating an imperative: "Only let your *manner of life* be worthy of the gospel of Christ."

Philippians 2:5, while perhaps textually more ambiguous, in all renditions seems to be agent-oriented. The King James Version records it: "Have this mind in you which was also in Christ Jesus." The Revised Standard Version says: "Have this mind among yourselves, which you have in Christ Jesus"; this rendition makes the reference more corporate in character. Vincent translates it: "Cherish the disposition which dwelt in Christ Jesus."[7] *The New English Bible* reads: "Let your bearing towards one another arise out of your life in Christ Jesus." Lohmeyer puts it: "*Also seid gesinnt.*"[8] The English terms "mind," "bearing toward one another," and "disposition" all suggest aspects of the agent. As in 1:27, the gospel provides a norm for the sorts of persons Christians are to be. Their manner of life, their dispositions, their bearing toward one another is to arise out of their life in Christ Jesus, and is to be worthy of that gospel.

The manner of life, the bearing, the disposition, clearly refer not only to individual members of the community, but also they are to characterize the relations of the members of the community to each other, and thus characterize the manner of life of the community itself. Thus, the individual members of the community participate in a manner of life that is both gift and task (the well-worn German *Gabe und Aufgabe*). The community, however, could not bear the marks of a particular manner of life without its individual members having certain characteristics.

In the context of the letter to the Philippians the manner or bearing that is counseled is one of humility, self-abnegation, self-emptying. We have one of the most striking passages for an *imitatio Christi* ethic that there is in the New Testament. It is not my intention in this chapter to focus on a single mark of the "bearing" toward one another, such as humility, but rather to indicate that there is warrant in the New Testament for examining the relation of the gospel to the persisting tendencies, dispositions, and intentions of members of the community.

Our interest is not only in finding a New Testament warrant, however, but it is also in addressing the questions raised from the point of view of ethics about the significance of the characteristics of the moral agent for his moral actions. Extensive theological and philosophical justification for such interest cannot be developed in this chapter.[9]

II. The Gospel and the Gospels

If it can be granted that the Philippians texts give warrant for discussing a "manner of life" that is "worthy of the gospel of Christ," or a "bearing toward one another" that "arises out of your life in Christ Jesus," we face, for our purposes here, the question of the relation of the gospel to the Gospels. Such a persistent and difficult theological problem, however, has to receive brief attention here, pivotal though it is. I would make the following assertion: the *gospel* provides a new and characteristic orientation toward God, toward the world, and toward other persons. It provides a fundamental intentionality, or directionality for the person and community of faith. The *Gospels,* in their literary unity as well as variety, provide the engendering provocation, the efficient cause, which brings this new orientation into being, and also provide in the narratives of deeds, in the language of commands, in the illustrative and parabolic discourses, a depiction of the manner of life and the bearing toward one another that arises out of and is worthy of the gospel. The Gospels function in the formation of the Christian as a person in the way that Sallie TeSelle suggests that all literature does: they provide "concrete, varied, and creative depictions of the basic structure of human experience," they create a "vision of life" in relation to God, to the world, and to other persons.[10]

It is increasingly common in contemporary moral philosophy to write about a "way of life," which is beyond full rational justification, and about which, for some persons, decision is king. For example, R. M. Hare, in discussing the justifications for moral decisions, writes:

> Thus, if pressed to justify a decision completely, we have to give a complete specification of the way of life of which it is a part. This complete specification is impossible in practice to give; the nearest attempts are those given by the great religions, especially those which can point to historical persons who carried out the way of life in practice.[11]

What I am suggesting here is that the gospel enables a "way of life," an orientation, intentionality, or directionality toward God, the world, and other persons. Depictions of that way of life are given in the Gospels, which also depict the "engendering deed" (to use Joseph Sittler's term) that makes the way of life possible. There is a significant coherence or consonance between the patterns of life that are depicted and the gospel, the event which brings about the fundamental orientation. The varieties of literature in the Gospels, the Beatitudes and the commands, the parables, the narrations of the actions of Jesus, line out the manner of life that is worthy of the gospel of Christ, the bearing toward one another that arises out of life in Christ Jesus. Since the coherence or consonance exists between the engendering or enabling deed on the one hand and the depiction of the manner of life on the other, there is also a normative or obligatory character to the way of life. Persons whose intentionality is reoriented by the gospel ought to have its marks on their manner of life, their bearing toward one another. Thus, in the scheme, there are three ways that characterize the relation of the Gospels to the manner of life: (1) they enable or engender it (not as final, but as efficient cause); (2) they depict it; and (3) this depiction is, in some sense, normative or obligatory.

To launch into these waters is, I recognize, historically, theologically, and philosophically treacherous. Research on the Gospels by biblical scholars has achieved a high degree of precision and refinement in analysis; yet on crucial points for our purposes, such as the interpretation of particular parables, consensus is limited. How this research is to govern the uses of the Gospels by theologians and Christian ethicians remains a disputed question. Also, in recent decades Protestants have been particularly fearful of saying too much about the manner of life that is worthy of the gospel for fear that the gospel becomes limited to, or primarily an account of, a particular kind of morality. There is an understandable revulsion against those less historically and theologically sophisticated treatments of "Christlike character" or "qualities of life" that are presumably enjoined by the Gospels which had wide popular appeal earlier in the century. Catholic theologians properly raise the question of whether the "manner of life" that is depicted has its authorization only on positivistic historical grounds, that is, on the grounds that Jesus was the founder of a historical community to whose "ethos" Christians bear a loyalty for only historical religious reasons. They are rightly concerned about whether that manner of life does not have to be grounded in "true humanity," in the ontological structures of human existence. And certainly many efforts to delineate a Christian bearing have excessively concentrated on particular characteristics, even as particular New Testament books seem to concentrate on those characteristics that were appropriate under particular circumstances, such as humility in the situation of the church in Philippi, or submissiveness at the time in which 1 Peter was written. Granting the problematics involved, the journey on which we have begun is important to take.

III. Manner or Bearing:
Dispositions and Intentions

To provide some specification to the terms "manner of life" and "bearing toward one another," I shall concentrate on two terms: disposition and intention. The discussion of the nature of the person as moral agent that is involved in this explication is derived from contemporary philosophical literature that deals with the questions of the person as an agent and with the questions of the nature of human acts, though I do not follow any particular philosopher in the way in which I am here working.[12] Simply put, my point is that when one chooses to generalize empirically about a person's or community's manner or bearing, one is likely to point to certain characteristic intentions of their activities and to certain dispositions to act in these particular ways. Generalizations about a manner of life are inferred from characteristic actions; actions are governed by dispositions and intentions.

For purposes of this chapter, I am using the term disposition to refer to a readiness or tendency to act in a certain way. A disposition is a qualification of a person which makes him tend to act in one way rather than in another. There are obvious affinities between my use of the term disposition and the concept of "habitus" in the theology of Thomas Aquinas, particularly when it is recalled that a distinction is drawn between an automatic motor habit that appears to determine an action on the one hand, and those habits which maintain a dependence on consciousness and volition on the other. By disposition I do not intend to suggest an automatic determination of particular acts, but a preferential readiness to act in a certain way, a readiness which requires confirmation and specification by practical moral reasoning.

I am using the term intention with two different references: one is the fundamental directionality of intentiveness which gives coherence and "identity" to a particular person or to a community. The other reference is to the specification of purposes, ends, or directions of particular actions under specific circumstances. As some philosophers put it, intentions are one's "forward-looking reasons" for acting, for exercising one's capacities and powers in a particular way. We shall use primarily the second reference in this chapter, and will note particularly when it is the first, more general reference, that is intended.

IV. The Gospels and Man's
Dispositions and Intentions

How do the Gospels affect the Christian's dispositions and intentions? What sorts of dispositions and intentions do the Gospels form? In our exposition of the ways in which the Gospels affect the "sort of persons" Christians become, we will keep these two questions in mind. Underlying this exploration is the assumption that Christian faith is properly, though only partially, spelled out in terms of trust in and fidelity to God through Jesus Christ.

The person of Jesus Christ is the paradigm for the life of the Christian community and of individual members of the community. It appears to me that this is what Paul assumes in the letter to the Philippians, and what other occurrences of the motif of Christ as pattern or example in the New Testament also assume. Thus, in a sense, the Gospels portray the paradigmatic person, not by stipulating a set of virtue-adjectives for his character, but by depicting the sorts of actions and relations that were thought to be characteristic of him in the community's memory and imagination, and by recording the teachings he was remembered to have delivered. In him there was the embodiment of a way of life, a coherence between his teachings on the one hand, and his person and his actions on the other, that depicts what man is meant to be in his faithfulness and love to God and to others. He was one of those "historical persons who carried out a way of life in practice."[13]

Some attention must be given to the use of the notion of paradigm. In the context of this chapter paradigms refer primarily to examples of a way of life.[14] Paradigms are basic models of a vision of life and of the practice of life, from which follow certain consistent attitudes, outlooks (or "on-looks"), rules or norms of behavior, and specific actions. As I am using the term, the function of a paradigm is not to provide an extrinsic *goal* for a "style of life" toward which one strives in order to embody an increasingly perfect approximation of it in the course of the self-development of his character. Nor is it to provide a timeless *ideal* to which particular actions, dispositions, and intentions are to be conformed. Nor does it function as a universal *rule* of conduct. Rather, the paradigm *in*-forms and *in*-fluences the life of the community and its members as they become what they are under their own circumstances. By *in*-form I wish to suggest more than giving data or information; I wish to suggest a formation of life. By *in*-fluence I wish to suggest a flowing into the life of the community and its members. A paradigm allows for the community and its members to make it their own, to bring it into the texture and fabric of life that exists, conditioned as that is by their historical circumstances, by the sorts of limitations and extensions of particular capacities and powers that exist in persons and communities.

Thus, the paradigm of Christ does not require uniformity among all members of the community; it does not create perfect copies of itself, as if Christians are clones from the genotype of Jesus Christ. Rather, individuals, with their uniqueness and particularity, are informed and influenced by the paradigm of Christ as they live out and develop the capacities that they have acquired through the processes of natural and cultural development. Similarly, the paradigm does not require uniformity in persons or in the community in its attitudes and actions through all times and in all places. For example, there are conditions in which the paradigm informs a response of boldness and those in which it informs humility and even submissiveness. The paradigm does not function as a totally self-sufficient reality which dictates precisely which actions, intentions, and dispositions are right and good under any or all sets of circumstances. Rather, Christ as paradigm, the paradigm of true humanity, of life as its creator and redeemer intends it to be, of life which is lived in perfect trust and obedience to God, *in*-forms and flows into actions, intentions, and dispositions which are governed also by many other specific and situated realities of human experience.

To make a case for Christ as the paradigm of the way of life of the Christian community and its members does not require one to make a case for the *absolute* uniqueness of his teachings relative to rabbinic teachings of his time, or the *absolute* uniqueness of his actions relative to actions of prophets and other religious leaders, or the *absolute* uniqueness of his virtues or dispositions relative to those of other "paradigmatic individuals" in history. The scientific establishment of the absolute historical uniqueness of Christ is not necessary in order for the Gospels to provide paradigms of actions, intentions, and dispositions for the community and its members. Nor is it necessary to depict a single, total por-

trait of Christ out of the several Gospel accounts, though the imagination is prone to develop certain generalizations drawn from his
separate deeds and teachings.[15]

It remains for me to attempt to show how the Gospels provide
three sorts of paradigms for the moral life of the Christian community and its members: paradigms of action, intention, and
disposition.

The narratives of the deeds of Jesus provide the community examples of the sorts of actions under particular circumstances that
are consonant with complete trust in God. Thus, they have a normative force for the community whose own trust is evoked by the
gospel. Through sensitivity to the specificity of the narratives, and
through the exercise of imagination evoked and guided by them,
the members of the community are informed and influenced in
the determination of their own actions by the records of the deeds
of Jesus. The form of their actions is *in*-formed by the actions of
Jesus.

This can be illustrated by one of the Gospel narratives that is
read during Holy Week in the church, namely, the account of
the foot-washing in John 13. The action and dialogue in the
story of Jesus' washing of the disciples' feet is at one and the
same time a paradigm of three interlocking actions. They depict
God's own love for man, his giving of himself for the salvation
and well-being of his people. That depiction is at the same time a
paradigm of the *kind of action that reveals* God's love through his
Son; it is an account of Jesus in word and deed that reveals him
to be the agent of God's love. It also, at the same time, provides
a paradigm of action for members of the community who know
the love of God through the words and deeds of the Son in this
very earthy activity. The love of God enacted in the deeds of the
Son provides the form of action for those who know God's love
through the Son.

The account in John 13 is not primarily written for a moral
purpose. Yet it is an account that flows into and informs the
bearing toward one another that arises out of life in Christ Jesus
and the manner of life that is worthy of the gospel of Christ. It is
one of the most beautiful accounts in the Gospels, evoking an
enabling and compelling power in those who read it and participate in its dramatic reenactments. It depicts the sort of action that
those whose lives are oriented by the gospel ought to be engaged

in, not only in relation to each other in the community's liturgical life, but in relation to others in the world.

From the action and dialogue, one infers the appropriateness of a basic intentionality or direction that is consistent with God's love. Christians ought to have an orientation toward others that issues in actions which meet the needs of men through humble and loving service. As a paradigm of action, the narrative makes its point more concretely than does a statement of the command to love the neighbor. Not only is the appropriate intention pointed to, but an example of what that intention might require under particular circumstances is portrayed. This paradigmatic intentionality can be distinguished in its function in the determination of actions from the provision of a precise rule of conduct. Rather than binding the community and its members to precise rules of behavior, the paradigm flows into and informs them as they are in their own bodily and social particularity, as particular moral agents with particular capacities and limitations, existing in different particular circumstances. Its function can also be distinguished from a strict process of analogical reasoning; it is not as if one can move by analogy (in a strict sense) from the account of John 13 to the particular intentions that are appropriate for the community in its own present circumstances. Rather, moral sensibility and the imagination are exercised in the movement from this paradigm to other occasions of action. The intention inferred from the narrative flows into both the basic orientation of the community and its members and into the formation of their particular purposes or intentions, their "forward-looking reasons" for action under other specific circumstances. It bears upon the decision of what goals are to direct action, and what sorts of consequences ought to be sought in the course of events or the state of affairs in which the action takes place.

From the action and dialogue one also infers the appropriateness of certain dispositions for members of the community. The gospel both enables and requires a readiness to act in the manner exemplified in the account of the foot-washing. The account depicts, evokes, and even commands a qualification of the sorts of persons that those who follow Jesus are to be. Jesus, in his speech and action, expresses dispositions which are consistent with God's love for the world and which are exemplary for those who know the love of God through the Son.

From this narrative a case can be made for at least two of the "virtues of Christ," as H. Richard Niebuhr calls them in a section of his *Christ and Culture* that has rarely been discussed.[16] These are love and humility. "Having loved his own who were in the world, he loved them to the end (John 13:1)." The actions are expressions of a loving disposition, of a tendency in Jesus as a person to do that which makes specific the meaning of love. "If I then, your Lord and Teacher, have washed your feet . . . (vs. 14)." "Jesus, knowing that the Father had given all things into his hands, and that he had come from God and was going to God (vs. 3)," is the sort of person who washes the feet of his followers. The dispositions of love and humility that are pointed to in the actions and dialogue are paradigms both of God's own readiness to loving and humble service and of the manner of life, the bearing toward one another that is to characterize the community and its members. "For I have given you an example, that you also should do as I have done to you (vs. 15)."

The crucifixion of Jesus can be shown to function as a paradigmatic action in a way that is parallel to what I have done with the story of the Passover meal. Jesus acts in perfect obedience to the Father, in perfect fidelity, and in love. To live by the form of the cross is to be enabled to be oriented toward God, the world, and others in a characteristic way. The gospel is, in part, the gospel of the crucifixion. The accounts of the crucifixion are also paradigms of intentions and dispositions that ought to characterize the manner of life, the bearing of the community and its members. They are called to fulfill those purposes which are faithful to the love and purposes of God, to give themselves sacrificially for the sake of the well-being of others and the world. The cross stands as a paradigm which flows into and informs the purposes of the community and its members in their own capacities and in their own circumstances. They are to have a readiness to be faithful to God and to others, to be loving and merciful toward others, to sacrifice their own interests and even lives. Indeed, the apostle Paul suggests the meaning of the paradigm of the cross in his explication of the content of the "mind of Christ." Philippians 2:5-8 in the Revised Standard Version reads:

> Have this mind among yourselves, which you have in Christ Jesus, who, though he was in the form of God, did not count equality with God a thing to be grasped, but emptied himself, taking the form of a servant, being born in the likeness of men. And being found in

human form he humbled himself and became obedient unto death, even death on a cross.

Further development of the thesis of this chapter would require an exploration of various teachings of Jesus—commands, parables, his teaching about the kingdom of God—as paradigms which suggest the appropriateness of certain intentions and dispositions among the community and its members. Time does not permit extension at this point. I hope that at least I have provided a plausible and discussible thesis, namely, that the Gospels provide paradigms of action, intention, and disposition which flow into and inform the manner of life, the bearing toward one another that arises from and is worthy of the gospel.

8

Spiritual Life and Moral Life

Among the many objects of attention for the theologian is the Christian life. It opens itself to all sorts of investigations: empirical studies of its marks have been attempted; somewhat phenomenological accounts of its "style" have had a recent vogue; its social setting in both the church and the world are objects of concern. Traditional theological doctrines open up: man as sinner and yet forgiven, man as graced and in some sense transformed. Its practice in worship and prayer, in institutional organizations can be described.

Moral theologians have often been too busy attending to the demands for rigorous thinking about practical problems to reflect much upon the wellsprings of disposition and action in the Christian community and its members. Ascetic theologians have often been so occupied with the opening of man's vision of God that they have not said much about the relation of the mystical to the moral, of the practice of corporate and private spiritual discipline to the practice of the moral life. It is, however, the "interface" between ascetical and moral theology that I wish to exam-

Originally given as the Sixteenth Annual Robert Cardinal Bellarmine Lecture at St. Louis University School of Divinity, Oct. 20, 1971. Reprinted from *Theology Digest*, XIX, No. 4 (Winter 1971), 296-307. Used by permission.

ine; or perhaps more accurately, it is the relationship of man's orientation to God and his moral orientation to the neighbor that I want to explore.

These are odd terms for a Protestant theologian to be using. And, indeed, they might well be used in the context of this chapter in such a way that Catholics find their precise and traditional meanings warped. Perhaps some novel language, more neutral, would be better. Yet I wish to look at something that Catholicism and Protestantism, and Judaism as well, have assumed all through their histories, namely, that there is an intrinsic and significant relation between piety and morality, between the spiritual life and the moral life, between the practice of one's devotion to God and his service to his neighbor. It is interesting to note that the book whose title comes closest to what I wish to examine, *Worship and Ethics*, is Max Kadushin's account of their relationship in rabbinic Judaism.[1] The apparent reason for writing this book, which is important for our understanding of Jewish ethics, is that, left to philosophical and legal minds, the *halachah* loses its vitality and communal significance as engendering the worship of God as well as right behavior to others.

Worship and Morality

Scripture provides ample evidence that the people of God could never separate what philosophers sometimes wish to distinguish as "religious acts" and "moral acts." That the community and its members were doing something different at the altar than they were when they justly paid the hireling his wages at the end of the day is clear, but it is also clear that they assumed a significant connection between the two. (I have, in a paper, "Religion and Morality from the Perspective of Theology," sought to indicate that the facile distinction between the two made by contemporary philosophers simply founders on the texts of the great Western religions.) Both the most sophisticated theologians of the Christian tradition and the writers of the manuals of piety and devotion, though not all in the same way, assumed that there are reciprocal relations between the spiritual life and the moral life. We might find the claim of Bishop K. E. Kirk to be too sweeping, but his great book *The Vision of God* is a major source in non-Roman Catholic theology for grasping what these relations are. Kirk wrote:

> The doctrine "the end of life is the vision of God" has throughout
> been interpreted by Christian thought at its best as implying in
> practice that the highest prerogative of the Christian, in this life as
> well as hereafter, is the activity of *worship;* and that nowhere ex-
> cept in this activity will he find the key to his ethical problems. As a
> practical corollary it follows that the principal duty of the Christian
> moralist is to stimulate the spirit of worship in those to whom he
> addresses himself, rather than to set before them codes of behavior.[2]

Too sweeping indeed. But if the *principal* duty of the Christian
moralist is not to stimulate the spirit of worship, perhaps in fact
it is the *most neglected* among his duties.

Experience of and Orientation Toward God

The more problematic that God as an object of belief and experience for man becomes, the more meaningless that worship
becomes. The more problematic that experience and belief in
God become, the more fragile the tone and quality of the moral
life of the Christian community become. Indeed, the moral arguments and actions of the community and its members take place
in a different context when awareness of the transcendent is lost:
persons become means rather than ends, sin becomes infraction
of moral rules rather than a denial of God; the end of action becomes an increased quantity of moral goodness rather than the
glorification of the goodness of God; casuistry becomes computer-
like problem-solving rather than man's earnest search for God's
will and purposes; the spirit of technical logic and technical
manipulation evaporates the spirit of awe, of wonder, and of mystery. Man loses his sense of finiteness, not to mention sin, and dis-
places God the Absolute. Without the experience of the Holy,
Christian moral life withers.

The principal point of distinctiveness for the moral life of religious communities is precisely their openness to and awareness of
God. It is the recognition that man's dependence is not merely on
other persons, on the world of nature of which he is a part, on
legal and social institutions, but also in and through these on the
power and goodness from which all things flow, in which all
things are grounded. Man's gratitude is given not only to those
whose love and care bring him into being and sustain his life,
but to God who brings all life into being and is its ultimate sus-

tainer. Man's guilt is caused not only by the suffering he causes others through his misdeeds, but by his failure to relate himself conscientiously in trust and in faithfulness to God's purposes for him and for all of creation. Man's repentance is not only before those who are the victims of his heedlessness, his insensitivity, and his overt and selfish wrath and destructiveness; his repentance is before God who wills and enables that he be other than as he is. Man's obligation is not only to those who have some social authority over him, or those whose very being in dependence upon him makes a moral claim; his obligation is to God as God's deputy in the care and nurture of life. Man's orientation is not only toward what will restrain evil in the world, or what will bring moral well-being to his fellows; his orientation is toward God that his goodness might be glorified in the order of life in the world and in the deeds of individual men. Man's love is not only for his wife, his family, his friends, his country, his church, the beauty of nature and of humanly created things around him, or even for humanity itself; God whose love makes possible all other objects of human life is the ultimate object of man's loves. Man's respect for the rights of others, his concerns to overcome injustices in the world, are grounded not merely in his perceptions that human well-being will come from adhering to these, but also from the conviction that others have rights because they are creatures of God's goodness, and that justice is a fundamental requisite for human peace because it is in accord with God's purposes for man.

Thesis

It is the single and simple thesis of this chapter that, apart from the individual and corporate disciplines of the spiritual life of the Christian community, its sense of the Holy, of the transcendent, withers; when its sense of the transcendent withers, the distinctive tone and quality of its moral activity is lost. Indeed, not only *how* it decides and acts is altered; the ends that it seeks to achieve and the limits on means that it imposes on itself might also be altered. *What* it does might also be altered. I am not prepared to assert and argue that a "spiritual" community is necessarily a better moral community, or that the "spirit of worship" (to use Bishop Kirk's terms) is in itself the sufficient condition for a morally praiseworthy Christian community. The history of piety and morality in the Christian community is replete with evidences that would counter such assertions. Too often a consciousness of orientation toward God has led to insensitivity to the needs of men; too often men who have claimed a special and privileged access to God have claimed also a moral certitude which has often been distorted and even perverse. Nor am I prepared to assert and argue that the moral conditions of the world—the injustices in social structures, for example—would be rectified if only the spiritual life of the Christian community were vivified. That would make the worship of God a technique for moral improvement, which is clearly a distortion of the reasons for worship, and would also be a mistaken prediction.

Basic Assumption

It is clear that the resolution of the problematic of "God-talk" (the term is itself a trivialization of the seriousness and passion that I would assume it would have for anyone for whom much is at stake) is crucial for the thesis of this essay. Minds of far greater power and learning than mine have addressed and continue to address that issue. If unbelief turns out to be truer than belief, if atheism turns out to be more honest than trust in God, all I will have said in this chapter could be subsumed under "the consequences of a useful fiction for the moral life." Similarly, it is clear that if persons who have an awareness and experience of the transcendent are merely the victims of their individual or collective unconscious, and that the spiritual life is "caused" by culturally available symbols for controlling and directing psychic drives, all I will have said could be subsumed under "the consequences of a relatively harmless neurosis for the moral life." We shall beg these prior and important questions. We work from the platform assumption that experience and awareness of the transcendent is a real relationship between human subjects and the reality of God, a "power bearing down" on them.[3]

The focus of our attention, in any case, is primarily upon the human subjects, that is, on the significance of their spiritual lives in their awareness of an orientation toward God for their moral lives. That the meaning of God is given in Christian and Jewish terms is, of course, crucial. To be aware of and oriented toward God as known in Hindu tradition leads to different sorts of both spiritual and moral life. But that is not our primary concern.

A Correlative Enterprise

In developing the theme more specifically, I wish to correlate three points of reference in the Christian life. The central point is certain senses, sorts of awareness or qualities of spirit, which the spiritual life engenders, sustains, and renews. The terms that I use here are not exhaustive: they are neither precisely fixed on the theological virtues nor on the gifts of the Spirit as these have been developed in Catholic theology. Nor is there time to develop all the ramifications even of the terms I choose and their relations to each other. But central in our correlative enterprise are the following sorts of awareness and/or qualities of spirit: a sense of radical dependence, a sense of gratitude, a sense of repentance, a sense of obligaton, and a sense of direction. It is my primary assertion that the life of worship and devotion to God as he is known in the Jewish and Christian tradition, that the Christian experience of the Holy, engenders and nourishes these senses or qualities of the human spirit.

While I desire not to be mechanically schematic about things which are organic in their relationships, for purposes of clarity I shall correlate each of these senses with the second point of reference, namely, certain experiences of God and beliefs about God. Thus, to provide an outline: the sense of radical dependence is correlated with our experience of and belief in God as creator; the sense of gratitude is correlated with the experience of God as beneficent, as good, in his creation, sustenance, and redemption of the world; the sense of repentance is correlated with the experience of God as judge; the sense of obligation with the experience of God as orderer and sustainer of life; the sense of direction with the experience of God as the end, the telos, of all creation.

The excessive schematization of this, it must be forewarned, is humanly and theologically dangerous, for on the theological side it is *one God* whom we experience, whose being, presence, activity, and relatedness to man cannot be separated into discrete aspects of creator, judge, end, and so forth, and into distinctive moments of being creator at one time and end at another. Theology, and even morality, often get into trouble when useful distinctions become separate aspects or moments, such as those that are made between God as creator and God as redeemer, between moments of his activity as being creative at one time and being redemptive at another. The schematization is humanly dangerous as well, and in principle for the same reason, namely, that while there are moments when the sense of gratitude is more overwhelming than the sense of repentance, the two are intrinsically related to each other in the experience of God.

The third point of reference in our three-way correlation is the predispositions to view life and to act in certain ways morally. Precision and clarity of terminology is extraordinarily difficult at this juncture. There are certain dispositions or tendencies which have significant consequences for how one lives morally that are correlated with these senses of dependence, gratitude, and so forth; "how one lives morally" not only in terms of what one does, but in one's perspective, outlook, deliberation, and motivation. Again, schematization is dangerous, but it provides an outline for further development. The sense of dependence is correlated with awareness of both finiteness and trust. Finiteness engenders self-criticism, knowledge of limitations, recognition of relativity, reins on claims to moral certitude. Trust engenders confidence even within finiteness; it engenders responsibility as deputies of the creator. The sense of gratitude engenders both a reason to be moral and a movement of the will to do: it provides a reason and an empowering of the will to be imitators of God, to be doing with and for others deeds in accordance with what God has done for man. The sense of repentance engenders again self-criticism, but also a returning toward the moral purposes that are in accord with God's will. The sense of obligation engenders awareness of both duties and opportunities in the moral sphere, and an awareness of the accountability of the community before God. The sense of direction opens the path through the thickets of human moral experience toward an end which is both spiritual and moral at once.

Our task now is to develop briefly, but hopefully in a suggestive way, each of these correlations, and finally to indicate that the disciplines of the spiritual life, individual and collective, are a necessary condition for them all, and thus for the Christian moral life.[4]

A Sense of Dependence

Man's situation is experienced as one of being dependent upon the author, power, and purpose of life, that is, on God. We have not chosen to be; we have come into being. To be sure, there are increasingly precise explanations of how not only we as individuals, but also of how the world itself came into being. The significance of our sense of dependence is not that of a causal explanation of how we and the world have come into being. Rather, it is in the experience of necessarily being reliant upon others than ourselves. We live in reliance upon our parents, upon our families and friends, upon the order of nature, and upon the cultural order that men have developed. In the Christian experience of life these are experiences which open our awareness of the Holy, of our reliance upon a power and purpose on whom all things depend.

The sense of dependence, it must be admitted, is a morally ambiguous one. It can become oppressive if it entails a coercive domination of the dependent creature by the one on whom he relies. It can stifle initiative and freedom of action by providing subtle life-destroying forms of paternalism. It can foster immaturity. It can paralyze a needed sense of self-confidence, for with it comes awareness of human limitations.

The experience of God in Jewish and Christian traditions is construed, however, in ways which can engender a morally worthy sense of dependence. The creator who brings into being and sustains the world is one whose creation is fundamentally good, whose purposes are the well-being of the world and of persons. Our experience of God creates and preserves a double response: first, that God is God and man is man, that his ways are not our ways, and his thoughts our thoughts; but also that God is worthy of our trust, our confidence, for his power and purpose ultimately favor the fulfillment of creation. Thus, our moral lives are lived in awareness of our finiteness, but also in a sense of trust and confidence.

Our awareness of finiteness keeps us from falsely absolutizing any of our moral values and principles, from claiming for ourselves as individuals or for our communities and institutions a dogmatic moral certitude that cannot err, and to which all men are obligated to pay homage. Our finiteness forces upon the community constant critical self-evaluation, constant need for the use of the subjunctive mode, constant willingness to admit moral mistakes. But it also creates the resources of openness to change, the readiness to learn what are the moral requirements under new and changing conditions in our lives and in the circumstances in which we are called to act. In short, it restrains our tendency to impose uncritically upon tomorrow the moral certitudes that fill another time, another cultural place, another historical condition; yet at the same time it evokes the disposition to search for the moral requirements that are concretely related to our conditions, the developments in our society and culture, the path through the entangled moral forest in which we live.

But dependence also evokes trust or confidence. The biblical pastoral imagery may still resonate the point better than more abstract terms. To be dependent upon God is to be like the sheep who can rely upon the sheepherder; it is to live in a confidence that there is one who accepts accountability for their conditions, who wills to provide their care, who seeks their well-being. Indeed, as the Christian community is reliant upon God, so are others reliant upon its members, that is, not only is there a ground for confidence, but (to indicate the interrelation of things) obligations to others come into being as we are obligated to God in whom we have confidence. Confidence in God provides a ground for living morally, even in finiteness, with courage, with willingness to risk, with a sense of inner freedom to seek the good and the right even under the conditions of finiteness.

A Sense of Gratitude

It is difficult in our experience of God to speak of dependence without at the same time speaking of gratitude, for the reality on whom we ultimately rely is one whose purposes for his creation are good, who wills the fulfillment of that which has been brought into being. If the experience of an ultimate power were not the experience of a beneficent power, there would be no occasion for gratitude.

There is in this particular aspect of believing and experiencing, as in others, a matter of trust and of hope which is only in part confirmed in human experience, both individually and collectively. Honesty requires the admission that it is difficult to be grateful to God for life when it gives no concrete opportunities for human fulfillment, when those who have been sustaining and meaningful to us are brutally taken away, and when whole communities are suppressed and destroyed by the demonic and destructive activities of men, and indeed, of nature. Conscientious religious men have a quarrel with God not only after Auschwitz but after earthquakes, not only in the midst of an unjust war but after assassinations of leaders who have symbolized hope and justice and peace. Like Job and Jeremiah, we too have occasion to curse God for the day that we were born. To gloss over such human experiences would be to engage in cheap religious rhetoric.

Nonetheless, the occasions for gratitude, though they come in small sizes and with less frequency than we might desire, remain as some testimony to the goodness of life and even evoke our celebration. For all our anxieties and struggles, we are grateful to be, to exist. Most of us have been loved beyond our deserving, forgiven when we dared not believe it possible, sustained by the patience of others when they have had grounds to reject us. We have received from the sustaining powers of the sun and the earth, the social order and the culture, more than we could ever claim to deserve. These experiences point to the goodness of God, and they confirm the goodness which we dimly apprehend. And we are grateful.

Gratitude, like dependence, can be oppressive and destructive if it carries also an obligation to cower before those who have given life to us. But it can be liberating if the gifts we receive are given freely, graciously, and in love, rather than as bribes or for the self-glorification of the giver. This is the importance of the experience of God as beneficent and gracious: what is given is freely given in love. It is not merely what we earn by our accomplishments, but it is already there for us to respond to, to appropriate, to participate in.

The experience of gratitude is a pivot on which our awareness of God's goodness turns toward our life as moral men and communities. What is given is not ours to dispose of as if we created it, nor ours to use to serve only our own interests, to mutilate, wantonly destroy, and to deprive others of. Rather, if life is given in grace and freedom and love, we are to care for it and share it graciously, freely, and in love. I believe this is at the heart of religious morality in the Western world; God has been good to us, and in gratitude to him we have reason enough to seek the good of others, and are moved to do so. This is a central theme in the ethics of both Judaism and Christianity: the imitation of God, "Go and do likewise."

A Sense of Repentance

Throughout the recorded history of man's experience of God

there are indications of man's need for, and experience of, repentance. We have denied our dependence on God and his goodness, and have used his gifts not only for our own interests, but to destroy and cripple the lives of others. We have assumed dominion over the earth, as we are called to do, but have ignored the dependence that is involved in this vocation: we have been the spoilers rather than the tenders of nature, we have been dictators rather than deputies in our relations to others, we have acted as masters rather than as servants, we have put other gods before the beneficent creator. In this God is experienced as the judge. Life is wantonly taken that God wills be treated honestly, the teaching which shows a way of life has been violated, injustice in both the patterns of life and in individual deeds is dissonant with the justice of God. The call of the prophets, of Jesus, of the Jewish and Christian communities is a call to repentance. It strikes a responsive note, for there is already in man an awareness of the abrasiveness between what he has done and the goodness of God. We experience God as judge.

The sense of repentance is not only a sense of guilt; it is a call to return to the Lord, to the purposes of personal and common life that are consonant with God's goodness. It is a turning to those ways which sustain and enhance the moral well-being of the human community. Like the sense of gratitude, it grounds not only a reason for moral concern and action (I ought to be reoriented toward those ends which are in accord with God's goodness because God wills and enables not only my forgiveness but my renewal), but it also grounds the will to act. Like the sense of gratitude, it has an existential or sense aspect that has moving power.

A Sense of Obligation

The experience of the reality of God engenders a sense of obligation in persons and in the religious community. In part this arises out of the sense of dependence. To be reliant on God whose goodness is experienced is not only to be grateful to him, but to recognize that one has obligations to him for sustaining and caring for life. But the particular aspect of the experience of God that evokes a sense of obligation is that of an ordering and sustaining power reflected in the ordering and sustaining requirements of creation both in nature and in human societies. In more specifically profane experience we gain the recognition that there are obligations and duties that we must fulfill in order for personal and communal well-being to exist. We know, for example, that if we do not order the common life in such a way that justice prevails more than injustice, persons and whole communities are deprived of the opportunities to share in the benefits of creation, and in their frustration are rightfully moved to unpeaceful activities for the sake of their common good. We know that the presence of others in our relationships in family, or in academic communities, or anywhere, whose well-being depends upon us is itself a claim of obligation upon us. We recognize that we must conform our actions to that ordering of life that is required if we are not to destroy the natural world upon which our lives and those of future generations depend. While we cannot say that evidence of the need for sustaining and ordering activities and structures is evidence for God's reality, we can say that in our experience of God, we recognize that he is present in such ordering, and that we are obligated to him to attend to the proper ordering of life about us.[5]

We must acknowledge that the language of duties and obligations is often resisted in our current culture. There are ample evidences that many persons believe they ought to do only what they immediately desire to do. And there are good as well as bad reasons to support such an outlook; the moral life has too frequently been taught to be one of bending one's desires and wills to the extrinsic authority of others, who by reason of their social position or claims to absolute moral truth have dictated what ought to be done and have demanded obedience only by threat of punishment. Consciences have been deformed, spontaneity has been repressed, and morality has been seen to be negative rather than positive in its ultimate aims. The Eichmanns of this world have claimed moral rectitude because they obeyed orders.

In the face of this a claim is made in the religious moral life that the ordering and sustaining forces to which man is called to conform seek the well-being of persons, human communities, and the whole of creation. We are obligated and accountable to God, the power and purpose who grounds life, as he is experienced and known through the developments in understanding that come through historical experience. Thus, order*ing*, rather than order. His purposes do not come with full clarity in a single moment of history but through our participation in life together with our conscientious wrestling with the moral purposes of God. We are obligated to seek to discern God's ordering and sustaining purposes and to shape our moral intentions in their light. We are obligated to seek just orders because God's purposes are just, and justice is a requirement of the fulfillment he wills for man. We are *obligated* to seek justice, even when it obstructs our own immediate interests, or those of our people, or even our generation. To experience God as orderer and sustainer is to have a sense of obligation, not only to him, but to the creation he orders and sustains. It is to be morally conscientious in developing and preserving those human orderings which sustain the good of man. It is to be obligated to the one to whom we are grateful, of whose love we are the beneficiaries; it is obligation within the context of grace and love.

A Sense of Direction

If a gross distinction is at all warranted between the Catholic understanding of the moral life and that which came from Luther (Calvin is more complex), it is that for the Lutheran tradition the moral life of the man of faith was an expression of his trust in the graciousness of God and took the form of an inwardly motivated love of the neighbor, whereas in the Catholic tradition man's natural orientation toward his end and his graced orientation toward the vision of God both motivated and directed the moral life of the community. Put even more crudely, one can conceive of moral life in Lutheran terms as being moved from within to do expressive acts of love with little attention given to the object of the act; one can conceive of moral life in Catholic terms as being drawn by the object toward those acts which are appropriate to it, the ultimate object being God.

The experience of God as the end and as the object toward which life is oriented provides a sense of direction. Insofar as each of us has coherence and integrity in our lives, it is in part dependent upon a consistency in his intentions, an orientation of his will toward certain ends. We look forward toward an end, as well as backward toward the antecedents of our actions. We are creators of vision, drawn by aspirations for the future of man; we are creatures of love drawn toward the objects of our deepest desires. In our behavior over a period of time we express to others what our visions and aspirations are, what the objects of our most profound loves are. In the experience of religious men there is an awareness of aspiration to fulfill the vocation of humanity in accord with the purposes of God; there is a love of beings which opens to a love of Being itself, to allude to the vision of Jonathan Edwards. Indeed, we can sing with Charles Wesley of a "Love divine, all loves excelling," which we have received and which evokes in turn our love of God, our orientation toward him. God, as the ultimate object of our love and loves, is the end toward which our lives are oriented, our intention turned, our desires directed. And not only individual loves and desires—since we are members of a community, he is the object of our social actions as well.

Catholic theology has long understood that the wrong object of our intentions and our loves leads to wrong actions in the moral life. If the fundamental purpose of life is to fulfill maximally the desire for sensual pleasure, and persons are means to that fulfillment, life may have a consistency, a sense of direction, but it does not redound to the benefit of the human community, but only to that of the individual. If one is driven by the aspiration to tyrannize over others, to dominate as much of the world as one can, there might well be a consistency, but its end does not lead to the fruits of justice and peace and love. If the ultimate objective of our scientific enterprises is to bring all things under our control, to be God, then our actions are likely to be destructive. We can then learn from the aphorism of Paul Ramsey, "Men ought not to play God until they have learned to become men, and when they have learned to become men they will not play God." The object of our deepest longing, the object of our most pervasive desire, our ultimate end, is to a great degree determinative of the moral worthiness of our acts. It is not that man is a creature oriented toward an end that is important to consider, but that the end toward which he is oriented be the proper one for him and his community.

The experience of the Holy, of the presence of God, in and through others whom we more immediately know and respond to, is central to the religious life. Beyond the good of the human community which we seek is the goodness of God to which we respond in love for him. Beyond our orientation toward the needs of the neighbor is the presence and power of God which is glorified in meeting those needs. The experience of God as the end of all our actions, as the object toward which life is oriented, provides a sense of direction.

If nothing could be affirmed about his reality and characteristics from the religious life of the ages, there would be little we could infer for our moral direction. But in the history of our community's life with him, in the moments in which there is an acute disclosure of him, there is insight into what is ultimately a mystery. To be oriented toward God is to seek those moral ends which are consistent with his reality, with our knowledge of his purposes for creation. As the Johannine epistles make so clear, to love God who loves us, and yet to be creatures whose acts are those of hatred is a lie. Put positively, to be oriented toward God who is loving, who is just, who wills the fulfillment of his creation, is to be oriented in our moral lives toward the needs of near and distant neighbors, to seek justice for all men, to be aimed in our actions toward what benefits the well-being of the human community in its interdependence with nature.

Worship, Meditative Prayer, and Moral Life

I think it is abundantly clear how these explorations will be completed in this chapter. The existential question is how to keep the experience of the Holy alive and vital in our preoccupations with all the specific activities that conscientiousness requires from day to day. It is how to keep that sense of reverence and respect for other persons and for nature alive when most of our relationships are those of use. It is how to maintain a sense of awe in the midst of cultural successes in which we manage and manipulate everything from human genes to arriving on the moon. I hope I have established that the awareness and experience of God is important as a ground for these "senses" of which I have spoken, and that these "senses" are significant for our moral lives. I am not prepared to say with Bishop Kirk that "the *principal* duty of the Christian moralist is to stimulate the spirit of worship in those to whom he addresses himself," but I am prepared to say that worship and meditative prayer are fundamental requisites of the Christian moral life.

It is in worship and meditative prayer (or prayerful meditation, if you will) that the presence of the Holy, the sense of the sacred, the awareness of the transcendent, can be evoked and renewed in individuals and in the community. It is in the freedom from immediate demands that one is open to the reality of God in a compelling and moving way. It is in the focus of attention upon the Reality in whom all realities exist, upon the

Power on whom all powers depend, on the events in which God's love has been peculiarly disclosed to men, that the community is renewed and nourished in its spiritual life, and thus in its moral life as well. The senses of dependence, gratitude, repentance, obligation, and direction become atrophied, warped, under-nourished, apart from their evocation and refreshment in attentive meditation, and worship of God. This is not to make worship and prayer means to a better moral life. But it is to affirm that apart from worship the spiritual roots of the moral life of the Christian community, the spirit out of which and in which its members act, loses its disinctive character.

After writing this essay I participated in an unusual and confusing evening. It was the program for the presentation of Kennedy Foundation Awards for contributions to the cure and care of the mentally retarded. We honored the achievements of B. F. Skinner in reinforcing useful behavior in homes for the retarded, we honored the achievements of the developers of rubella vaccine, and others. We heard Donovan sing folk songs, Loren Hollander play a Prokofiev sonata, Beverly Sills sing operatic arias, David Frost crack jokes, Joan Kennedy play Debussy. But if a standing ovation is an expression of respect and honor, it was only the humble Mother Theresa of Calcutta who moved a diverse crowd to its feet. Why? No doubt for different reasons, among them sentimentality, but surely chief among them was the awareness that her piety and her moral activity were one and the same, and that her laudable activity could not be understood apart from her devotion to God. For her, spiritual and moral life were demonstrably unified.

9

The Relevance of Historical Understanding

Students of ethics, whether Christian ethics or other sorts, have a strong inclination to neglect history. Critical moral philosophy, almost by definition, is concerned with formal questions—with the structure of arguments, with issues of logical consistency and precision of thought. As the New Critics in literature counseled their students to go to the texts rather than to the biographies of authors or to the study of their times, so the students of ethics have also tended to study texts as if they were not conditioned by the life history of their authors and the social conditions under which they were written. How many articles does one read on the just-war theory, for example, which do not consider the political and military situations in which the theorists existed when they wrote? To be sure, there is a weightier pressure on the practical moralist to consider the contemporary historical conditions about which he makes judgments and in which he counsels certain forms of action; but even such writers sometimes are limited by the lack of awareness that these moral issues, or similar ones, have been addressed in particular historical contexts in the past.

Reprinted by permission from *Toward a Discipline of Social Ethics: Essays in Honor of Walter George Muelder*, ed. Paul Deats, Jr. (Boston: Boston University Press, 1972).

An intellectual giant now dead for half a century, namely, Ernst Troeltsch, made clear to his readers that historical understanding was important for the study of ethics, and particularly the study of Christian ethics. This great historian, philosopher, and theologian had more impact on Christian ethical thought in America than he did in his native Germany. One looks in vain for a successor to Troeltsch in German theological and social ethics; that is, one does not find in the German literature anyone whose major efforts were directed toward assessing the interactions between cultural developments, historical circumstances and events, theology, ecclesiology, and ethical teachings. The reasons for this would make an interesting investigation, but would take us far afield.

In the United States the impact of Troeltsch has continued through the influence of some of the most important teachers of Christian theology and ethics during the past fifty years. H. Richard Niebuhr at Yale and Walter Mueder at Boston University both wrote dissertations on Troeltsch, and both were teachers of many persons working in the field of Christian ethics today.[1] Troeltsch's impact on their writings was persistent; for both, the sociohistorical matrix of Christian ethical thought was kept in view, although each of them resolved the Troeltschian theological problematic in a different way. James Luther Adams, at the University of Chicago and at Harvard University, led many students, including this author, into serious encounters with Troeltsch and his patterns of thought, not only in *The Social Teaching of the Christian Churches,* but also in important essays in the other volumes of the *Gesammelte Schriften.*[2] Adams' own interests and scope have been as broad as Troeltsch's, and he has sponsored English translations of many of Troeltsch's essays. Wilhelm Pauck, the only one mentioned here who was actually a student in Troeltsch's classes—at Chicago and at Union Seminary in New York—always made it clear that he stood for the historical rather than the dogmatic method in theology and had many students read Troeltsch on that issue. His classroom claim during the height of the influence of Karl Barth—that Barth failed to come to grips with Troeltsch's problematic—is probably borne out by recent developments in theology.

The purpose of this essay, however, is not to discuss Troeltsch or his influence on American theology and ethics. Rather, it is to look at the continuing importance of the Troeltschian perspective, namely, the relevance of historical understanding for scholarly work in Christian ethics. Three aspects of this relevance are attended to in this essay: (1) the importance of knowing the historical context in which religious ethical ideas were formulated in order properly to understand them; (2) the importance of, and difficulties in, using historical analogies in formulating constructive ethical positions; and (3) the freedom to be historically situated and aware of the press of historical circumstances on one's own ethical judgments.

The Importance of Historical Settings

Historical studies of themes in Christian ethics are lamentably few in number and do not begin to attend to all the facets that are interesting and important. Studies of teachings about particular moral problems are a case in point. There are useful studies, for example, a volume edited by Joseph Fletcher on property, the work of Roland Bainton on war, religious liberty, and sex, Schillebeeckx's study of marriage, the treatments of usury by Benjamin Nelson and John Noonan, Noonan's work on contraception and abortion, and others.[3] But with occasional significant exceptions, these are sketchy treatments, and the range of topics by no means exhausts the possibilities for research. Studies of theological ethical themes are also few in number, and none of them is very recent: Anders Nygren's *Agape and Eros,* Newton Flew's *The Idea of Perfection,* K. E. Kirk's *The Vision of God,* and N. P. Williams' *The Ideas of the Fall and Original Sin,* are perhaps most prominent.[4] But many comprehensive studies are lacking; for example, there is no first-rate history of natural-law theory available in English.

Many of these books are written in the mode of the history of ideas; indeed, they are literary histories of ideas, histories which study documents but do not set the documents in the historical contexts out of which they emerged. While some of them engage in the historian's task of analyzing the influences of antecedent texts upon subsequent ones, others are more clearly ideal-typical in method. No demeaning of the significance of these approaches is intended by observing that they might lead to seriously mistaken impressions: for example, that a theologian's writings about love or property were not reactions to events in his time as well as to other writings of his time; or that one can understand teachings about war or property without understanding the sorts of wars and the economic conditions that existed when the teachings were articulated. Many of these studies need supplementation from the Troeltschian point of view that ethical ideas are formulated in a complex historical matrix—a culture, a society, historical events, theological polemics, an ecclesiological and ecclesiastical setting, philosophical currents, and other matters. Ethical thinkers, perhaps by predilection oriented toward abstract ideas, are prone to deal with texts as if the historical context is of little significance for understanding them.[5] A reader may know, for example, that Augustine's *The City of God* was written while the Roman Empire was under its most severe threat; but he probably does not know much about those historical events or what their import is for accurately understanding that classic in Christian theology and ethics.

Two important studies of the ethics of birth control are illustrative of our concern: David M. Feldman's *Birth Control and Jewish Law* and John Noonan's *Contraception*.[6] In some respects it is unfair to compare these two. Feldman's method is the *halachic* one, and is appropriate to both the subject matter of Jewish law and to his own profession as a rabbi. Noonan's work is a study of the Christian Catholic tradition by a historian of law. But they do invite comparison for a number of reasons: birth control is their common subject, the Western religious traditions have a common root, and the role of law—Jewish and canon— is central to both. Each has made an indispensable contribution to our knowledge of the historical background of matters of contemporary importance. But there are differences in their uses of historical contexts which illustrate our concern.

Both Noonan and Feldman have texts as their basic data. The extended subtitle of the Jewish study is: "Marital Relations, Contraception, and Abortion as set forth in the classic texts of Jewish Law. An examination of the relevant precepts of the Talmud, Codes, Commentaries, and, especially, rabbinic Responsa through the present day, with comparative reference to the Christian exegetical tradition." Noonan's briefer subtitle is: "A History of Its Treatment by Catholic Theologians and Canonists." Both are clearly literary histories. It is the difference in approaches to literary history that is important to note; a richer and more intensive use of a broader historical context characterizes Noonan's work, and thus enables the reader to understand not only what particular canonists and theologians said, but the reasons for saying what they did at the time that they said it.

Perhaps Feldman assumed that the reader, or at least the Jewish reader, of his book was familiar with the detailed contexts in which the writers he cites produced their works; and thus the issue is not the character of the writing, but the ignorance of the reader. Perhaps also Feldman works within an accepted and acceptable tradition of Jewish scholarship; nonetheless, this reader consistently finds himself puzzling about issues not explicitly dealt with. Feldman is generally careful about identifying the dates and places of rabbis he quotes: for example, at the end of a chapter on non-Jews and the commandments he introduces Yechiel M. Epstein and informs the reader that he lived in Navarrodok, Russia, and died in 1908 (p. 58). Rabbi Epstein's contribution was made in a restatement of the *Shulhan Arukh,* the great code of Joseph Karo. This information entices the reader. Why did a nineteenth-century rabbi restate a great fifteenth-century code? Granting a great degree of continuity in Jewish religious life, were there nineteenth-century currents of thought which prompted a restatement of the code? Particularly, were there reactions to Gentile communities at that time which prompted the particular passage that Feldman quotes? Among the currents of East European Judaism of the nineteenth century, was Rabbi Epstein particularly influenced by one of them? Over and over again, given his own ignorance and the absence of an explication of the historical context of the writing, the reader is uncertain of whether he comprehends the particularities of the contribution acutely and properly.

To be sure, it would not be possible for an author who has as much material at his command as Feldman uses to satisfy the questions of the reader at each point. And it is clear that the rabbis themselves worked within a literary tradition which was composed largely of responses to previous texts received as authoritative and important to varying degrees. Within the tradition itself the historical conditions under which certain texts were written were not judged to be as important as modern curiosity finds them to be. But it is apparent that one would have a different and, presumably better, understanding of the texts and the moral teachings if one knew a great deal about the historical background of the authors and their times.[7]

Noonan's work, by comparison, is more in a Troeltschian

spirit, although there is no explicit reliance on the great German for authority or inspiration. For example, in Part 2, which covers the years 450–1450, he establishes many reference points by which the reader can orient himself to the intent of specific teachings. One finds accounts of the means of contraception used during the period, descriptions of the motives of those who used them, the views of heretical and other groups on the issue of contraception, the state of sexual morals, and the ecclesiastical situation in which teachings were established, as well as the theological warrants for them. The moral teachings, under Noonan's historical examination, are seen to be not only later responses to earlier texts, but also responses to a variety of conditions. The reasons given for the teachings of a particular person or for a certain period of the church's history are many, and the reader is able to read the texts as quoted in a much more penetrating light. A better grasp of the author's meaning is thereby possible.

Of course, recognition must be given to the different cultural and historical situations of Christianity and Judaism and to the different internal traditions of the two streams of biblical religion, in looking at the differences between the works of Feldman and Noonan. Indeed, there are theological differences as well as historical ones that require a different sort of historical writing: Jewish ethical teaching is, with reference to specific issues like contraception, developed in a legal tradition; Christian teaching came from more speculative theology, from the penitential concerns of the church, as well as from canon law. Historical precedent has a more important function in the Jewish tradition, although it is of great signficance in the Christian as well. Granting these and other conditions, it remains possible, at least for the modern reader, to read more accurately the ethical teachings of the past when they are set within the wider historical context.

The issues here are not, of course, confined to the best way to read religious ethical texts; they are present wherever historical texts of any sort are used by scholars. The problem is that of understanding and interpretation; it is the hermeneutical problem. What is the significance of a biographical and historical context for the proper understanding of a text? Does one have to know Gnosticism and Hellenistic Judaism in order to understand the texts of the New Testament? Does one have to know Luther's biography and the political and social conditions of the sixteenth century in order accurately to understand Luther's teachings? We are beginning to scratch against the thorny hedge of both the formal and material problems of historical literary scholarship, where general theories compete with each other at levels of ideological abstraction and where practitioners disclose different aspects of meaning from different perspectives. Abjuring such discussion will be excused, I hope, in order only to make a modest claim pertinent to the study of Christian ethics. Religious ethical texts and, more particularly, the material moral teachings of the churches, have arisen within complex religious and cultural circumstances. In order properly to understand these texts and teachings it is necessary to understand the circumstances. As trivial as this sounds, as often as one has heard it since his first course in history, it bears repetition, if only to encourage more studies in a Troeltschian mode. Perhaps historians are to be admonished as much as scholars of ethics; the professional group to blame is a matter of indifference.

The Uses of Historical Analogies

In popular moral exhortation, as well as in certain more sophisticated Christian ethics, historical comparisons are often made in order to convince the reader or hearer of a moral point. Vivid recollections come to my mind of a conference on ethics sponsored by the World Council of Churches in June 1960. Anti-Gaulist French Protestants were passionately comparing the situation in France at that time to the situation in Germany in 1932. The parallels that they drew were political, cultural, spiritual, and moral. One speaker indicated that the sermons and other discourses of Christian resistance that appeared early in the Nazi period in Germany had a particular ring of authenticity when read in the light of the events in France in 1960. Contemporary prophetic and moral discourse in the United States abounds with similar formal comparisons. The American situation is like situation x in the past; we can see in retrospect what moral actions should have been done in situation x; we ought to engage, because of the similarities of our situation with situation x, in such actions now. Thus the argument goes.

A different use of historical analogy occurs in Christian social ethics. Its fundamental premise is that certain historical events are normative, or revelatory, for Christian interpretations of the meaning of history, including contemporary history. The Old

Testament accounts of certain events in the history of the people of Israel have come to function in this way in recent decades. For example, in the exodus of the Hebrew people from bondage in Egypt there is a revelation of God's activity as a liberating force; there is thus a theological authorization for liberation as a social moral value. Where liberation is going on in the world, God is at work, and men ought to join in those activities which foster that social moral value.[8] The critical questions that can be raised about this procedure are many. Which historical events, and which accounts of these historical events are theologically and ethically normative? What justifications would be made for the choice of one event over another, or one account over another? Would one give a theological ethical reason, for example, to show that the exodus account is normative but the conquest of the people of Canaan is not? Is the theme of liberation more consistent with Christian theology and ethics than the theme of conquest? How does one proceed to apply the normative account of a normative event to a present-day event? What aspects of the historical and social situations of the present are similar enough to those of the past to give some warrant for the analogy? Answers to these questions are assumed, often uncritically, in all normative uses of historical events, and readers need to be alerted to the importance of teasing them out. (A complete argument about how they can best be answered lies outside the bounds set for this essay.)

Whether done as a popular exhortation or with scholarly sophistication, the use of historical analogies for the purpose of clarifying how one ought to do ethics and what one ought to do in the present situation at least presupposes a continuity in history, a significant similarity between the past and the present. Such a presupposition need not entail a high level of theory of history, such as a cyclical one. If such a theory were accepted, one could presumably read present events about which there is moral consternation as the return to the fundamental order of previous events; thus one could act to conform to the inevitabilities of such recurrences. Nor does one need to presuppose a natural moral order embedded in the structures of being which takes on historical manifestations of similar sorts from time to time in order to make comparisons that would shed light on contemporary issues. It is quite possible to eschew speculative philosophies and theologies of history and, in the interests of practical moral reasoning within the Christian community, to reason directly from history. Indeed, most persons who engage in such practical uses of historical analogies would be surprised to be pressed into a clarification of their assumptions about the fundamental nature of history.

These are, however, significant issues for the theologian of social ethics, and there are arguments which suggest that where one stands on the map of theologies of history makes a difference in how one functions in practical moral discourse. As we shall see, the issues are more complex than some theologians of history and political theologians seem to realize; they also involve the question of what the practical task of the theologian addressing social issues, or of the social ethicist, is. Jürgen Moltmann's essay, "The Understanding of History in Christian Social Ethics," provides a basis for adumbrating some of these concerns.

Moltmann's concern is to develop the proper theological understanding of history and briefly to indicate what its consequences are for the social ethics of the Christian community. The first assumption in his argument is that one will find out what reality is by looking to the scriptures. Within the scriptures, "the reality of man is understood through an eschatological disclosure to be 'history.'" The familiar polemic against "Greek" views of time and history from the standpoint of biblical views is at the heart of the matter. God's action is not seen in natural eternal laws, but "in the unique and unrepeatable quality of temporal contingency." The

> Israelite-Christian man . . . experiences a truly "open," namely an eschatologically open, world and he experiences his reality as a history which is unique and unrepeatable, irreversible [sic] and oriented towards a goal; he does not experience his reality as eternal nature which always remains the same in the cyclical pattern of its process.

Such a view would, on the face of it, preclude significant use of historical analogies in moral reasoning, for in Moltmann's view to be human is to have a history and not a nature, and to have a history is to be involved in the unique and unrepeatable.[9]

While Moltmann is concerned to undercut "Greek" views and the social ethics that come from them, he is also concerned to define his position against remnants of that position in the theologies of orders of creation, the idea of spheres, mandates, etc. But he must also define his position against views in which contingency and uniqueness preclude any sense of what one ought to do in the eschatological openness, that is, from views in which there are no bases for identity and continuity in historical and personal experience. Indeed, in the passage quoted above, the phrase "oriented toward a goal" already qualifies the sense of contingency, which other terms Moltmann uses lead one to believe are more important for him. Such continuity, identity, and "determination" stem from eschatology, as readers of Moltmann's other writings are aware.

> Theologically, we may say that man is an eschatologically determined being and that his history is controlled by eschatological transcendence in its unique aspect. Determined by eschatological revelation, he experiences the future of truth as history. . . . Consequently, nothing can be acquired from Christian faith for the stabilizing of normative conceptions of order in an unstable world. There is, however, the wider horizon, an eschaton of all history which is itself historical and yet no longer historical. There is no security in history, though there is an eschatological horizon for all historical processes.[10]

In order to develop a social ethic which in any sense proposes, however modestly, to render moral judgments about the ways in which events are carrying mankind or about the ends and purposes of social action, that horizon of the future must be given some material content, some substance. Moltmann recognizes this when he writes: "If, however, the future is not to be made unreal as empty openness for the arbitrary character of every new plan, one must talk about a concrete future."[11] What makes the future concrete? How do the moments of ethical particularity achieve continuity? How does one come to some understanding of a process of history within the discrete events? Moltmann's answer to these questions is more psychological than ethical or theological. It is that "definite hopes arouse definite remembrances" and that "traditions are alive when hopes are aroused." So hopes arouse memories and traditions. But, for Moltmann, there is a normative history that is remembered; it is not that hope can justify any tradition or any memory. The history to be remembered is "the history of the promise." Thus, if any historical analogies are to be used in making moral judgments about contemporary events or in giving direction to contemporary activity, it would appear to be those biblical accounts of a promise.

What Moltmann derives from this rather elaborate theology of history for social ethics confirms the impression that there is little of positive and constructive significance in making practical and material moral judgments about particular conditions. The people of God who "travel in hope" become a "source of eschatological unrest" in society. They bear witness to the openness of the social process when the culture would seek to close it in various ways. Moltmann, however, wishes to claim more, namely, that the people of God also provide a directive for the society, which otherwise seems to sink into "the trauma of resignation in the face of meaningless determinism." There is an appalling paucity of content to that directive; in the end it functions in a way similar to the "eschatological impatience"; namely, it shows that "social institutions can be made obsolete by being questioned about their final purpose and their eschatological justification." In sum, it appears that the social ethics which comes from this theological interpretation of history and of hope rest primarily, if not exclusively, in the provision of a stance for a prophetic critical response to institutions or movements which seek to absolutize themselves or to foreclose the future. Even Moltmann's essay on "Hope and Planning"[12] becomes another occasion for elaborating a theology of history and of hope, and functions more to counsel an attitude than to provide the basis for moral reflection about what plans might be in accord with the Christian hope.

In introducing this excursus on Moltmann it was noted that one issue that had to be raised was the practical task of the theologian who addresses social issues, or the question of what social ethics is. One answer to that question is that the social ethicist's vocation includes the obligation to make particular moral judgments about particular social proposals and to suggest optional courses of moral action which might be judged morally approvable. This has been at the heart of the American social ethical tradition. The most valid criticism against this answer is that often such a definition of the task has led to premature acceptance of the institutional frameworks within which particular issues are raised, and thus the sharper prophetic criticism of the institutions themselves gets blunted. That is not necessarily the case, nor has it actually always been the case.

Troeltsch's understanding of the relativity of all historical movements in relation to the Absolute probably contributed to the capacity of some Christian ethicians to keep two points in mind. First, that given the historical character of ethical issues, no values involved can be absolutized. Thus, there are grounds for the sorts of radical critiques of politics, religion, and morals such as one finds in H. Richard Niebuhr's *Radical Monotheism and Western Culture*. Indeed, Niebuhr's unrest with established institutions is as deep as Moltmann's, but is developed from a Troeltschian base rather than from a theology of hope. Second, that at the same time, Troeltsch's ethics of social and cultural responsibility within historically relative institutions and movements have led those who learned from him to be deeply concerned with the moral requirements of specific and concrete circumstances. Niebuhr's ethics of the "fitting response" is a case in point.[13] Walter Muelder's work taken as a whole is another example of the readiness to make more fundamental criticisms while at the same time dealing with particular problems in a constructive way.

Theologies of history and hope and of politics, such as are currently being proposed from Europe and by Americans who take their cues from the continent, attempt to move from theology to history or to politics without going through a stage of more careful ethical reflection—both about why certain things are judged to be bad and about what concrete proposals are necessary to make them better—that characterizes the social ethical tradition in America.

There are, no doubt, different theologies of history involved in different conceptions of social ethics. In characteristic German fashion, Moltmann and others begin with the big ideological issue—the proper theology of history—and move from that to social ethics. The more pragmatic mentality of much American ethics often leaves the big issues implicit rather than explicit and does not feel an obligation fully to expose and expound what are considered prior questions from another point of view. And it may be that when persons from the two traditions work together to resolve practical issues, the ideological differences will appear to be of little significance. The use of historical analogies in ethics in the ways suggested in the first paragraphs of this section, however, does presuppose the existence of historical continuities in events and experience and presupposes that there are significant similarities, as well as differences, between the events of one time and the events of another. If the exodus of the Hebrew people is to be used to indicate the theological ethical direction for black Americans today, there must be similarities between the conditions under which the Hebrew people lived in Egypt and those in which black people live in America. If liberation, as a social moral value that has a particular theological justification, was an end under the conditions of slavery in Egypt, the conditions must be similar today if it is to be judged to be God's moral purpose for suppressed people.

Indeed, a case could probably be made on biblical grounds (if one feels compelled to look to scripture in order to understand reality rightly) that such continuities and similarities of historical experience are assumed in the Bible. Without denying the eschatological expectations present in many parts of the Bible, one can also note that frequently recollection of a past event provides a clue to the understanding of God's purposes (including his moral purposes) in contemporary events. While the uses of remembrances do not take a precise analogical form (stating that present conditions are similar, for example, to the exodus conditions in ways a, b, and c, but differ in ways x, y, and z, and therefore what was applicable under the exodus conditions would appear to be applicable in certain limited ways to present conditions), nonetheless, the past events are used to interpret the significance of present events and to shed light on what men ought to do. This seemed to be possible without defining a consistent theory of history. It is, after all, systematizers who push for consistent theories of history and seek to justify them either biblically or philosophically.

Does the use of historical analogies beg a prior question of some continuities in human nature? Does it suppose that man has a nature as well as a history? Or at least that there are universals in human experience, which, while not denying the uniqueness and precise unrepeatability of events, nonetheless are a ground for continuities? These are questions raised by the natural-law tradition, and a full answer to them would require a critical account of that movement. Suffice it to say that I believe that uses of historical analogies, given their tenuous character and expressing the caution that is required in using them, do assume continuities of experience which presuppose that man has a nature as well as a history. One cannot dispose of such continuities by appealing to the authority of scripture as the source of the proper understanding of reality. Other evidences and arguments than scriptural ones are required to settle issues as complex as this.

Historical analogies about contemporary events are often used in Christian ethical reflection with less than proper awareness of the perils of such an enterprise. What appears to be rhetorically persuasive does not always stand up under rigorous scrutiny with regard to the assumed similarities of circumstances and the rectitude (or fault) of actions taken under past circumstances deemed to be similar. Nonetheless, there is limited but important value in such efforts. If under the past circumstances, conscientious, religious men, Jewish or Christian, perceived God's purposes to be of a certain character, it is certainly worth considering whether under similar circumstances his purposes might not be similar today. If in past circumstances men misjudged the purposes of God in a disastrous way, under the present circumstances the same course of action might also be a disastrous mistake. At least the discipline of such historical reflection will help one to avoid the error of assuming that every occasion is unique in all its respects and, therefore, that the ways in which men have thought in the past are of no significance in the present. The assumption of absolute novelty in history is at least as great a mistake as the assumption that history flows in cycles, or that inexorable laws govern the development of history.

The Freedom to Be Historically Situated

A sense of man as historical being, and of the way in which ethical ideas are related to particular historical conditions, can lead to quite different attitudes, depending to some extent upon one's personal background. For example, one finds that writers in Roman Catholic ethics, both fundamental and practical, have become freshly aware of historical as against ontological ways of thinking. One response to the discovery of man as a historical being is an attack upon all moral absolutes. The older, "manual" moral theology assumed the immutable and eternal moral order and trusted the inferences drawn from it for all sorts of issues without taking the historicity of man adequately into account; so the charge goes. When one sees that man is better understood as a historical, psychological, and social being, a new way of ethi-

cal thinking emerges which avoids entanglement in moral absolutes.[14] Ethical arguments begin to rely more heavily upon the
historical and empirical elements in man and his circumstances
than they do upon principles or values judged to have been endur-
ing, if not eternal and immutable.

Another response in Catholic theology is more moderate; it
seeks to incorporate into fundamental moral theology a more historical understanding of natural law, without giving up the interest in lining out the ontological structures of human nature. This
is done in part by emphasizing in natural-law theory the dynamic
and personalistic aspects of man; aspects which, it is sometimes
argued, are present in the work of Thomas Aquinas himself but
were lost through a static and absolutistic interpretation. The
point is to find in human nature a dynamic aspect which is historically developed. Bernard Häring is an important moral theologian who has sought to make this turn. He has written:

> The rationalistic understanding of natural law started with ab-
> stract principles; and, finding that these principles remain always
> the same "truths," this understanding admitted variety only in
> different "applications" according to the varying "circumstances."
> Our approach starts with the real man, as a historical being, with
> his real capacity for understanding himself in his essential relation-
> ship to his fellow men, to the world around himself, and to God.

In this way Häring and others have sought to overcome the
"physicalist" bias of the tradition in favor of a view that understands the nature of man more in terms of his personal and historical being than his physical being.[15]

Persons from traditional Catholic backgrounds who have tasted
the wines of historical understanding in one way or another,
then, find themselves directed toward overcoming static absolut-
ism. The excesses of moral certitude, of depersonalized rationalism,
of rigid mentalities, and of ecclesiastical authoritarianisms built
upon such foundations, are the objects of criticism. From a modern Protestant background, however, which has assumed the historical stance for some generations, the response can often be
quite different. While there are Protestants who take historical
understanding to provide license for radical relativism, there are
others for whom the task of constructive ethics is overcoming historical relativism, at least in part. We have noted that Moltmann,

whose theology of history (except for the insertion of history's orientation toward a goal) would seem to lead to radical relativism in ethics, has a way of giving some closure to the openness, some identity and continuity to that which is also claimed to be unique and unrepeatable. The work of Paul Ramsey during the past decade, beginning with his *War and the Christian Conscience* (in which he announces that he is seeking to overcome the "wastelands of relativism"), has been increasingly directed toward the development of unexceptionable moral principles.[16]

As Walter Muelder and others note, the relativism of much contemporary Protestant ethics is not grounded in historicism alone; but there are ways in which Christian theology itself is formulated which provide a warrant for relativism. Muelder breaks through the relativism in his *Moral Law in Christian Social Ethics* by developing further the moral laws stated by E. S. Brightman and L. Harold DeWolf, following the tradition of personalistic idealism in philosophy. The development of these laws does not move one away from concerns for the concrete and the historical, as Muelder works them out; indeed, his sixth law, "The Law of Specification," moves one toward

> concrete relevance. . . . It states: *"All persons ought, in any given situation, to develop the value or values specifically relevant to that situation."* . . . This law is a corrective against abstract laws, against mere idealism. It is a law that recognizes the unique and unrepeatable in social process. . . . [it] forbids escape from existential decision.

The classical doctrine of prudence is invoked as necessary in its application; one discerns what is fitting in the historical circumstances. But by making this one law among fifteen, a great deal of general guidance is provided in coming to that discernment.[17]

An understanding of both the historical aspects of persons and of circumstances—whether hedged by the development of moral laws or by other devices—does provide a freedom to work within the particular historical situation in order to provide constructive proposals or relevant principles for dealing with the moral issues which arise in one's own time and place. This is the warrant for the sorts of continuing commentary on the political and social events that have characterized Christian social journalism in this country, such as one finds in *The Christian Century, Christianity and Crisis,* and *Commonweal.* It is also the warrant for more systematic investigation of one's historical situation through the uses of the social and behavioral sciences. Muelder's work is again instructive, for he has consistently insisted that social ethics is an interdisciplinary task which requires the uses of economics, political science, and sociology. The task of Christian ethics in its "applied" forms (as well as in its constructive theory) demands intelligent and thorough immersion in the data of the problems that one seeks to address.

Risks are involved in exercising this freedom. Of least significance is the fact that within a short time what one has written may be outdated; one's successors can look back with critical derision and assert that the author was timebound and culturebound. The risks of being bound to time and context are sometimes more formidable than the risks of irrelevant abstraction, and they are more formidable in certain periods than in others; in the very determination of the historical situation to be addressed there are often errors of shortsightedness, limitations of vision with reference both to problems emerging on the historical horizon and to persistent and deeper issues embedded and nearly hidden in the data of a focal concern. The practical moral theologian is forced also to make judgments that have heavy empirical weight, judgments about precisely what the historical situation is in which he is counseling some form of policy or action. Since often the experts do not agree on what the historical situation is, the social ethicist finds himself assuming the burden of giving the empirical dimensions of the problem a configuration which makes it an identifiable object of thought and action. And clearly, if he feels the obligation to make specific moral judgments about a historical situation, he has no guarantee that they will turn out to be right in the light of future developments.

The freedom to be historically situated does not, as Muelder and others remind us, mean that there are no continuities in history, persons, and experience. Nor does it entail the stance of an existentialism which abjures serious critical reflections and serious empirical inquiry. The awareness of the individuality of historical occasions does not rule out the necessity for serious study of ethical traditions. Yet it does free one from the paralyzing effects of excessive scrupulosity, from the emasculated idealism that retreats to the eternal verities and universal values and principles in order to avoid the possibility of being culturebound or mistaken in a particular judgment.

Conclusion

For some persons who discover the insights of historical understanding, particularly if they are in reaction against an absolutist tradition, they issue in an extreme relativism. If, for example, one is persuaded that the truth or validity of an ethical teaching is bound to the biography of its author and the historical context of his life, what the church has taught about contraception, or war, or any other matter is valid only for a particular author, or for his time and place in history. The warrants for historical analogies are weak because of a persuasion that historical individualities are more dissimilar than similar. What one is left with is only the third aspect of this essay, namely, the freedom to be historically situated. Often this leads to a severe weakening of any objective moral discourse and to an acceptance of whatever moral standards prevail. But such relativists respond to different present circumstances in different ways. They do not uniformly accept what currently is to be the "ought." They operate with hidden criteria. While they may affirm the "sexual revolution," they deny the legitimacy of the current war. In our time a principle of humanization, generally not developed with precision, often is appealed to in order to justify the distinctions between what they accept and what they reject in the present historical situation.

The story is often different for those who have lived with the insights of historical understanding for a long time. Troeltsch's own intellectual biography is a case in point; toward the end of his life he was almost plaintively seeking a framework for greater universality.[18] The task of theological and ethical work becomes that of finding justification both for religious belief and for moral decisions which do not deny the relativities of history, but which provide an objectivity short of absolute claims. In ethics the task is to find some degree of order, continuity, and structure within historical change. If the absolutist has morality conforming to an immutable order and thus has difficulty in coping with historical change, the relativist has an openness to change but a difficulty in developing the criteria of purpose and action to guide choices and give direction to moral activities.

Some activities of historical understanding are useful in the relativist's pursuit. To see how moral questions were framed in the past, and why they were framed as they were, provides insight into his present situation in which the same general issue arises. He can see not only what is valid in the teaching, for example, about contraception, but also what was mistaken and how present conditions alter our understanding of the problem. He can carefully formulate analogies between present and past and gain insight into what might now be required.

But larger philosophical and theological issues remain. In a sense, the debate between realists and nominalists continues, and the question for the relativist is how to retain universality in the context of historicity. This surely is the question at the heart of the ethical thought of Catholics like Karl Rahner and Bernard Häring; and it is the issue under debate in both popular and scholarly Protestant treatises. Does man have a nature? Or only a history? Are there abiding moral principles and rules? Unexceptionable ones? Or only individual intuitions of the ethical demand in particular circumstances?

We have inherited Troeltsch's problematic; we find some value in his dealing with it. But the debates and discussions continue and will for the foreseeable future.

III

Ethics
and
the Sciences

10

Man–In Light of Social Science
and
Christian Faith

What one understands about man depends upon the particular light in which he is seen or, more precisely, upon what vocabulary and relationships one chooses as the framework for interpretation. In theology, man is interpreted in his relationship to God the creator and sustainer, to Jesus Christ the Son, and to the presence of the Spirit in the church and the world. The fact that man is seen in this relationship (the one in which is seen the *real* man, according to Karl Barth and other theologians) predisposes the writer to use language appropriate to it. Man is seen as creature of God; he is seen as fallen from a state of faith and trust in God; he is seen as sinner in relation to God and to other men; he is seen as responsible to God in all his words and deeds; he is seen as participating in new life in Christ; he is seen in Christian freedom. All these things that can be said about man in relationship to God, however, obviously do not exhaust what can be said about man in other relationships.

The secular philosopher of ethics has another light to turn upon man, different from the theologian's. He asks about man's moral action: Is it determined by his sentiments and his emotions?

Reprinted from *Conflicting Images of Man,* edited by William Nicholls. Copyright © 1966 by The Seabury Press, Incorporated. Used by permission.

Or is it determined by a fundamental moral law that is grounded in human nature? Does he decide what his conduct ought to be in relation to the prevailing moral consensus of his community? Or is his behavior basically determined by some fundamental drives for self-preservation that reside in his psycho-physical being? Can he perceive values in things? Or does he act according to some rules of conduct set up by society?

Theological language and the vocabulary of ethics by no means exhaust the ways we have to describe and interpret man. There is political language, psychological language, aesthetic language, and many other forms. In this chapter, with an opening confession of necessary oversimplification, we are concerned to see what man looks like in the light of social science. The task is appallingly broad, and justice cannot be done to refinements in viewpoints, and to competing forces at debate within the sciences that deal with social behavior. To make it manageable, three themes have been selected as fairly pervasive in the social sciences: (1) man is viewed genetically—that is, in terms of the causal processes, and thus there is an emphasis on the determination of his present state by past events; (2) man is viewed functionally—that is, in terms of a creature with needs that seek fulfillment in various ways in order to survive; (3) man is viewed as researchable—that is, he can be defined in terms measurable by contemporary social research procedures.

Throughout the exposition of these themes, certain contrasts will be drawn with theological and moral interpretations of man. This is done not to demonstrate the superiority of theology and ethics to give the picture of "real" man, but to indicate the differences in frame of reference, and thus in the characteristics that are accentuated in the portrait of man. Nor is the procedure of contrast used to demonstrate the greater adequacy of social science themes about man; they will always be inadequate taken in themselves for those who think of man in relation to God, and who think of man in relation to moral responsibility. Actually, however, most Christians have absorbed much of the fundamental vision of man that is embedded in studies of his social behavior without consciousness of discrepancies between that view and those provided in the Christian tradition. Most of us act as if social determination is the whole story of man. Finally, however, both our action and the views of social sciences need to be questioned in the light of our Christian confession.

Behavior Is Determined

One of the oldest arguments among Western views of man deals with the extent of man's freedom versus the extent of his determination by forces outside himself. This has been an issue in philosophy: at one extreme Spinoza seems to say that the only freedom man has is his acquiescence to necessity; in his acceptance of the fact that he is determined by other forces, he finds the measure of freedom that he has. In contrast, Kant, who was interested in preserving a strong sense of moral responsibility, asserted that the essential character of the human self was outside the realm of the effects of causal factors, and could exercise reason and free will to determine behavior. The issue of freedom and determinism also has a long history of theological debate. Finally, is each man predestined? Or does he determine his own destiny? If he is predestined, are all the detailed decisions of life governed by God's power? Or is there a realm of responsibility for the exercise of free choice? This debate continues in theological discourse: Christian existentialists stress the capacity for a free response of faith and obedience to God, and thus the ability to shape life and events. Theologians who still desire to interpret the providence of the almighty God are forced to find qualified ways to deal with freedom.

The social scientists have not taken part in this debate in philosophical and theological terms. Indeed, they tend to eschew such language, and aver that they are concerned only with such generalizations about human behavior as can be developed from observation and from refined empirical evidences. But social scientists do belong to a community of scholars who seek to understand what now exists in the light of cause-and-effect analysis; they look at the self in an effort to find out what conditions, causal factors, relationships, and occasions are most important in shaping behavior. Thus, there is in the social sciences a predisposition to think in "behavioristic" terms, that is, in terms of the determination of human selfhood and action by turning to the antecedents of the present experience. There is a tendency to view the present self particularly in relation to its past experiences, and in relation to other selves, cultures, and institutions that presently exert decisive influence on behavior.

In Freudian psychology this is clearly the case. In order to understand the present condition of a personality, whether a healthy or an unhealthy one, the interpreter turns to the early experiences of the child. It is assumed that the decisive factors in the shaping of behavior characteristics occurred in the relationships of son to mother, of father to daughter, of siblings to each other. It is also assumed in the orthodox forms of this view, that the human sexual drive is of unique significance in determining how a person thinks and what a person does. Fascinating biographical interpretations have been made from this point of view: Erik Erikson's *Young Man Luther* deals with an important religious historical figure; Ernest Jones's *Hamlet and Oedipus* uses psychoanalytic language to understand two great characters in literature.[1]

The social psychologists have tended to think a different set of factors to be more important in the determination of behavior than do the orthodox Freudians. They look to the effects of belonging to certain social groups, such as an ethnic immigrant community or the "middle class." Cultural anthropologists among them look at what the "ethos" and values of a culture do to the development of personality. Some of the writing in this vein is done in the manner of grand theorizing; in others research is done with great precision of measurement and analysis.

One of the early formulators of the general view of social behaviorism was the Chicago philosopher-psychologist G. H. Mead, whose *Mind, Self, and Society*[2] remains a landmark of fundamental theory of a social view of selfhood. Mead sees the self coming into being in two general stages. First, the child organizes in his own experience and behavior the attitudes that others have expressed toward him and toward each other in their gestures, their speech, and their actions. Self-identity comes into being by virtue of the internalization of the meanings of expressions that occur in the primary social relationships. The second stage is that of absorbing not only individual attitudes, but social attitudes of groups to which one belongs. Particular groups—the family, the social class, the church, the peer group—are "generalized others" to which a particular person responds, and to which he conforms to some extent in the organization of his own behavior.

This view of Mead's assumes that there is always an "I" that cannot be totally explained on the basis of past experience, and continues to be the organizing center of all the influences exerted upon the self. But there is also a "me" that is the fundamental core of identity resulting from the accruing effects of social participation in various groups. Thus, the analytic procedures can be crudely stated: If you want to understand and explain a person you know, turn to the various groups to which he has belonged and continues to belong. You will find that what is identifiable about him is the result of these social relationships. In the less precise words of a contemporary of Mead's, Charles Horton Cooley, the self "mirrors" other selves and groups to which it is related. In distinction from Cooley, Mead stresses the organizing center, the thinking self, as a factor that brings all these past influences together into some integrated unity.

Most cultural anthropologists and sociologists operate in the same basic frame of reference. Ralph Linton developed a general viewpoint in his *Cultural Background of Personality* that states the case as accepted with variations by many anthropologists. To be sure, there are "innate factors" that are not culturally determined, by which one can understand some of the differences between persons who share a common culture, but personality is largely shaped by the people and things that form one's environment. "The behavior of the members of any society and the forms of most of the objects which they use are largely stereotyped and can be described in terms of culture patterns."[3] It is through these stereotypical culture patterns that personalities take shape. Thus, in the famous study *Patterns of Culture* by Ruth Benedict, one finds "Apollonian" traits of personality, stressing rationality, self-control, and the like, to be characteristic of such a tribe as the Zuni Indians of the Southwest United States, and "Dionysian" traits, stressing competitiveness, aggressiveness, violence, and the like to be characteristic of Indians in the northwest. The patterns of culture developed in relation to cultural heritage, physical environment, and social conditions become internalized in the individual members of particular societies.

The grand generalizations of earlier writers have provided a viewpoint, and certainly give insight to the observer. But they have been qualified and carefully refined by contemporary research. The blanket statements have been transformed into verifiable evidence of statistical probabilities that allow for exceptions to the general case. A recent study in the sociology of religion illustrates some of the refining process. Gerhard Lenski, in a study of people in the Detroit, Michigan, area, demonstrates that religious affiliation is a significant factor in the determination of attitudes and behavior of people. But rather than make a point as general as "if a child is raised in a Catholic home and church, he will reflect the patterns of Catholicism in his behavior," Lenski suggests that the religious "variable" has to be seen as one among many: the racial, ethnic, social class, and other factors. On the basis of a refined research procedure he seeks to indicate the strength of the religious-group determination by sorting it out in reference to other factors, and then provides a statistical probability that can be stated in "more likely" types of generalizations such as "the middle class was more likely than the working class to believe in the availability of opportunities for workingmen's sons and in the importance of ability." Or, "white Protestants were more inclined than others to believe that the sons of workingmen have good chances for advancement."[4] The basic thesis remains the same, however, namely, if you wish to understand a person's attitude toward work, look at the groups to which he belongs, and you are likely to find the decisive influences.

The interpretation of the self as conditioned, or determined, results from the kinds of questions that the social scientist asks: "What factors seem to cause behavior? How is behavior to be understood in relation to its antecedents?" Thus, with these questions in view, the analyst sees the continuities of human behavior within one person's life, and between the action of a person and the characteristics of the group to which he belongs.

In contrast to these questions, others can be asked about the self, in different languages, with different intentions. The ethicist might ask: "Given a self that is facing the present and the future, how does he decide to act? What does he do?" He is not asking, "How did the self get this way?" but rather, "Where does it go from here?" The social scientist, with his generalizations about behavior, might venture to predict what a person or a group will do on the basis of their knowledge of the past. But the moralist, by virtue of being oriented to the present and future in his questions, stresses the unpredictabilities of selfhood, the possibilities for doing the novel, the creative thing.

The theologian might find the analysis of human behavior given from the viewpoint of social science to be interesting, and even helpful, in understanding the characteristic continuities of behavior. But his questions relate to another object, the divine Being. He might, however, wonder what patterns of Providence can be interpreted as present in the ordering of life that the student of social life describes. Or he might question whether both the continuing patterns and the particular actions of a person are in accord with what God has meant man to be in the world. The theologian's questions are governed by his concern—man in relation to God. The social scientist's questions are governed by his concern—man in relation to factors that condition or determine his behavior.

The response of some theologians to the social scientist's interpretation of man has been one of critical dismissal. The grounds for this seem to be the excessive confidence that many scientists have had, particularly in their assumptions that what they have known provides grounds for predictability of behavior. Certainly most social scientists are now cautious about predictions, though they would affirm that their studies enable one to project certain probabilities with reference to future behavior, both of persons and of groups. Theologians also believe that the most important questions about man cannot be answered by science, namely, those that pertain to man's status before God and to man's moral obligations to his neighbor. This is no doubt the case, but within their limited sphere of concern, the scientists of behavior offer illuminating evidences.

Indeed, for the religious person one of the functions of genetic interpretations of man is to unmask illusions and pretensions to which our faith tempts us. Christians are often likely to assume that their behavior is governed by their trust and loyalty to Jesus Christ, when the larger part of it is actually determined by their relationships to parents and to social groups. They are likely to assume that in faith they are freed from bondage to their personal histories, to ideologies and groups, when in actual behavior they are not. Indeed, the amount of light that social science can shed on behavior, including the behavior of Christians, ought to chasten believers; it might lead them to self-examination and repentance. As Hannah Arendt, no friend of behaviorism as a general philosophy, has observed, one reason the social scientists are so effective and popular in North America is that so much of what they say about American behavior is true. We do "behave" as conditioned, rather than "act" in the light of reason or faith.

Man, the Creature of Needs and Desires

A basic model for the interpretation of human behavior in a number of the social sciences has been taken from the field of the biological sciences. It is the language of "organism," and if this word is rejected, part of its meaning is carried over into a "functional" theory. These terms point to a view of both individual selves and societies as entities that live for the sake of surviving with the least possible strain within and between persons and groups. Persons find ways of "adjusting" to what is happening to them, just as animals adapt to a changing physical environment. Societies seek to approximate a status of "equilibrium" in which the elements of conflict and dissent are reduced to a tolerable point, and something approaching harmony exists, just as in nature the various forces relate to each other in such a way that most beings and plants can survive. There are needs that have to be met, and human beings find ways to meet these needs. Indeed, for many sociologists, psychologists, and anthropologists man is finally an organism in an environment, seeking to establish those patterns of life that make for survival under the most harmonious conditions possible.

This view has been particularly offensive to many Christian interpreters of humanity, for it posits man and his survival as the final reality to which all things refer. Behavior has reference to God who created man, who requires man to meet certain conditions if life is to be sustained, who demands a faithfulness that might well bring the denial of harmony and equilibrium. Behavior is finally explainable with reference to need-fulfillment.

Functionalism readily becomes itself a pseudotheological doctrine insofar as it provides a fundamental principle in the light of which almost everything is interpreted and understood. Religion itself, not to mention other phases of life and culture, is often explained on functional grounds. This has been done by a number of cultural anthropologists, and the viewpoint is by no means confined to the practitioners of that academic discipline or field. Bronislaw Malinowski was a major formulator of a functional theory. It is his view that man has a series of basic needs— for food, reproduction, bodily comfort, safety, growth, movement, and health. These needs in turn evoke developments in society and in culture. The need for food is at the root of agriculture, hunting, and fishing. These become the centers around which increasingly complicated institutions emerge: refinements in agricultural technology, development of marketing institutions, emergence of advertising, and many other things that a brief exercise of the imagination could enumerate. Even certain religious actions are related to this: in the uncertainty of the hunt or of crops, primitive tribes seek to relate themselves to the mysterious animistic powers that move all things, in order to remove obstacles that might hinder the enterprise. The need to reproduce evokes the intricacies of family systems, marriage, wider kinship groups, etc. These in turn find, among other things, religious sanctions; and ritual acts and beliefs like marriage services are brought to bear on sex and family life. Religion, like all other aspects of culture, is a human invention by which people manage to meet needs, and come to grips with the strains and tensions of life.[5]

Religion has also been interpreted in terms of society being "the substance of God." This view is associated with the name of Emile Durkheim,[6] and in a modified form has recently been developed in a book by sociologist Guy Swanson, *The Birth of the Gods*.[7] The God, or gods, function to provide a point of coherence, integration, and sanction for a society. A god is a projection of the "spirit" and the values of a society, and is given a reification in order to become an object of worship as well as a norm for behavior. Man, as religious being, then, fulfills a social need by the creation of religious rites and beliefs, which provide for the continuity of society as generations die and which become "collective representations" of the values and life of the community.

The notion of need-fulfillment also appears in treatises that deal with economic life and policy. In a very important study on *Politics, Economics, and Welfare,* Professors Robert Dahl and Charles Lindblom find it necessary to state the basic ends that are to be achieved in the policies of Western governments and societies. This obviously moves them into the realm of philosophical, ethical, and perhaps even theological questions. In accord with the general functionalism of the American human studies, however, they settle for "prime goals" that are basically need-fulfillment in their statement of them: "existence or survival, physiological gratifications (through food, sex, sleep, and comfort), love and affection, respect, self-respect, power or control, skill, enlightenment, prestige, aesthetic satisfaction, excitement, novelty and many others."[8] From these "prime goals" certain "instrumental goals" can be designated that define the particular ends to be sought through social policy, as well as the means to be considered in their achievement.

To what does economic behavior finally refer? To the needs of men. This, patently, is sensible. In the spheres of economics, politics, and much of social organization, all of which are in the realm of what theologians call "life in creation," the human needs have significance as a starting point, if not the point of final reference. No Christian interpreters of man would object to the value of preserving what is human, nor would they seek to divinize the natural in such a way that everything ought immediately to be related to the divine Presence and activity. Yet this "functionalism" often tends to become the sole basis for the derivation of goals and norms for human behavior. If one wishes to find out what the proper goals for human life are, one looks to the things that people believe they need, to the things that they desire, to find them. If human beings desire variety in their sexual experience, then the order of sexual relations in which this is possible with the least stress and strain on their lives is the good order of human life.

Some critical moralists would acquiesce to the assertion that human needs form the fundamental basis of human morality, but would quarrel with particular determinations of what these needs are. A Roman Catholic might agree that what is right and good is what fulfills the deepest human needs, but he would hardly take a poll or rely only on his observations of current behavior to determine what these needs are. He has a conviction that determines his definition of need, and in turn the ordering of life: namely, that man finally seeks the good and avoids evil; but the good is not simply the fulfillment of every desire or the realization of impulses. To think about it properly one must introduce terms like justice, the virtues of prudence, temperance, and courage, and other things that are not derived from assessments based on analysis of behavioral evidence in some simple way.

The Roman Catholic, like other Christians, also would see the realm of human needs within a framework of God's creation, and of purposes that exist because God has so ordered human life. The point of stumbling is that most functional interpretations of man believe that there is no point of reference beyond the self or beyond nature, to which life refers. This becomes clear when a functional interpretation of religion comes into view. Religion has no point of reference that is objective to the needs of self and society. To speak of God is to speak of something that is incapable of empirical verification, whereas to speak of human needs is to define something which, men can agree, does exist. There is a "positivism" that informs functional views of man: only the observable, measurable man exists; he is not related to anything beyond himself. Man, in functionalism, is viewed only with reference to nature, and to nature defined in a particular way. Societies, like individual persons, seek an adjustment not to the will of God but to a state of equilibrium in which strains and tensions are reduced to the point of toleration.

The Christian might be most offended when he sees religion reduced to a human need, but he also ought to wonder whether economic and political life do not have some purpose with reference to the kind of life that God has created for men, to the kind of order through which God can sustain human societies. Where the functionalist stops is but a station in the Christian interpretation of man: God's work is done through the orders of preservation, the establishment of justice, the fulfillment of human potentialities.

Functionalism, however, cannot be lightly dismissed. Human needs are a kind of prism through which all light goes; for this reason functionalism can become an inclusive principle of explanation for human existence. Faith, Christians affirm, relates men to God, but faith in God also fulfills human longings and needs. Thus, even faith goes through the prism of human need, man's need for God, and this provides the temptation to explain all that is involved in faith by that through which it is refracted. Further, when functionalism is applied to the interpretation of behavior, religious included, it has an unpleasant unmasking effect on the pretensions of Christians and other moral men. It enables men to see how much of action reputed to be engaged in for lofty purposes is really a matter of adjustment to the world. The functionalists provide a point of view for a critique of much religious life: We like to believe that men worship to praise God, but many of us worship to get a psychic serenity we need to adjust to the ambiguities of daily life. We like to believe that confirmation is a rite in which a child's reception into the Body of Christ by baptism is really confirmed, but for both parents and children it is often a puberty rite in which a new stage of physical and social maturity is celebrated. So much of behavior can be accounted for on functional grounds that it is no wonder the point of view has a persuasive power in contemporary culture.

Behavior Is Researchable

It is obvious that for many centuries scholars and poets, as well as businessmen and farmers, have been making observations of human behavior in which they have confidence, and from which they make certain generalizations. Aristotle made many shrewd remarks that seem to penetrate human behavior, such as "man is a political animal," and so have most philosophers. The fact that man can be "researched" is not novel. But some of the procedures used to research human behavior are increasingly refined in character. Among social scientists—sociologists, psychologists, political scientists, and others—the current effort is to find ways in which human behavior can be converted into numerical terms, can be recorded on IBM cards, and can be delineated in highly precise generalizations as a result of these refinements. One symptom of this is the way in which a course in statistics is required for most graduate students of society, persons, and politics. It is as if the way to reality was by the quantification of things, and unfortunately, in some instances, the assumption is that if something is not reducible to number it is not researchable, and therefore (almost) it is not real.

These refined measurements of behavior are not without significant value, although they are probably overvalued by some of the researchers. Certainly they are a rigorous check upon impressions; persons who assume that they can perceive and generalize on human behavior have often merely projected what they wish to see onto the world around them. No longer need this be the case; the perceptions and imaginative generalizations can become the hypotheses for more careful assessment of what is and is not the case. For example, for generations there have been assumptions about the political behavior of various social groups in the United States, based on impressions from election returns. If a particular ward was heavily Democratic, and there was a large Roman Catholic church in the ward, men felt rather secure in saying that Roman Catholics vote Democratic. And they were probably correct. But with various sampling techniques, refined schedules of inquiry, etc., one can find out not only how many Roman Catholics vote Democratic, but whether other factors are not more important than the religious one, e.g., the income status, the ethnic group identification, the family system, and the like. General impressions are corrected and refined by research into political behavior.

The measurement research into behavior professes to be interested only in accurate description of what exists. Description includes not only an account of what is at any particular time and place, but also an analysis of the correlation of factors that enable one to begin to understand some reasons why "what is" is. Thus, there is an easy movement from description to causal analysis, and at this point other questions sometimes need to be raised. First, if the methods of measurement begin to dictate what can be researched, can one be sure he is finding out the most important things that need to be known about behavior? This question might be answered by various social scientists in different ways. The more modest and self-critical might suggest that all one gets at are certain indices of behavior, and that these are limited to some extent by the number of variables the researcher seeks to ferret out in his research design. Even when one can make significant correlations between aspects of human life, one has not yet proved a causal sequence. Less self-critical practitioners of the measurement procedures often claim more for what they find out; crudely stated, they assume that if something is not quantifiable it is not real, and in effect rather than conforming method to the human behavior to be studied, they rule out the significance of all behavior that cannot be reduced to their methods. At its worst, this kind of work is mechanical, presumptuous, and "genius-proof."

Second, there is a great deal of dubiety in assuming that correlations declare unambiguously clear assertions of causation. Robert Merton, in refining the procedures for the sociology of knowledge, suggests some of the words that need to be carefully selected in determining the character of the relationship of things that are correlated: they "correspond" to each other; or one is the "condition" of the other, or there is a "functional interdependence" between them, or one "determines" the other.[9] In the selection of appropriate words, there is a heavy weight of philosophical decision, of predisposition, that is not necessarily verifiable, or requires even more refined studies to validate accurately. For example, juvenile delinquents in one area are Negroes, Protestants, come from lower-income families, have a high incidence of broken families, live in slums, and are poorly educated. In another area they are white, Roman Catholic, of Italian extraction, from families with lower incomes, have traditional Italian family systems, etc. How does one assess which factors are "causally" most significant in delinquency? There are refined ways to proceed with such analysis and, without doubt, through social analysis one can be surer about which factors are more important than one can be without social analysis. But judgments have to be made, even of the data, and these obviously require more than measurement—a fact social scientists would agree to. But social analysis of behavior is not prejudice-proof; one can be disposed to look at Protestant religious behavior, for example, as the result of large segments being members of the middle class; but a case is also made for the fact that Protestant religious faith and life tends to push people toward middle-class goals and behavior. I merely wish to indicate the complexity that is involved in making judgments of causality between factors of behavior that are significantly correlated statistically.

The Christian interpreter can be informed about what is actually taking place by the work of social research. He often wonders if what he finds out is worth all the time, effort, and money that went into such study, but that query is not so much the result of his Christian viewpoint as it is of other bases of judgment. But the Christian interpreter generally wonders whether the most significant dimensions of human behavior can be reduced to the measurement procedures. Some things that formerly seemed out of the range of research now are coming into it, for example, research on the "values" that people hold, and the extent to which behavior is governed by them. But can something like loving the neighbor be measured? If one could get consensus on which acts are "loving" acts, which attitudes are "loving" attitudes, etc., something might be done. But insofar as love of neighbor is a spontaneous act, stemming from God's gracious love and freely given to the other, perhaps the task is more difficult if not impossible.

Further, Christians have believed that man is related to God (a "nonempirical factor" for social research). There are dimensions of the meaning of human behavior that are governed by faith in God. It is at this level of the framework for interpreting the *meaning* of human existence that Christians part company with the social researcher. This parting of the ways does not mean a rejection of what research has found out, but a critical approach to it, seeking to make clear the assumptions of such research. It also requires that the Christian interpreters carefully develop the significance of what is known about man through research, for the moral and theological purposes that are given in the Christian community. The data are interpreted with reference to the knowledge of God and his will and work.

Similarly, the secular ethicist might be grateful for information on voting behavior, but he necessarily incorporates other bases for judgment and interpretation into his efforts to define what political and social policies are "good" for a given society. The research may help him at the level of tactics for achievement of moral ends, if he wills to put policy into action, but he has other purposes in view and thus reinterprets what is known. Max Millikan, in an essay "Inquiry and Policy," suggests that what the researcher comes out with in his conclusions is not so important for the policy-maker as are his arguments. "The purpose of social science research should be to deepen, broaden, and extend the policy-maker's capacity for judgment—not to provide him with answers."[10] Obviously, then, the measurement research into behavior is worthwhile if the problems to which it is addressed are important, and if it needs to be used by Christian and secular interpreters of man. But the moral judgments that go into policy judgments cannot be derived from research.

What is the Christian's response to the general views of man in the social sciences? Properly, first it is gratitude for the kinds of knowledge and understanding of human behavior that can be derived from the perspectives and procedures that inform the social scientist. He sees things because he has a particular view; he depicts behavior because he has refined procedures to use. But the Christian's response is also critical—though certainly not rejection. He is critical of claims made indiscreetly that all there is to know of man can be known from the scientific perspective and method. But such a critique must be discriminatingly applied only to those social scientists who assume the posture of omniscience. The Christian claims the right to interpret man from the Christian perspective as well, and he sees things in this light that the lights from social science do not expose. Finally, the Christian carefully interprets and uses the knowledge from the social sciences in his own particular interpretations of men and in his ethical considerations. For the Christian is interested in the quality of human life and in the moral character of human action.

11

The Relationship
of
Empirical Science
to Moral Thought

The extensive development of empirical sciences in the United States and abroad has had several consequences for moral thought, particularly for practical moral theology and ethics. The range of empirical sciences that impinge upon moral thought is almost as extensive as the range of actual problems that are discussed. Moral theologians have become intrigued with the rapid development of the social and/or behavioral sciences. It is no longer possible to discuss economic ethics, for example, at the level of generalization used in the great social encyclicals. Now one must have technical knowledge of the gross national product, the economics of development, the function of monetary and fiscal policies, etc. Nor is it possible to discuss political ethics without awareness of the structure and the functions of various political systems, the ways in which they operate in relation to law and constitutions, and even the behavior of voters. Sociology provides a basis for the critiques of moral thought itself, as one finds in Karl Mannheim's essays on sociology of knowledge, and particularly, for example, in his essays, "Conservative Thought."[1] Sociology also provides concepts and data about social behavior, institutions, and class

Reprinted with permission from *The Proceedings* of the Catholic Theological Society of America, XXVI (1971), 122-37.

structures. Psychology is used to understand the nature of moral agents, and also increasingly to assist in the definition of moral norms of fulfillment, happiness, and well-being.

The harder data of the biological and physical sciences impinge on other areas of concern to moral theologians. The science of fetology bears in many ways upon the ethical arguments about abortion. The technology developing from the science of genetics has attracted the attentions not only of moral theologians such as Paul Ramsey, but also of the dogmatic theologian Karl Rahner.[2]

Further suggestions about the general impingements of the empirical sciences on moral thought are not necessary. In this chapter I shall address several foci of the relationship. The assigned task is a large one, and thus the essay is more an exercise in clarification and exploration than a thorough study. The relevant literature is relatively sparse.[3] Philosophical issues whose development require more intensive development than is possible in this chapter will be alluded to.

The order of discussion in this essay is as follows: (A) The areas of moral thought in which one finds significant use of empirical sciences. These are (1) the understanding of the nature of persons as moral agents, (2) the understanding of the circumstances in which decisions and actions occur, (3) the prediction of potential consequences of various courses of action, and (4) the development of moral norms. (B) Major problems involved in the use of empirical sciences in moral thought. These all affect the selection of empirical materials: (1) the judgment about what data and concepts are relevant to the moral issue involved; (2) this first raises the issues of the principles of interpretation in the empirical studies, of what are involved in the selection and significance of the data used; and (3) it secondly raises the issue of the normative biases built into the empirical studies.

A. Use of Empirical Sciences in Moral Thought

1. Psychological, sociological, and anthropological studies have had a very significant impact in recent decades on the *understanding of persons*. The question to which these sciences have offered tentative answers is this: How can the behavior of persons be explained? Included in human behavior is moral action. Explanations are offered not only to account for particular acts, but also for the kind of person an individual has become, which in turn conditions, if not determines what one does. The central concern

that erupts in these accounts is the degree of answerability that agents have for their conduct. It is not as if the question of free will and determinism is raised for the first time with the development of social and behavioral sciences in recent decades. The question has been answered by philosophers and theologians in different ways throughout the history of Western thought. But the discussion of answers has shifted from the realm of metaphysics to the realm of descriptive and analytical accounts of human persons and their behavior. Indeed, one might begin such an account at the presocial level of the genotypes of individuals, which have some determinative significance on their capacities to become and to act.

Another concern that emerges from these accounts is the extent to which individual differences between persons have to be taken into account in moral judgments. One can ask whether on the basis of empirical accounts of individual differences, one does not have to make moral judgments about actions with reference to the specific persons who have acted, rather than to a class of actions. For example, would we morally excuse one person for committing adultery, while morally blaming another?

In general, it is clear that the persuasive power of scientific accounts of the development of persons and explanations of their actions have deeply affected moral thought with regard to these two concerns. There has been a major trend toward the willingness to excuse persons from moral accountability for their actions in the light of knowledge we have about their relationships with their parents, about the moral values of the communities in which they grew up, and the social circumstances in which they have been nurtured. In the arena of legal accountability one sees that psychiatric data are used to warrant an excusing condition. Data and concepts from psychiatry (or other fields) are used to make a case for the limitations of answerability. Men are not as prone to believe that an agent has "free will" in the strong sense that they once believed, and thus in some circles there is an erosion of the notion of moral responsibility itself. Although the concept of causality employed in the social scientific account of behavior has been subject to rigorous philosophical criticism in recent decades, partially in the interest of retaining a meaningful concept of moral responsibility, "blame" is often laid for moral faults not so much on the agent, as on the conditions over which he presumably has no control.

The accounts given of the formation of persons and of their actions also, quite consistently, have led to a trend to make judgments of moral actions increasingly specific with reference to the individuals who engaged in them. While this trend is ambiguous, it is nonetheless present: there are moralists who would suggest, for example, that adultery is morally indifferent, if not approvable, for two individuals who have particular needs under particular circumstances, while it is morally wrong for other individuals with other needs in other circumstances.

Thus far we have assumed that there is a vague and general agreement among the empirical sciences about the determination of human persons and behavior. It would appear at this point that one could speak of "the contemporary scientific understanding of man."[4] That such a generalization is not warranted is apparent to the critical reader of psychology, sociology, and other fields. Thus, our later discussion of critical problems in the employment of empirical sciences can be anticipated here by indicating that any moral theologian chooses from a number of renderings of the explanation of persons and behavior. Let us hypothetically suggest that he has read Freud, B. F. Skinner, and Rollo May, and has thought about the implications of the writings of each of these three persons for understanding the moral agent. The critical questions are which one should he choose, and why choose the one he does. It is likely that the moralist will choose the one whose interpretation is most in accord with his philosophical, moral, or theological predilections. If this is the case, one can ask whether he can claim "scientific" authority for the view of the agent that he adopts. If he chooses to claim such authority, he obviously has to make his case on scientific grounds, which implies that he will have to adjudicate between the scientific claims made by each of his three authors. The moral theologian could, however, make a weaker claim for one or more of the authors, namely, that the authors are sources of "insight" into the nature of persons and into human behavior. If such a claim is made, he bears his own authority for the way in which he combines or uses the insights he gleans from one or more of the authors. He might take recourse to the justification that his own combination of insights "makes sense" to him, and hopefully to others—a justification which has its own implicit empirical references, but which does not rely upon the sorts of scientific evidences offered by Freud, Skinner, and May.

The choice actually is more difficult than we have thus far suggested, for it involves not only some selection of empirical data, but also the selection of certain concepts and principles of explanation. In each of the authors the data, concepts, and principles of explanation have been systematized to the degree that there is coherence in the overall position. Thus, as we shall note more extensively, the concepts and principles of explanation are already involved in the isolation of certain data about persons and behavior as being significant and the ruling out of other data.

Enough has been said to rule out the simple use of a simple notion, namely "the contemporary scientific understanding of man" in developing a view of the moral agent. Here we only note the complexity of the issues involved in the use of empirical sciences in this area of moral thought.

2. The social and other sciences are often used to get a more precise and complete *understanding of the circumstances* in which a moral problem occurs, and thus in defining both the causes and options for action. This has been clear for a long time in the arena of medical ethics. For example, Catholic moralists have long been schooled in the biological processes of conception and birth, and have argued their moral cases using the best available scientific data that pertain to the related moral issues. In areas of social morality some Protestants and Catholics have been operating in a similar way.

Let us take the interest in developing a social ethics for urban problems as a general instance in which empirical sciences would pertain. All ethicians would readily admit that a study of the history of cities would not provide sufficiently accurate and insightful information for understanding contemporary urban existence, though Lewis Mumford's *The City in History* might provide insight and perspective.[5] All would also admit that cities are much too complex for any one person to have a full range of experience of their life; each person is likely to have a partial experience of urban existence, as a participant in its productive economy, a resident of a particular neighborhood, a driver on its expressways, etc. Thus, some supplemental information, some concepts for ordering it, and some principles for interpreting its significance are necessary beyond reliance on the knowledge of history and personal experience.

Among other things, one needs to know something of the structure and dynamics of the social order, the political order, and the economic order, to name but three factors. On the face of it, to turn to the social sciences makes sense. When one does, however, he is faced with choices comparable in principle to those above between Freud, Skinner, and Rollo May. Let us confine ourselves simply to the question of how best to understand the distribution of power in the city. A few years ago, for example, the social ethician had choices to make between the model of *The Power Elite,* described by C. Wright Mills with reference to the nation as a whole, which had structural similarities to Floyd Hunter's *Community Power Structure,* a study of Atlanta, on the one hand, and on the other hand, Robert A. Dahl's widely acclaimed study of New Haven, *Who Governs?*[6] Hunter and Mills found evidence for the existence of interlocking elites who by virtue of social and familial connections, responsibilities in industrial, political, military, and other institutions, seemed to be in control of what was going on in American urban life. Dahl explicity challenged this interpretation with evidences he gathered for the existence of much greater diversity of centers of power in a city. (The issue of locus and distribution of power is complicated even more by the shifts that are rapidly taking place; all the books I refer to were written before the emergence of black power, chicano power, and other ethnic developments in American cities.)

How would the moralist decide between the option of Hunter and Dahl? First, he might review the evidences of each author, and seek to determine what evidences were omitted. He might assess the methods of research that were used, and judge which has the greater degree of sufficiency for the study of urban power structures. If he finds one to be a superior scientific study, he might use its authority for his work precisely on those grounds. But second, he might probe behind the scientific work to inquire into the concepts, the principles of interpretation, and indeed, the basic assumptions about the political and social process that inform each of the studies. Are there reasons why Hunter is predisposed to a power elite model of analysis? Is there a view of man involved in his choice? One which, in a sense, sees men as power-seeking (in a quiet conspiratorial sort of way) in their efforts to retain control of urban institutions for their own class interests? Are there reasons why Dahl is predisposed to an analysis which finds power more widely dispersed? Does Dahl's empirical work rest on confidence in the liberal democratic process, and does this confidence affect his analysis in crucial ways? Does it shade his awareness of power elites? Does it heighten his awareness of pluralism? If the moralist finds answers to these questions, he makes not simply a choice of the best scientific study, but a choice of a point of view that involves philosophical commitments, and that leads to certain predispositions in the area of morality. The choice of model will have a significant influence on the kinds of social ethical policies he develops and supports; if these policies inform institutions and programs, they will in turn affect actions and their consequences.

3. Max Weber, in his sophisticated studies of the methodology of the social sciences, long ago indicated that one of the functions of such research for moral and policy choices is to assist one in *predicting the consequences of certain choices.*[7] His argument is part of a larger concern, namely, one that attempts to limit the value biases in social sciences. Whatever one thinks of the total effort in this regard, one would have to admit that social and other empirical research can make the prediction of consequences more accurate. The point is this: if on moral grounds you choose course of action a under the known circumstances, then consequences l, m, and n are likely to occur; but if you choose course of action b, consequences o, p, and q are likely to occur.

The arena in which the moral choices are made is significant for the degree of accuracy in prediction. In the situation of a dying patient, predictions can have a high degree of accuracy. If a physician decides that patient x no longer has any right to use artificial life support systems, there is no question that by "pulling the plug" one creates the circumstances in which he will die. In the arena of social problems, however, the accuracy of predictions is not as precise. (I once read an article which indicated that the Ford Motor Company developed the Edsel on the basis of potential markets that were indicated by social research. As I recall, the research suggested that persons who moved from lower- to higher-priced cars tended to stay in the same automobile "family." Thus, it was predicted that by building a car in the Ford family that was more elaborate than the Ford, the company could increase its share of the total auto market. The illustration is trivial, but it makes the point.)

The moralist can make certain maximalist or minimalist claims for the authority of empirical research in the prediction of consequences for moral action. Hypothetically, he might establish a set of ends to be "good," and on the basis of social research define the policies and actions that would guarantee the achievement of those ends. (Max Millikan, in his essay on the uses of research in policy, in Daniel Lerner's *The Human Meaning of the Social Sciences* indicates that researchers are often frustrated because persons who formulate policy and engage in the exercise of power rarely simply follow recommendations of the research. Millikan argues that policy-makers have other matters to bring to bear than those in the purview of the researcher, and that the contribution of research is "to deepen, broaden, and extend the policy-maker's capacity for judgment—not to provide him with answers."[8]) The moralist, however, is not likely to have so mechanistic a view of social developments that research would permit him to function as a social technocrat or engineer who can control events to guarantee their outcome.

A more modest claim is likely. In the light of empirical research the moralist is likely to gain insight into the potential consequences of various courses of morally determined action. Insofar as the consequences of action have moral weight, that is, insofar as they can be judged to be morally good or better, evil or less evil, calculation of consequences is of major importance. In this regard social research can fulfill an important role in more precise calculation. This is possible without accepting a view of absolute determinism; what one accepts is at least the degree of determinism that is assumed in all views of human action, namely, that to initiate an act is to intend certain consequences and to exercise such powers as one has to make those consequences most likely to occur.

4. The more problematic use of the empirical sciences is in the *development of moral norms*. It is problematic because it raises the philosophical questions of the relations of fact to value, of the *is* to the *ought*. Our concern is not to rehearse that question in terms of the logical problems involved, or to review the hundreds of pages of discussion about it in the past seventy years. Rather, we shall indicate some of the problems involved in the relation of empirical sciences to moral norms. Since the range of such sciences is so wide and the applicability so multiple, our investigation takes on even more of an outline form at this point.

First, let us examine the possibility that the moral norms for economic justice might arise out of economic science, out of economic data. In the introduction I indicated that one no longer finds the level of generality of the great social encyclicals to be satisfactory for social ethics. Thus, it is clear that I am positive about the contribution of economic science to economic ethics. But one immediately is pressed to ask: what are the principles used to judge a "good" economic system from the standpoint of economics? Not being well versed in economics, I can only indicate some hunches in this area; but it does not take much reading to find out that there are differences of opinion about what constitutes a good economics system. Clearly, the science seeks *to minimize radical instability* in the economic system when economic knowledge is applied to policy. However, there are differences of opinion about how much instability is tolerable, and at what costs to whom in the society. Certainly *growth* has been a factor in recent decades in judging a "good" economic system. Growth clearly affects stability, and depending on where the growth is, it affects some persons adversely and other persons advantageously.

The more clearly ethical questions emerge when a word like *distribution* is introduced into the discourse, for it immediately evokes tones of justice. But it also calls attention to differences of opinion within the science itself. For example, I believe there was a strong opinion a few years ago that the way in which the economy might best grow would be for some persons to have sufficient resources beyond their needs in order to plow the surplus back into the economy in the form of capital investments. There was alongside of that the opinion that the pump should be primed at the other end, that is, by increasing the consumer power of the masses sufficiently to create increased demands which in turn would call forth increased capital investment. (I do not mean to suggest that these two opinions were not reconcilable at some levels.) My point is to suggest that the question of how wealth should be distributed is a factor within the development of the system, and does not necessarily, from the standpoint of the economist, immediately raise the questions of justice. But the question of distributive justice with all its ramifications does enter rather quickly into a critical discussion. If one takes either of two famous formulas, "To each his due," and "Equals shall be treated equally," one quickly sees that economic science alone cannot determine what is due to each person, or who are the equals who ought to be treated equally, except on the assumption that the free market system takes care of the question of justice—that is, in a free market system persons would receive what was due them, and if they did not receive much they were not due much.

I hope it does not enlarge issues too swiftly or too much to suggest that when economists address policy questions (and the purpose of their science is in large part to contribute to policy and the direction of society), the themes of liberty, justice, and power are always latent. Indeed, one difference between state-controlled economies, such as that of the Soviet Union, and freer economies, such as that of the United States, is the difference between the allocations of liberty, justice, and power. One might argue, I suppose, that from an economic standpoint one reaches decisions about these distributions; that is, one might develop norms for the distribution of liberty, justice, and power out of assessments about what it takes to make the economy function with a minimum basis of instability and a necessary rate of growth. Yet what might be judged to be best for the economic system to function as a system does not from various moral points of view satisfy, for example, the concern for distributive justice. What determines the norms of justice are noneconomic judgments about whether persons are to be rewarded according to need, or according to productive contribution or other criteria of merit, or according to ascribed status due to inherited social class. Clearly, if need were the criterion, it would have significant consequences on the allocations of power and liberty in the society. These would be different from the consequences that occur if one or several criteria of merit were used, or if there were a mixture of need and merit. The moral norm of distributive justice does not arise from economic science, but is independent of it.

When one is addressing questions of economic *policy,* one is in an arena in which ethical considerations and economic science interact with each other. At this level a case might be made that policy norms, used to determine the exercise of economic power, take on a character that is both empirically and ethically informed. (In a sense, the encyclicals have not been policy statements, but guides for policy; the policies illumined or directed by them had to be worked out under particular economic, not to mention political and other social conditions.) Yet even at the level of economic policy it is not possible to say that good economics is good ethics, since the reference of the word good in each case is different. Good economics usually refers to the successful functioning of an economic system as this is interpreted from a particular point of view in that science, and not to concepts such as distributive justice. Policy norms are informed by economic science, and refer to a given set of conditions in which the ends of human and moral values are sought, but policy norms are not in a restrictive sense purely moral norms.

In an essay, "What Is the Normatively Human?" (see chapter 12), I have addressed the question of the relation of empirical sciences to the answer to that question in more detail. One example from that essay might be instructive at this point. In the area of obligations to keep life alive, at certain points the statistically human functions to establish the moral norm. These points pertain to birth defects. Birth anomalies of the grossest order are often called "monstrosities," and no moralist questions whether an obstetrician has the right not to sustain such living matter. Such monstrosities deviate so significantly from the statistical norm of the physically human that they are not judged morally to be human. At the other end of the spectrum are the "normal" infants, who are within the statistical range of the descriptively human, and here there is no argument about the obligations of obstetricians to sustain the life of such infants. Increasingly, questions are being raised about genetically defective fetuses, and about the relation of the statistical norm to the moral norm, or put in the form of a question, how defective (statistically deviant from the norm) does a fetus have to be before it is judged not to be normatively human from a moral point of view? Is the mongoloid fetus to be so judged? Is the fetus that has the dreaded Tay-Sachs disease? It is clear that the statistical norm refers not only to individual humans in such cases, but also to a normative conception of the human gene pool. A judgment about the benefits or cost to the future of the human race is based upon statistical extrapolations.

Clearly, in the cases purported to be ambiguous the moral norm of the right to life is determined not merely by empirical evidence, but also by what the human community values as normatively human. There are appeals to moral values which are not embedded in the empirically (physically) normative in all the instances in which the moralist would insist upon the right to life of fetuses or infants who deviate. Yet it should be clear that by permitting a judgment in cases of gross deformities that is based on empirical evidence alone, the moralist has opened the door to the use of such evidence in other cases as well. There might be several responses to this dilemma. One, it could be argued that even in the cases of gross deformities there are appeals to moral values which enter into the judgment, and these support the contention that there is no obligation to sustain the living matter. Another might be an elaboration of the first, namely, that there is a dialectic between the empirical and the ethical, and that this must be worked out with references to particular instances or to classes of instances. If this is granted, however, one must accept a degree of necessary uncertitude of moral judgment, for one would be appealing both to "facts" and to "values" which do not cohere perfectly.[9]

B. Major Problems Involved in the Use of Empirical Sciences

The purpose of this part of the essay is to specify some of the issues previously suggested. This can be done by formulating three major questions.

1. What data and concepts are relevant to the moral issue under discussion?

The answers to this question involve a number of difficult considerations. First, responses to "moral" problems are made in terms of the delineations of what empirically is the issue; such delineations are made in terms of experiential or empirical data. Thus, what is included and excluded is crucial to what the actual moral issue is. One simple example will make the point clear. What is the situation of a dying patient? One has a different definition of the moral issues if the financial circumstance of his family is included in the situation than if it is excluded. If the use of artificial life support systems is draining the family resources, is this a relevant consideration in the determination? From some moral points of view it is not, from others it is. To include such information reflects a moral point of view; at the same time the exclusion of the information would state the moral issues in a different way.

Second, in many instances the empirical studies used in moral theology and social ethics were not designed to help the moralist answer his questions; the studies were not done to resolve the moral questions. Thus, the studies are in a profound sense "translated" from their own arena of purpose to another. Certain information which is crucial for the moralist might not have been crucial for another purpose. Great care must be taken in acknowledging the limitations and difficulties of this translation process, for it might not only distort the data used, but also require a reformulation of the moral questions in such a way that crucial aspects from an ethician's point of view are ignored.

Third, it is possible that a predetermination of which data and concepts are relevant to the moral issue might foreclose awareness of other studies, points of view, and information that are in the end of equal, if not greater relevance. For example, as one proceeds with a question of economic ethics, he might foreclose it if he is not aware that political and social issues studied by other sciences are at least as significant, if not more so, in coming to a resolution. The ethician clearly needs to be open to a wide range of studies that might possibly pertain to the issues he is specifically attending to. The peril of openness should also be noted: since most human problems defy the boundaries within which research is conducted, it is possible to develop a degree of complexity of information and concepts that makes thinking unmanageable and resolution impossible.

2. What interpretation of a field should be accepted? And on what grounds?

This question has been addressed at several points previously, and the considerations need only to be summarized here. If the moralist accepts an interpretation on its "scientific" adequacy, he has the burden of making his case for his choice on scientific grounds. Clearly, most moralists are in no position to do that. Yet a counsel of despair is out of order. There are ways available to the moralist for determining which scholars are more reliable, and which interpretations are at least most questionable. The moralist clearly needs to be in communication with scholars in the areas from which he borrows in order to avoid horrendous mistakes of judgment, but he has to accept responsibility for making choices within the best of his knowledge.

If he chooses those studies that have an affinity with his own philosophical or theological point of view, he must be prepared to defend such decisions. In such an instance he would argue for the researcher's philosophical point of view as being more adequate, accurate, or at least plausible with reference to the understanding of man and society. For example, if he has a preference for social research that maximally takes into account man's capacity to choose, decide, and act (in short, a high measure of free will), he is in a sense not only under obligation to defend that philosophically, but also to argue that studies done from such a position are more likely to be empirically adequate.

The moralist's third possibility is more eclectic, namely, to use empirical research for sources of "insight" into the nature of man and society. Here he takes full responsibility to be his own thinker, and not to borrow authority from the research. To defend such use he will probably make claims for interpretations and data on the basis of the "sense" that they make to him and to his purposes. His uses are subject to critical judgment and to revision when the insights appear to be inadequate or the data invalid.

3. How does the moralist deal with the value biases of the studies that he uses?

If it is conceded that value preferences are involved in many dimensions of empirical research, this question can be difficult to answer. The researcher's choice of an area of study at least refers to his interests, if not to what he values as being significant for the human good. Thus, there is a reference to value in the choice of what to study. In addition, his preference for certain values is likely to have a considerable measure of effect on how he defines his research problem, what he is looking for, and what he consequently sees. This has become clear in the conflicts within some of the social sciences between those who have revolutionary tendencies and those who are "liberal reformers."

Again, a counsel of despair is out of order, for while the post-empirical and even postethical (in the sense of decisions about values or ways of life that can never be fully defended on rational grounds alone) are at work, there are canons of evaluation about good research which mitigate some of the potential idiosyncratic consequences of these assumptions. As empirical sciences become more sophisticated about these matters, there is greater articulation of them by the researchers, and this facilitates the moralists' discourse.

The moralist has to accept responsibility for his own way of answering all three of these questions. He is, after all, finite. He can, after all, only do what he has the capacities to do. Within awareness of these questions, he is more likely to be a better moralist by being widely and deeply informed from the side of empirical research. But empirical research will never replace ethical arguments in the resolution of moral issues.

12

What Is
the
Normatively Human?

The word human is read and heard in discussions of moral issues more frequently as each year goes by. Fifteen years ago it was seldom used; today it is broadly used as if its meaning were clear, its references universally understood, and its persuasiveness unexceptionable. After all, who would want to support something that is "inhuman"? One finds it in theological discourse about the ethical. Paul Lehmann's phrase "to make and keep human life human" has become common parlance among Protestant academics, and William Van der Marck's "The human is the Christian and the Christian is the human" speaks for a considerable body of Catholic ethical thought, whether it takes the form of highly technical discourse or popular exhortation.[1] Robert Johann develops the significance of notions of "wholeness" and of "community" in a particularly insightful way under the general title *On Building the Human*.[2] In popular rhetoric we have all heard over and over that urban technological society is "dehumanizing," that repression of the poor and the Blacks is "dehumanizing," and the positive correlates of these observations

---

Reprinted from *The American Ecclesiastical Review*, CLXV, No. 3 (Nov. 1971), 192-207. Used by permission.

set the direction for reformist and revolutionary activity. We are concerned to humanize society.

The drift of both the academic and the popular discourse is to be affirmed; something sound is being said, and the moral passion with which it is said reflects the finest and noblest moral sensibility. But precise specification of the meaning of the human cannot be avoided when we confront issues such as abortion, genetic manipulation, and behavior control through manipulation of the brain. The question that cannot be settled to the satisfaction of all disputants in the abortion issue is at what point the fetus is considered to be human or to have human rights. In genetic manipulation there is a concern both for the means of research and for possible consequences of it which might violate the human as we have known it. In brain manipulation the question is whether something human is being abused by the uses of electrical and pharmaceutical means to control human behavior. When one gets to the hard cases, the drift of rhetoric and discourse requires specification, unless one has confidence in the intuitive powers of all men to feel and know what the truly human is under every possible circumstance.

The difficulties of such specification provide not just an academic puzzle to be resolved; rather, the effort is important for the clarification of practical moral discourse, for the specification of moral judgments and decisions, and for the evaluation of the consequence of scientific endeavors. It would be folly to assume that one could answer in a few pages the question which provides the title to this chapter, but some clarification can be provided of how we might go about answering it. Indeed, this attempt is, on the whole, a prologue to the answer, rather than a ringing and persuasive settling of the question. We are particularly concerned to look both at the contribution of scientific data to the answer, and at the limitations of such a contribution. The comment that "good science is good ethics" is, in the end, rejected— but to assume that we can answer the question without consideration of empirical observation and data is equally to be rejected.

The Concept of the Human

That most of us resort to *description* of certain conditions of life when we think about what is *in*human is clear, and our commonsense approach may provide important insight. We assume to a great extent that there is a common understanding of at least which conditions are extremely antithetical to the human. For example, it never occurs to most of us to dispute the allegation that the ways in which black people are treated in America is dehumanizing. We do not dispute this because we are afraid that to do so would make us look terribly out of style in the company of persons of moral refinement; rather, we do not dispute it because most of us agree that the conditions in which many black people live are, without a doubt, dehumanizing. Yet let us imagine a tabula rasa, or a being from some other realm of life engaging in the conversation. He might ask *what* conditions in which black people live are dehumanizing, and *why* we call them inhumane. How would we answer? We would range over a great number of aspects of the black experience in a descriptive way. The physical conditions of ghetto life in which most black people live would be described, the psychological consequences of centuries of repression in a status of inequality would be enumerated, and so forth. Or, for another example, if confronted with a birth anomaly in the delivery room of a hospital, our very designation of such as a "monstrosity" packs in a descriptive element. It is monstrous because it diverges widely from the statistical norm of what human infants are. We would not call it "inhuman" on the basis of its parentage; both parents are human.

There are, however, borderline cases which are not so simply solved. We are not ready to say that the mongoloid infant is "not human." It, too, has human parentage, and most of us would be offended if someone called it a monstrosity. Physically, it is closer to the statistical norm. But let us suppose that Mr. A would assert that the mongoloid infant is "not *truly* human" and thus we have no responsibility to keep it alive. What grounds would be given? A different judgment would be made about the degree of divergence from the statistical norm that marks the line between the human and the nonhuman. But I suspect another element would come into the account, namely, the capabilities for development into what Mr. A would judge to be "fully human" existence. This observation is important, for it indicates that there is a *teleological element* in the judgment, and the argument would occur not only on the basis of divergence from the statistical norm, but also on what constitutes the meaning of "the human," or the "truly" human, or the "fully" human. We must underscore a point: that argument would not take place without some reference to the empirical and the descriptive, though it would never be resolved simply on empirical and descriptive grounds. One can readily imagine occasions in which two persons would agree that physicians are under no obligation to keep alive a particular "monstrosity" that has some physical processes functioning; it is more difficult to imagine agreement on the borderline cases. Descriptive and empirical elements would be data in their arguments about the borderline cases, but they would never in themselves settle it. Simple logical distinctions between descriptive "factual" statements and moral "value" statements do not resolve such practical dilemmas, at least not in the first instance.

In the light of this, our question can be specified a bit more: What is the relation of the empirical and descriptive elements to the ethically normative elements in concepts of "the human"? Just as I have become persuaded that the major question about moral value in the sphere of biomedical developments is "What do we value about human life?" so I have become persuaded that the major question in how we proceed to answer that question is the relation of the empirical and descriptive elements to the ethically normative elements.

Let us engage in a thought experiment in order to pursue the question of the relation between empirical and the ethically normative in notions of the human. Consider Dr. José Delgado's use of electrical impulses transmitted to the brain through electrodes implanted in its various regions as a means of evoking the desired reactions from the experimental subject. Presumably, the experimenter could control a great deal of human behavior through widespread use of such a procedure. This brief description of Delgado's work gives us sufficient information to raise a number of questions.

First, do the results of his work tell us what it is to be human? It all depends on what we are willing to settle for as the referents for the concept of the human. What sorts of data count, and how are they to be used with reference even to the descriptive aspects of the human? Would statistical evidences which warrant generalizations about what actually causes human behavior provide us with the substantial content we need to determine what is "truly" human? Imagine that as a result of research by biochemists and others it is "proved" that behavior is absolutely determined in a cause-effect mode, that so-called mental activity is merely the epiphenomenal consequences of biochemical and electrical processes in the brain. What is human is then only a more intricate development through evolution from other forms of life, and there is no significant discontinuity between what one would describe as human and what one would describe as animal behavior. If this were the case, what would it mean to say that we are to make and keep human life truly human? That we are to build the human? It is clear that persons who speak about the human in a moral frame of reference have something in mind other than the generalizations made from biological experimentation on the brain or elsewhere. What would be "normatively" human surely could not go against whatever is known of men from scientific evidence. Indeed, in the history of moral development we have seen occasions in which we no longer hold persons accountable for deeds that in former times were presumed to be subject to full control by the "will." But most persons who now speak about the human in a normative context would still hold that the capacity to respond, to govern one's actions in accordance with decisions and purposes, to be accountable for what one does are part of the human in distinction from the animal.

Consider another sort of thought experiment. Suppose the sociologists are able to conclude on the basis of refined sampling techniques that the majority of persons desire, or prefer, that other persons make their decisions for them, and that others tell them what they ought to do. Suppose the subjects of such opinion research indicated that life for them is more pleasant and freer from anxiety in circumstances in which they are not given the freedom to determine for themselves what they ought to do. Suppose that the statistical evidence showed that most persons wish to "escape from freedom" (to use the title of one of Erich Fromm's earlier books). Would we be prepared to say that because the majority prefer such a life, that mode of life is more truly human than a mode of life in which there is a minimization of social control, in which there is a maximization of personal accountability for what one does? Probably most persons would not. But what if we publicly announced that the escape from freedom was an inhuman way to live, that its effects were dehumanizing? In many ways we do make such an assertion about such conditions. But then, suppose those who like to live that way retort that it is inhuman to expect men to be something other than they are, and that not only are men statistically in favor of the escape from freedom, but that these persons enjoy life more than those who are trying to be creative, responsible, and free? It is clear that the pending discussion will not be settled on the evidences of statistics, and yet those who wish to say that to be human is to maximize freedom would hardly wish to say that those who cannot bear such a mode of life are less than human.

Now, let us introduce a third thought experiment. Theologian X comes from a Protestant Kantian theological tradition. He tells us in a lecture that the Christian view of man states that "each man is the author of his own acts." He then expounds on the implications of this affirmation, telling us that it testifies to the vocation of man to be morally accountable for his deeds, that it is the presupposition of human guilt, and that men are indeed guilty since they know that they are responsible and yet fail to fulfill their obligations to others. I suppose that most of us would want to qualify such a view of man, or at least refine it in some ways, but how would we go about it? We might ask on what grounds he asserts that each man is the author of his own acts. If he says this on theological grounds, we would presumably have to argue with him on theological grounds, or else proceed to indicate that his theology is deficient in not taking into account many things we know about human action. If he says it on the grounds that it is an empirically, factually true statement about the nature of man which is to be adhered to not only because it is "Christian" but also because he can prove it philosophically, or biologically, or some other way, we would have a different sort of quarrel with him. We might wish to find out what the word author is supposed to indicate—whether its references are in the direction of "creator" of his acts (in a strong sense) or in the direction of "putting together things in a different way." I suspect that our argument would begin to use descriptive evidences to indicate that if by "author" he means something like "creator ex nihilo," it simply cannot be the case. If his claim that "each man is the author of his own acts" is even a normative statement of what it means to be human, would all sorts of descriptive evidences modify, if not subvert, that as a statement of what man truly is? We would marshal evidences from genetics that might indicate that a person's acts are limited in a significant way by his genotype; or we might cite evidences from psychoanalysis, cultural anthropology, social psychology, or sociology. The point is that even if on some ethical grounds we might say that a normative statement about the human would include the assertation that "each man is the author of his own acts," we would bring empirical evidences or descriptive accounts both to sustain and to clarify the assertation.

Further thought experiments could be introduced that would suggest other sorts of ways in which the descriptive and empirical is and is not used in the formation of a normative concept of the human. Sufficient churning of the matter, however, has been done. It remains to draw together some responses which will mark the way toward an answer to the question of the relation of the descriptive to the normative.

Relation of the Empirical to the Normative

The first response is that another question is appropriate, one already suggested in the course of previous discussion. When we are examining the relation of the empirical to the normative in a view of the human (our own, or another's), *what counts for evidence* even in the descriptive reference of the concept? Any answer to this question involves judgments that have far-reaching significance for any further discussion. A prejudgment about what is and is not "truly human" probably lurks in the judgment about what data to use in describing the human. From our three thought experiments we can indicate at least three answers to the question.

In the first, the neurophysiological study of the brain, it might be said that one would arrive at the nature of the human by giving a scientifically verifiable account of the neurological processes which govern human behavior. The descriptive or empirical data of the human would result from rigorous scientific procedures and a plausible interpretation of the significance of them. Is there a prejudgment involved? If there is not a prejudgment, there is at least a preference for an hypothesis that, no doubt, emerges from other data. That preference might be stated as such: To be human is to have a neurophysiological system in continuity with but in many respects more highly developed than other animals. Dr. Delgado is particularly interesting since he is more willing than other experimenters to speculate about what can be done with such knowledge for what he considers the "well-being" of the human race. Using such knowledge one could achieve a "psycho-civilization" in which there is reduction of anxiety and aggression and other sorts of pleasant prospects.[3]

In the second thought experiment, someone might claim that what describes the human is the statistical evidence drawn from a study of the preferences of people. To be sure, if only 51 percent of the people preferred to "escape from freedom" one would not be able to make a strong case for a generalized view. Social scientists are sophisticated in their treatment of data; they might project only that certain statistical probabilities will be verified with reference to the preferences of persons. But from such a view one might infer that no normative concepts of the human are possible other than the statistical norms, and that such norms are bound to change with changing social and cultural situations. An admittedly gross generalization might be made to illustrate this: two decades ago one might have said that a normative view of the human would include man's need or vocation to achieve; perhaps opinion studies would have given support to such a view—it would have been close to a statistical norm. Yet today, particularly in the "counter-culture," one would hardly suggest that to be human is to achieve or to be goal-oriented. A new norm is arising that could be supported in part by a new statistical study. What role does statistical evidence play in determining even the descriptive references of the human?

In our third thought experiment some method other than statistics seems to be involved in order to establish even the descriptive references of the claim that each man is the author of his own acts. One would not arrive at such a view without some reference to experience, but obviously the deductions, transcendental or otherwise, that are made from experience lead to a special sort of conclusion. Perhaps the route taken is that which Kant took in order to establish that man is free. But one has a right to question whether there is not a preference involved that selects and orders elements of experience in such a way that the conclusion is almost foreordained.

I would conclude from this cursory examination that the use of empirical data either in refined form or in the rough form of descriptive accounts, in the establishment of a concept of the human is, indeed, a tricky business. I find it difficult to agree, at least on the face of it, with John Giles Milhaven when he suggests that "good medicine is good morality, and vice-versa," or that "the ethical question can be purely a question of economics."[4] The difficulty lies in the simple equation of good medicine with good morality, of ethical questions with economic questions. If Milhaven's comments were to be spelled out in terms of the idea that we could deduce or infer what is good morality from medicine or economics, it is too facile. Whose medical data and theories would we use? Which economic data and theories would we use? If, however, Milhaven is telling us that what is morally good cannot be medically or economically impossible, there are grounds for some agreement. But such an interpretation of his intention simply points to where the hard issues lie: What counts for data? Whose data are to be used? Which accounts of the human are most "accurate"?

The second response to the three thought experiments is this: How do we arrive at the normative concept of the human in an ethical sense in relation to the data? I shall outline five optional answers to that question in hopes of alerting us all to what is involved.

First, one could assert that the ethical norm and the statistical norm, or the most persuasive descriptive account, are one and the same. If, for example, an infant is reasonably close to the statistical norm of what infants are when they are born, it is judged to be "human"; and therefore it is treated ethically as a human. If, however, it diverges widely from the statistical norm, it is judged not to be human and therefore has no human rights. Or, if, on the basis of opinion polls, it is shown that most persons do not regard a fetus as being human, then ethically it has no human value or rights, and there are no moral questions about abortion.

I suspect that few people would accept such a procedure. One quickly asks how to judge what is "reasonably close" to the statistical norm with reference to infants. Would a high probability that an infant would be an epileptic constitute a significant enough divergence from the norm to let it be called "not truly human"? One also quickly asks whether all the forms of discrimination and repression are ethically right simply because a high percentage of the American people have regarded Blacks and Indians as not fully human.

For a second option, one could assert that we could find out what is ethically normative in the human through a process of empirical cross-cultural analysis. We could follow the efforts of those cultural anthropologists who have developed certain cultural universals, or certain prerequisites for human societies, and from this develop generalizations about what are at least the minimal conditions for human survival. We might find, for example, that rules against incest or patterns of social authority are present in all societies, and from these develop some ethical norms for the human. David Little has made such moves in his article "Calvin and the Prospects for a Christian Theory of Natural Law,"[5] in which he engages in a three-way discussion between theology, the social sciences, and contemporary analytical moral philosophy. Little, after an intricate discussion, writes, "We are, then, coming close to an empirical definition of 'humanity' as distinct from the primates (to whom man is obviously similar in many respects): *to be human is to order life cooperatively.*" In an important footnote he indicates that "cooperatively" implies cultural as well as other kinds of sharing. Little states a bit further on, "Beings become human insofar as they are capable of symboling and sharing. There is, as it were, a certain fixed design to the concept 'human' which designates what man must do and be, if he will survive as *man.*"[6] While the "empirical definition" is rather formal in character, it can be given substantial content from data of a variety of sorts.

This approach is characterized by induction from a wide variety of data. The status of the affirmation that "to be human is to order life cooperatively" is more that of a generalization based upon empirical evidences than it is an ontological statement. The approach shies away from the issues that other philosophers would raise about the ontological structure of human existence, about man's "being" in distinction from his existential and historical manifestations. No doubt others could use the same method that Little uses, and come to different, more elaborate conclusions. The move to the ethically normative follows; on the basis of cultural universals arrived at inductively, one defines what the human is. This definition operates, in turn, also as a basis for ethical norms of the human, and is brought into the processes of moral decision and judgment that are required to determine whether particular circumstances or particular acts are "human" or "inhuman."

For a third option, one might suggest a revision of the second, though the method used would be basically the same. One might read widely, conduct surveys, observe human societies and action, and come up with generalizations about certain things that most persons *value,* things toward which they aspire. On the basis of this, descriptive generalizations could be made about the sorts of goals, aspirations, and values, that persons most deeply share. If one wished to dignify this procedure, he might characterize it as an effort to develop a phenomenology of human values. I have attempted to do this in some earlier work, particularly in a paper done for a conference on brain research.[7] One seeks to determine what are the fundamental conditions for meaningful personal life, both in individual and social terms. For example, what apprehension of values lies within the disquiet most of us have at the prospect of manipulating human behavioral responses through electrical or pharmaceutical means? One is the capacity to be self-determining, not in an absolute sense, but at least in the sense of not being "thingified" to the degree that we are merely extensions of the power of others. We wish to be treated as ends, rather than as means; we resist becoming "its" rather than "thous." Perceptions of other areas of human experience, and reflection on such perceptions yield other values, other aspirations, which seem to be close to a normative view of the human based upon such perceptions and generalizations from experience.

Like the procedure that David Little uses, this one also eschews the ontological leap—i.e., to state that such insights yield knowledge of the nature or being of man—though it is not impossible to reconcile such a procedure with such philosophical intentions. As I have tried to work this way, a plurality of "values," or of "requisites" for the normatively human are developed. The apprehension and articulation of these in a pluralistic way is less than satisfying in some respects, for it does not settle the sorts of conflicts that are bound to emerge when two or more such requisites are abrasive to each other under particular circumstances. However, I would defend the plurality as being close enough to raw experience to be valid, and distant enough from it to provide clarification of choices about the human under particular circumstances.

For a fourth option, there are those who find a vision of the human, or a model of the human in ideal paradigms, or in imaginative constructions of what man's existence can and ought to be. Jaspers, for example, has suggested that in the cultural history of mankind Buddha, Socrates, and Jesus have functioned as such paradigmatic personalities. Prof. Antonio Cua has provided a suggestive account of the significance of such views in his article "Morality and Paradigmatic Individuals."[8] In social dimensions, myths of an idyllic past, a Garden of Eden, have functioned to provide visions of what man truly is meant to be; projections into the future of a kingdom of God, a "peaceable kingdom," and other visions have provided other clues to what is truly human.

What makes certain individuals compelling as examples of what it means to be truly human? What makes certain social visions appealing as representations of what a truly human community ought to be? When the individuals and the social visions have religious sources we have often heard them defended as revelations. But the notion of revelation is ambiguous. They can be revelations because people believe that somehow God dictated they come into historical reality, and thus their authority is extrinsic to their content. But they can also be revelations because in them there is an apprehension of what man can and ought to be which in turn resonates with the deepest human longings and appeals to the highest human aspirations. I take it that something of the latter notion of revelation is appealed to even in the Christian community when the paradigmatic figure of Jesus Christ is asserted to be true man. It is not that the truth of his humanity has to be authorized by some magical view of scripture or by some ecclesiastical authority. Rather, it is that the records, in all their fallibility, of his deeds and words, his life and death, portray something very compelling to many of us, for they portray the truly and fully human life of man with and for others, love which suffers and leads to death, freedom that is not license and hope that is not fantasy, obligation fulfilled in service.

But the historical presence of paradigmatic persons or of visions of the social good did not occur only once in human history. Not all the richness and nuances of human life could be portrayed in one life, or in one vision. There are frankly competing visions, and visions which supplement and complement each other. Indeed, there are visions which have a relevance to the struggles for humanity in one time that are not as pertinent in another, visions which show what human life can be to those groups and individuals who have one deprivation which does not mean as much to those who have another.

In the appeal to persons, and perhaps to occasional historical communities, there is also a relation of the descriptive and empirical to the normative. The case is often made less by conscious processes of argumentation than by a felt authentication. The reasons are more the "reasons of the heart" than persuasive logical argumentation. But the question remains as to how one moves back from the paradigmatic person or community to the struggle to determine what is truly human under the particular conditions of brain control, or genetic manipulation, and of abortion. For some, that too is a reason of the heart, an intuitive perception resulting from sensibility and imagination more than from rational discourse. For others the paradigms are but illuminations, not fully disclosing the meaning of the human, but giving insight which together with other insight and other wisdom provides some clarification of what it means to be a human person, or to be a human community.

For the fifth option, there is a great tradition that makes ontological claims. It claims, either through the Christianized views of Aristotle's nature, or through the Christianized views of existential phenomenology, or just through such views without baptism, that man's apprehensions of the truly human are not merely generalizations from experience, or visions of the good life, but are knowledge of the *being* of man. What is the normatively human? The normatively human is the true nature of man, man as he was created to be, man as his fundamental intentionality and tendency direct him to be. Clearly, knowledge of man's "true nature" does not come apart from sensitive observations of experience, or apart from full participation in human experience—but what is claimed to be known is more than the averaging out of experience, more than a polling of aspirations. It is the structure and dynamic of the being of the human itself.

The content of these apprehensions of the true being of the human is often highly formal; it is man's tending toward the good, or it is man in his corporeity and his sociality. The move is a familiar one. Van der Marck, for example, wrote that "the very essence and nature of man is intersubjectivity." This is not a sociological generalization that human beings tend to live together, be dependent upon each other, and enjoy each other; it is a statement about the "very essence and nature" of man. From this statement certain aims and ends follow, all of which tell us something about man. "The ultimate aim of man is none other than intersubjectivity, communication, community, a share in common humanity, love, justice."[9]

In particular decisions about what builds the human under specific circumstances, what makes and keeps human life human, the task is to draw inferences from these more formal apprehensions of man's essence which are pertinent to the choices that are forced upon one. The moves, crudely put, are from experience to the fundamental nature and structure of the human which becomes normative, and then back to experience again to judge and to direct it.

The first of these five optional answers to the question of how we arrive at a normative concept of the human is the easiest to reject. It is clear that the statistical norm is not necessarily the moral norm, and probably is actually never the moral norm. The other four are not necessarily mutually exclusive, and the importance of struggling for some workable concepts of the truly and fully human provides practical incentive for not ruling any of them out without further exploration of their contributions.

My third response to the question "What is the relation between the empirical and descriptive elements and the ethically normative elements in concepts of the human?" is that the context in which we seek an answer will be important both in the method of finding it and in what aspects are stressed. Two sorts of circumstances illustrate my point. One is the circumstances of the philosopher or theologian who is trying to state what is essentially human, or what is universally human. The effort to state the universally truly human simply requires a degree of formality which bears with it certain ways of working that are different from what the obstetrician is trying to decide when he has doubts about a specific obligation to seek to preserve the life of a significantly abnormal infant, or from the geneticist who is speculating about whether it is morally right to "clone" a human being. It is fitting and proper in the circumstances of the speculative philosopher, for his purposes, to come to such generalizations as "to be human is to order life cooperatively" or "the very essence and nature of man is intersubjectivity." But I suspect that a physician attending a dying patient and trying to decide whether he is under obligation to use extraordinary means to sustain life would be either angered or bemused if, in answer to his question "In what sense is this still a human person?" he got one of those answers.

The upshot of this last response is to suggest that the empirical data that the physician uses is of a *more specific character* than that which the philosopher uses, and thus the discussion of the relation of that data to the ethically normative has to take place with a specificity commensurate with the problems involved. The physician's question is likely to be "What is the significance of a flat electroencephalogram for judging whether this organism has the value of a human, is truly human, is fully human?" His circumstances are very different from the philosopher's and the theologian's when they are normally dealing with the question. We need to carry on our discourse in both sets of circumstances, in relation to both purposes.

Conclusion

In a discussion with a theologian who speaks a great deal about "the human," I once pressed the sorts of questions I have raised here. It is a compelling but difficult task to formulate clearly and precisely what the normatively human is. Thus, I turned to him, and asked, "What, then, is the human?" He turned to me and answered, "Jim, if you don't know, I can't tell you." I reject what is implied in his response to me, namely, that we have sufficient individual capacities to intuit the meaning of the truly human in each set of circumstances.

In a discussion with a philosopher who responded to a paper of mine in which I pleaded for some objective formulations of criteria of the human, he was worried that the criteria would become goals, and we would use various means to manipulate persons and communities to embody these goals. He properly pleaded for the "humility of ignorance," for the recognition that some things be left to chance rather than to deliberate action. Since we cannot define the human, he said, let us respect it and respond to it as a mystery. While agreeing with the caution, I reject the consequence.

I believe that finding what is the human is an ongoing process of discovery. It is never a search that is complete, but the process goes on for several reasons. One is that we as humans, individually and as a race, are changing and developing. New historical circumstances, new information about man's mind and body, new awareness of human aspirations and problems all compel a process of rethinking old norms (not their rejection) and discovering the import to be placed on various norms under various circumstances. The race has discovered, all too slowly, the inhumanity of slavery and war; it may discover the humanity of love, self-determination, of peace and justice as it develops.

Another reason for the continuing search is that no one of us, or no class of us, is sufficiently perceptive and wise to be able to give the answer. The insights come from poets as well as philosophers; they are made clear in narratives as well as moral principles; they emerge out of dialectic between scientists and humanists; they can be found in religion and in those who attack religion.

But the task is no less compelling because it is difficult and unending. Teilhard aptly reminds us that in the card game of evolution, we have become the players, as well as the cards and the stakes. The urgency should not overcome complexity in favor of rhetoric. We all have the task of pondering over two questions: "What do we value about the human?" and "What is the relation of the empirical and descriptive to the ethically normative in our concept of human?" My strong hunch is that to be human is to have a vocation, a calling; that it is to become what we now are not; that it calls for a surpassing of what we are; that apart from a telos, a vision of what man can and ought to do, we will flounder and decay.

13

Basic Ethical Issues
in
the Biomedical Fields*

The "new biology" and developments in medical science and technology have aroused a great deal of public interest. Nothing less than the future of human development seems to be at stake. Although men have always affected the course of evolution through such things as wars, the exposure of infants, and the use of natural resources, we are now able to intervene purposively in ways that did not exist before in the developmental process to prolong, shorten, and direct human life. Commentary on this new set of circumstances has come from scientists, social critics, journalists, philosophers, theologians, lawyers, and many others. The public is sharply aware of the growth of knowledge and understanding of the life processes, of the power that this provides for human intervention and control, and thus of the extent to which human destiny is in the hands of men themselves rather than being fated by natural evolution or immediately governed by Deity. Two Jesuit theologians have stated very well the human fact that

Reprinted with permission from *Soundings,* LIII (Summer 1970), pp. 151-80.

* This essay has had the benefit of careful critical reading by Julian N. Hartt, of Yale, Martin Golding, of Columbia, Karl Hartzell, of SUNY, Stony Brook, and most intensively by Dr. Leon Kass, of NIH in Bethesda. None will be satisfied with my efforts to take their criticisms into account; I am, nonetheless, much in debt to each.

bristles with potentialities for good and ill. Teilhard de Chardin, in *The Phenomenon of Man,* simply states, "We are evolution." He also makes the point more dramatically: "We have become aware that, in the great game that is being played, we are the players as well as being the cards and the stakes."[1] Karl Rahner, in an interesting and important essay, "Experiment: Man," asserts that "human self-creation means quite simply that today man is changing himself. To be more precise: Man is consciously and deliberately changing himself." "Man today finds that he is manipulable. A radically new age is coming–new in every dimension."[2]

These writers and others are responding to many scientific developments. Both negative and positive eugenics lie within the scientific capacities of man. The technical capabilities exist for family planning and population control. Artificial environments can be constructed so that human beings can exist where the natural environment is hostile to them. Chemical and electrical interventions in the human brain make possible states of euphoria, but they also create new possibilities of controlling the responses of others.

New human moral problems emerge in a sharp way. Who will determine how these capabilities are to be used? Do we have a right to experiment on human beings? What envisioned ends are sufficient to risk the use of destructive means? Are legal protections necessary to preserve existing rights and values? The body of literature that deals with the general syndrome encapsuled in the remarks of the Jesuit theologians is rapidly growing.[3]

I undertake in this chapter to distinguish some of the basic human moral issues* that arise in the situation created by developments in biology and medicine, and to suggest some ways in which we can deal with them. The task is too extensive and complex to be managed fully and satisfactorily in one chapter. There are several quite different matters involved in the differences of judgment that are being made. One is simply the matter of fact. What exactly are the present capabilities and what are their actual limits? Another is the matter of prediction or projection from present knowledge. Exactly what possibilities can be seriously en-

---

* I have not used "moral" and "ethical" in a restricted sense that meets the criteria set by some moral philosophers. The essay rather addresses what comes within the general range of "moral" in the vocabulary of most scientists with whom I have discussed these matters.

tertained? What new knowledge is on the horizons and to what might its uses lead? Another is the matter of the perspectives from which the human situation is understood and evaluated. Can we have confidence that men will use their new knowledge and powers wisely and for the end of human welfare? Or are human propensities for evil so great that we must protect the human race against its own capabilities? Another matter is more distinctively and narrowly ethical. Are there certain human rights and preroga- tives that cannot be infringed upon under any possible circum- stances? Or is a utilitarian ethic, calculating and weighing desired and undesired consequences, the proper one to adopt?

In the hope of clarifying this situation, and of suggesting some possible ways to move the discussion forward, I shall distinguish nine pertinent issues, and state some conflicting propositions di- rected to each. I shall develop these issues and propositions in such a way that some of the reasons for contrasting judgments become clear. In some instances, the reasonable position appears to be a dialectical one between two prima facie opposing prop- ositions. A fully developed constructive or systematic position cannot be elaborated here, but the direction which I believe a more complete development ought to take does become clear.

1. The same scientific situation generates opposing dispositions or outlooks toward the future. These dispositions can be charac- terized as confidence and hope on the one hand, and anxiety and fear on the other. The contrasts and the reasons that can be given for each can be developed in the following manner.

a. There are surely grounds for confidence and hope in the new biomedical developments. (1) Scientists have uncovered new possibilities for human health and welfare: certain genetic defects might be eliminated, suffering can be decreased, human life can be prolonged, and even a genetically superior human race might be developed. (2) Many of the possibilities that frighten the masses are the products of irresponsible speculation and science fiction. (3) Members of the scientific community are humane moral persons who can be counted on to restrict the uses of knowledge to what enhances human health and welfare. (4) Men, in general (whether scientists, politicians, administrators, or phi- losophers), can be trusted to seek and to do what is beneficial for all mankind. (5) There is a providential process, or a providential Deity, that is ultimately working out its purposes, and these are beneficial to the development of man. For example, Teilhard de

Chardin assures us that the developmental process is one of "hominization," "amorization," and "personalization," moving toward fulfillment in the Omega point. Or, Rahner assures us that God is "not only above us, as Lord and horizon of history, but also . . . he is ahead of us as our own future, that future which carries history forward."[4]

b. There is also a sharply contrasting outlook, for surely there are reasons for anxiety and fear. (1) Scientific developments now make it possible for human life as we know it to be altered radically, or perhaps even be destroyed. (2) Many of the most knowledgeable scientists are themselves alarmed by the growing destructive capabilities of science, and thus, on their authority, others ought to be deeply concerned. Gordon R. Taylor, for example, quotes Prof. Salvador Luria of MIT as having said that his response has "not been a feeling of optimism but one of tremendous fear of the potential dangers that genetic surgery, once it becomes feasible, can create if misapplied."[5] (3) Members of the scientific community tend to become so engrossed in the pursuit of knowledge that they do not always think about the potential human consequences of their work. (4) Even those who are very morally sensitive do not always have it in their power to control the uses of knowledge. (5) History testifies to the fact that scientists in the past have not been able to control fully the uses of the power they create, and certainly some of them tend to use their knowledge for their own self-interest, or that of their particular group, rather than for the benefit of all mankind. Thus, on very general grounds, we need to be careful about expressing confidence in the moral wisdom of men. (6) Evolution is not governed by a purpose. Or, even if it is, many mistakes are made in the process, and there is no guarantee that its end is the fulfillment and benefit of the human species. (7) There is no providential Deity working out his purposes. Or, if there is, he has granted man such a degree of autonomy and power for self-creation that natural and historical developments are to be held to man's accountability, not God's.

It is important to note the different kinds of reasons that are given as warrants either for confidence or for anxiety. Some of them involve *factual judgments* and the *predictive extrapolations* made on the basis of them, such as whether both potential benefits and harms are likely, and which is most dominant. Thus, some disputes could perhaps be settled by an objective assessment of the actual status of the biomedical sciences, though agreement on this will not necessarily lead to agreement on the most fitting outlook toward the future. Some reasons, however, are based on *evaluative assessments* of matters about which persons might have agreement with reference to the evidences. For example, does historical evidence support the judgment that men generally are to be trusted, or that we ought to be wary about excessive confidence in man's ability to know and to do what is good for all mankind? What one *believes about the human condition* makes a difference in his disposition toward the future, insofar as it is in human control. So also *theological* and *metaphysical* beliefs enter in, e.g., whether the evolutionary process is providential with regard to the human species, or whether there is a God whose purposes are to be trusted. Assessing the weight and functions of reasons like these is itself a logically complex task.

Obviously, then, the warrant for either hope or fear that a person might give consists in one, or in various combinations of the reasons suggested. A commitment to one of the reasons supporting an outlook toward the future does not entail a commitment to other reasons that also support it.

The bases for human dispositions or outlooks toward the future are indeed complex and are of different sorts. Most laymen, and perhaps also most scientists, move dialectically between confidence and anxiety, between hope and fear. Karl Rahner speaks for many who do not share his Christian beliefs when he writes that we

> must speak out with great determination against all abuses of man's self-creative power. There can be no toleration of latter-day forms of barbarity and slavery, nor of totalitarian subjection of the human person to mass society. But this danger does not warrant any precondemnation of the coming age of self-creation. Nothing is gained by retreating behind negative epithets of rhetoric about shameless barbarism and the destruction of "nature," and all this accompanied by dirges about the death of love in a technological era.[6]

For Rahner, this attitude is supported by theological arguments. It might also be supported by practical reason: to avoid panic and illusions. Whether other evidences would support it is a matter of dispute.

2. The issues of moral responsibility in biomedical develop-

ments are several, and they will concern us in a number of subsequent sections of this chapter. At this point our concern is to ask what lies within the bounds of the moral or the ethical, and what lies outside of these bounds. Is biomedical research ethically neutral? If it is, where does neutrality end? The answer given to these questions will begin to define where the researchers' moral responsibilities begin. Two contrasting positions may be taken.

a. Medical and biological research procedures and the acquisition of knowledge are morally neutral. Therefore, the scientist, qua researcher, has no moral responsibility for his work.

b. Moral issues are so intertwined in research, in the gaining of knowledge from it, and the uses of this knowledge, that it is not possible to declare research procedures and the acquisition of knowledge to be morally neutral. Therefore, the scientist, qua researcher, has moral responsibility for his work.

A little reflection on these alternatives makes it clear that the old term value-free is insufficiently precise to be of much use in dealing with the issue. It begs the question of what kinds of values, or of interests (and do "values" equal "interests"?) are involved in research. It is clear that research at least has a reference to the interests of the scientist. James D. Watson's widely read narrative of the discovery of the structure of DNA had a disenchanting, even demythologizing effect for many persons, for it demonstrated that scientists are motivated by a variety of interests in their pursuits even in the "purest" kind of research.[7] Research in that project did not have anything like the kind of disinterested rationality the scientist has in the widely popular stereotype. The motives of Professor Watson and others were not in any simple sense "value-free." They were in a highly competitive situation, seeking to gain the intellectual prize also being sought by others. But does the fact that the research had reference to the values and interests of the researcher in his pursuit of honor in any way involve a moral or ethical issue? Do we judge either the research or the scientists to be in any sense immoral because their motives are not as disinterested as common belief has assumed? It is by no means clear that we ought to. The fact that research is not "value-free," in the sense that it is motivated by the interests (including the self-interest) of the scientist, makes it neither moral nor immoral.

The fact that there is a morality of the pursuit and reporting of knowledge must be recognized. The biologist is at least obligated to conform to the rules of practice of his profession, whether or not he recognizes a wider sphere of moral responsibility. The rules include such things as being honest in reporting one's findings, acknowledging one's dependence upon the work of others, reporting procedures so that they can be critically examined by one's colleagues, and the like. The very possibility of a community of discourse among scientists is dependent upon a rigorous adherence to the established canons of practice in the field. While mistakes might be made and forgiven, deliberate deception leads to the immediate discreditation of the researcher. In the sense, then, that there is a code of rules of practice to which scientists have a moral obligation, no research is ethically neutral or "value-free." Thus, when the question of the ethical neutrality of biological research is raised, it usually refers to some realm of values or principles other than the rules of practice of the profession.

When, then, do the moral questions arise with reference to biomedical experimentation? Do they arise only with reference to the social *use* that is to be made of the findings? If they do, research and knowledge are in and of themselves ethically neutral; it is only in the employment of knowledge that questions of a moral nature arise. To make this claim is to take a position in favor of one major option involved in ethical theory. It is to choose a utilitarian view of ethics, and it opens the door to the intricate philosophical discussions of the viability and limitations of that view. Moral philosophers in the Anglo-Saxon world have for decades been arguing whether the morality of action is to be judged by its consequences, or whether other criteria need to be used. If one claims, for example, that because the transplantation of vital organs has led to the prolongation of life, transplant surgery is "good," has one made a *moral* judgment, or some other kind of judgment? How is the "good" known? How is it measured? Are all "good" consequences to be assumed to have moral value?[8] Although this is not the place to develop these questions, the main point is important: to choose to judge the morality of scientists on the basis of the consequences of the use of their research is to take on the task of defending a point of view about ethics. Much can be said in its favor. Certainly one advantage of the utilitarian point of view for biomedical researchers is that a clear line could be drawn between ethically neutral research and ethically laden uses of it. The scientist would not be held morally accountable for his research; others would be accountable for the uses made of it. Confronted with such a claim, however, many persons will quickly ask whether the scientist who makes certain uses possible by his research does not have some responsibility for their subsequent consequences. Certainly he has "causal" responsibility. But does causal responsibility imply moral responsibility?

Public clamor about the morality of science normally does not occur until after scientific knowledge has had some significant consequences for human welfare. Research in atomic and nuclear physics in the early decades of this century is a case in point; no one thought of making a public moral judgment about that work until it was used in military technology to develop weapons of mass destruction. Interestingly, theoretical physicists had different opinions about whether and, if so, where they were morally culpable for the development of those weapons. In the latter decades of the century, which reputedly "belong to the biologists" as the first did to the physicists, has it occurred to anyone to make a moral judgment about the Crick-Watson theory of the double helix structure of DNA? Surely not in and of itself. One can anticipate, however, that judgments will be made about the morality of genetic surgery and other forms of manipulation of the biological processes that the Crick-Watson theory and other information will have made possible.

The clearest difficulty in holding biologists culpable for their research lies in the fact that it can be used for both human good and human ill. Just as atomic physics made possible the destruction of Hiroshima and Nagasaki, it also opened a vast source of energy that is being used for socially useful purposes. Similarly, the same brain research that could lead to the control of human behavior by persons who gain control of certain resources can also make possible relief from mental anguish for deeply distressed persons. Is our only procedure one of ex post facto judgment? Do we calculate the benefits and the harms, and then decide whether research was morally justifiable? Even the entertainment of this possibility leads to the conclusion that the uses of biomedical research are morally ambiguous, and thus the research itself is at least morally ambiguous, if not neutral.

An alternative to the calculation of consequences in making moral judgments about scientists and their research would be to insist that certain things are morally right or wrong regardless of their effects. For example, Kant argued that it is morally wrong to tell a lie even from altruistic motives, with the intention of saving the life of a potential victim of assassination. But we will return to the consideration of this possibility in our fifth issue.

3. Even to raise the question of the responsibility of biomedical researchers is a process that demands clarification. In the most common forms of discussion two simple questions are asked. To whom are the scientists responsible? For what are they responsible?[9] The latter question has already been introduced, but it forces its way into our discussion at this point in such a way that it cannot be omitted. The contrasting answers to these questions can be stated as follows.

a. Biomedical scientists and technologists are responsible only to their employers or sponsors (government, private industry, universities), and they are responsible only for fulfilling the technical research task they have contracted to do.

b. They are also responsible to the human community (politically organized into states, or simply mankind at large), and also for both the ways in which research is done and its potential social and personal consequences.

c. They are also responsible to God, both for the ways in which research is done and for its social consequences.

Our interest at this point, primarily, is in the "to whom" rather than the "for what." Our list of propositions could readily be extended with reference to that question. For example, many scientists would be dissatisfied with being held accountable only to their sponsors; they also accept accountability to the community of fellow researchers who have a passionate interest in breaking through the barriers of ignorance simply for the sake of extending knowledge. This more extended position, however, would still retain the possibility of raising the second and third alternative stated above.

The issue of "responsibility to" is a complex one for researchers. Much of their work is under contract; they have committed themselves to resolving particular problems, either in "pure" science or in its technical applications. Some, no doubt, believe that their moral responsibility ends with the fulfillment of their obligations to their sponsors. Beyond that, they would say, other persons are answerable for the uses that are made of new knowledge. In addition, "the human community" is a vague and amorphous entity, comprising a great many interests and values, and it has no clear consensus about what is right and what is good. In the absence of such a consensus it is difficult to know to what moral principles and human values the scientist is responsible. To be sure, governments exist to protect and develop the "public interest" or the "common good," and there are instances in which laws and regulations are passed that function as precise duties and limitations whose violation leads to punishment. But scientists are rightfully wary of hasty crystallizations of a definition of the public interest into laws and regulations, for these often can be short-sighted or can be the result of uninformed fears and pressures, and they can stifle the freedom that is necessary for creativity and development.

The invocation of responsibility to God is meaningless to most biomedical researchers, since they are a highly secularized group and since this would only raise the difficult question of what it means for men to be answerable to him.

But despite the difficulty of making clear and precise a more universal object of responsibility than simply the sponsor of research, it is also the case that a significant and vocal number of scientists do acknowledge at least a "sense of moral responsibility" to more than themselves and their sponsors.

The issue of "responsibility for" cannot be as easily separated from that of "responsibility to" as our initial posing of the question appears to make it. To hold researchers responsible to the human community is to hold them responsible for the "goods" and "values" of that community. They often rightfully plead that their own control over subsequent uses of knowledge is very limited. It is difficult to predict what the uses of research will be, since isolated bits of information are brought together with information developed by others when research reports become part of the public realm. The contributor of one bit of information can hardly be held morally blameworthy for the subsequent decisions and actions of others who use his contribution. Also, there is a differentiation of roles in the society, so that other persons are charged with producing and marketing whatever instruments, processes, techniques, and products give research its social utility.

All this points to a pressing constructive task that will engage scientists and humanists together, namely, the clarification of the answers to both the questions of "to whom" and "for what." The reliance on "feelings" of responsibility apart from more specification of the objects of responsibility has become a luxury.

4. One particular aspect appears to loom more important for

this generation than it has for previous generations, and that is responsibility to and for "the future," or more specifically for the conditions under which human life will be lived in subsequent generations and centuries, as Martin Golding has made clear in his valuable contribution, "Ethical Issues in Biological Engineering."[10] Two contrasting positions may be taken.

a. Biomedical scientists are morally obligated only to the present generation for its welfare.

b. Biomedical scientists are morally obligated to future generations for their welfare.

This issue takes on a cogency and imperiousness that perhaps it has never had before. While men have always struggled to survive and achieve happiness under the conditions of limited resources, they have been occupied more with the means by which these resources could be used for human ends than with the possibilities of their depletion or radical alteration. There has been a sense that the natural environment was one of relatively high abundance, if only men could harness it to their purposes. And migration to areas less depleted has been a possibility in the past. Now, however, even while new sources of energy are being developed and migrations to outer space are being predicted, there is also a strong sense of urgency arising from the awareness that the conditions necessary for survival and happiness can be destroyed and depleted. Thus, choices made in this generation will have important consequences for generations that are to follow.

New issues must be faced. Morally sensitive scientists are in the vanguard of the growing public concern for the conditions of life in the future; they are leaders in the movements for both population control and conservation. But how this obligation to and for the future is to be spelled out is a matter of some intricacy. Does a researcher at the National Institutes of Health in Bethesda, Maryland, have a moral obligation to consider the consequences of subsequent events of which his work will be only remotely and partially the cause? We are now facing in the sphere of the sciences an issue that we have known best in the historical, political, and social orders. For example, in what sense could Karl Marx have been assumed to be responsible for future historical events that were in part "caused" by the publication of his ideas? Is he morally culpable for the terrors of Stalinization? Is he morally praiseworthy for the distributive justice of Sweden's social democracy? Was he causally, and therefore morally, responsible in any meaningful sense for the polarization of the nations in the middle of our century between the so-called "free world" and the Communist world? This example should make clear that the ascription of moral responsibility, insofar as it is bound to causal responsibility, to and for future scientific and historical developments is, indeed, no simple matter. Surely it would be an error to lay an undifferentiated moral obligation onto biomedical scientists for the future of mankind. While the sense of obligation to the future that many of them are willing to assume is morally commendable, part of a more carefully developed agenda of the ethical issues in the biomedical field will be a more precise development of the limits, as well as the extent, of this generation's responsibility to and for the future.

5.* Moralists have puzzled for centuries over the proper answer to the questions, "Are there any intrinsically morally evil acts?" and "Are there any intrinsically morally good acts?" With reference to biomedical research, some persons might argue that men have no moral right to conduct certain sorts of experiments, regardless of the potentially beneficial consequences, just as they would argue that it is morally wrong to torture a human being regardless of the value of the information that might be extricated from him through inflicting acute pain. This issue can be set in the following contrasts.

a. A scientist has the *right* to do anything he has the capacity to do in research, such as fertilize human eggs outside the uterus, "clone" a human being, alter the genotype of human beings, and manipulate brain responses. Various reasons might be given in support of this position, though most persons would not find all of them to be equally persuasive. (1) New knowledge is intrinsically valuable, and therefore worth getting regardless of the means required. (2) Men will do anything they have the capacity to do anyway, so it might as well be assumed that rights to do something arise from the capacity to do it. (Obviously, this would lead to negative responses from almost everyone if it were generalized; for example, the capacity of the American military technologists to make poison gases does not give them the moral right to make them, and certainly not to use them.) (3) The "right to know" is one of the basic human liberties, and any restraint of this is an infringement on the freedom of the scientist. (4) Intellectual

---

* This section has been refined and expanded in the next chapter.

curiosity and growth are some of the most distinctive characteristics of human beings, and thus unrestricted fulfillment of their
maximum possibilities is in accord with human nature. (5) If it
had not been asumed that man has the right to do anything he
has the capacity to do, many of the scientific and technical advances of the past would not have taken place. There have always
been suspicions and superstitions that have led to restrictions of
inquiry, and the effects of these have been to delay scientific advancement. Here one would be arguing that since the breaking of
taboos in the past has had beneficial effects (both the intrinsic
value of the knowledge secured and the beneficial uses to which
it has been put), the same would also be true in the present.

   b. A scientist has no right to intervene in the natural processes of human life because all life is sacred.

This position would not be advanced by any serious intelligent
person in the modern world. Obviously, men have intervened in
the natural processes from the earliest time of human development
in order to make human life more comfortable, healthier, and
more rewarding. Thus, once the right to intervene has been
granted, the lines of discussion can no longer be held to this
fundamental proposition. (This suggests one of the basic difficulties in Pope Paul's position on birth regulation. By granting
that the rhythm method is morally licit, the issue is no longer
the right to prohibit nature from taking its course. Rather, it becomes one of whether human self-restraint is the only morally
licit means for doing so.)

   c. A scientist has no right to intervene in the natural processes
in such a way that he might alter what men believe to be most
distinctively human.

This third proposition comes closest to the center of the anxieties of scientists and humanists alike. It assumes a distinction between the normal situation and the exceptional situation, and suggests that there might even be a different "logic" of rights on the
borderline or unusual cases. Also, it suggests that in our present
scientific circumstances one of the oldest issues of thoughtful literature again takes on importance, namely, the pursuit of a normative understanding of humanity. A question discussed by Stoic,
Platonic, Aristotelian, and ancient Christian thinkers takes on an
acutely exacerbated quality in our situation.

Various reasons might be given in support of the third proposition as it is stated. (1) A qualitative difference in the meaning of

human life would occur if the effects of research were radically to alter life as we know and value it. The risk is too great to give up the degree of certitude about life's meaning and values as we know them for the uncertainty of qualities and meanings that might emerge. (2) A qualitative difference in the powers to control human destiny would occur, and if these powers fell into the hands of those who do not share the same values most men share, they could lead to tyranny and worse. After all, it is not that "man" in general is in a new position to determine human destiny, an exaggeration made by theologians, philosophers, and popular commentators alike, but rather that *some* men will be in that position. (3) Man is made in the image of God, and to alter the fundamental image of man is to "play God," which is not only religious idolatry but also a movement beyond the healthy recognition of human finitude that keeps various forms of evil in check.

The important question raised by the third proposition is this: What constitutes the distinctively human? As we have noted, it is not a new question, but it takes on new importance now. On the surface this seems to be a factual question that could be answered through proper kinds of research. We might find that man has distinctive capacities for speech, for abstract reasoning, for intellectual exploration, for a qualitatively different kind of control over his destiny than other animals do, for certain kinds of aspirations, for a sense of moral responsibility, for love, etc., etc. But how would any such inquiries resolve the *normative* questions about what is to be most valued in human existence?

Some theologians are interested in arguing, for example, that what is distinctively human (and thus in the image of God) is the capacity for "self-creation," the capacity to control the development of life. If this is taken in isolation from other normative considerations, it might be inferred that it is morally right for man to do whatever enables him to further the control of human development. Yet it is precisely the haunting uncertainty of this that raises moral doubts of the most acute existential import, to which this chapter is one exploratory response.

Some might argue that man *intuitively* knows and values what keeps human life truly human, and therefore, excessive rational exploration of this question simply befogs what is essentially a simple matter. But the insufficiency of this response is readily seen when we find that there is no universal agreement about what is normatively human. Thus, different persons with different intuitions might well pursue different courses of action, unless some effort were made to formulate in a relatively objective way certain areas of agreement that might guide human actions. This leads to the statement of our next issue.

6. Can general moral principles or rules, or statements of normative humanity which might be developed, be applicable to the procedures and uses of scientific research? The question invites three sorts of more intensive inquiry. How would such principles, rules, or statements of human values be arrived at? What ought their content to be? And, if one had them, how would they be applied to particular circumstances? Thus, the question invites a comprehensive treatise on ethics; here our concentration is on the third question, the issue of practical reasoning. Some attention will be paid to the other two sorts of inquiry subsequently.

a. The decisions about the procedures and uses of biomedical research all depend upon the circumstances. It is useless to attempt to apply general moral principles and rules or general statements about normative humanity.

b. General moral principles and rules, and statements of normative humanity, can determine or (weaker) give guidance to the morally licit interventions in the life processes and indicate norms and purposes of human life that should direct the intentions of those who use biomedical research.

The first proposition suggests that each new development in research and technology raises significantly novel moral issues, and that any sort of ethical reasons used in previous circumstances is not readily applicable to the new ones. For example, it might be argued that the feasibility of transplantation of vital organs is not only a new stage in medical technology, but it consequently calls for an absolutely fresh rethinking of the problems of medical ethics. Or, in a different vein, it might be argued that reasoning from some traditional moral principles and human values when choices have to be made concerning which patient is to receive vital organs never settles the individual case in hand. Thus, one must rely upon the discerning intuitive judgment of the medical staff attending the case to choose what would be not only medically but also morally right in the particular circumstances. The medical, social, economic, and other circumstances of the particular case would be judged to be more decisive than any general principles or rules, or any statements of the priorities of values.

At least two important matters are at stake here. One is whether a high degree of novelty in the scientific and medical circumstances necessitates a high degree of novelty in the normative content of the ethical thinking that pertains to those circumstances. The other is how practical moral judgments ought to be made. This involves many problems of theoretical and practical importance, such as the place of reason, the place of emotions, sensibilities, and dispositions, the place of insight or intuition, the significance of technical data for the ethical determination of what ought to be done, and the authority and function of moral principles in a particular moral judgment.

The second proposition indicates the basic contrast between the stance that "everything depends upon the circumstances" and the stance that moral principles and statements of values ought to function in an important way in the determination of conduct. It does not settle two questions, as we have noted: how one derives such moral principles and statements of values, and what content they ought to have. Nor does it settle precisely how they ought to function in the process of making practical judgments.

Two important suppositions are present, however, if the second proposition is chosen. The first is that, regardless of the significant changes in scientific and medical developments, both certain *formal* and certain *contentual* ethics still pertain. Does transplant technology raise new ethical problems, or are persistent ones being raised in new circumstances? If it is the latter, one can define the ethical issues in more traditional terms. For example, the problem of to whom scarce resources (blood or organs) are to be given involves very seriously the issue of justice. The medical profession seeks to be just in the decisions it makes about the allocation of available resources. Two traditional concepts of formal justice might be recalled: "equals should be treated equally" and "to each his due." In the light of either of these, the determination of who will receive a vital organ raises the practical question of what constitutes a just claim to it. Should organs be available according to the principle "to each according to his need?" If they should, one must make precise what constitutes "need." Is it purely a medical need? Or should organs be available according to the principle "to each according to his worth to the community"? If this principle is used, a university president might be placed above an inveterate gambler on the preference list.[11] As the questions of transplants involve the choice of recipients, the questions of justice are indeed pertinent. New circumstances raise persistent ethical questions, and traditional concepts are applicable.

The second supposition is that rationality is of great importance in making practical moral decisions and in the determination of what possible course of events ought to be followed. The alternative to rationality might be the profundity and direction of one's immediate emotional response, or of one's steadier and more persistent sentiments. The possibility of intervening in the function of the brain to control responses through electrical stimulation might arouse anger, and this sense of indignation might be judged to be a sufficient basis for prohibiting such procedures. Or one's persistent sentiment of hopefulness might lead him to approve of anything that suggests promise for the benefit of mankind. Or the alternative might be more complex than either of these; it might be a kind of "perceptual intuitionism" that claims to discern what response is fitting in the light of the primacy and objectivity of the facts of the matter confronted.

To claim importance for rationality, of course, begs many questions. There are different uses of reason in making moral judgments. One person might have a deductive logic in mind, by which he moves from "first principles" to case judgments; another might mean to suggest that one is under an obligation to justify rationally the decision that has been made, or is about to be made. Still another might have in mind a complex process of drawing inferences from various points of reference involved in making a judgment: the facts of the matter, the applicable traditional principles, various beliefs, and the like. The point of the second proposition is a general one that would include at least these three; it is that moral reasoning is important in making decisions about the procedures and uses of research. Indeed, moral reasoning provides the basis upon which some measure of objectivity in discourse can be achieved in order for persons to overcome at least some of their disagreements, or at least understand wherein the disagreements lie.[12]

7. The sixth issue begged the questions how any statement of moral principles and human values could be arrived at, and what its contents would be. There is dispute about whether any widely acceptable statement of either the inviolable rights of individuals or of the common good is possible. If, however, such a statement could be developed and agreed upon by most persons, it would provide criteria both for the judgment of the morally licit proce-

dures of research and for its uses. We can formulate the following contrasting propositions.

a. There is no universally acceptable normative concept of what individual rights are inviolable, and what particular values contribute to personal and social well-being. Nor is it possible to formulate one, even if it were desirable to do so. Thus, it is futile to seek to state moral absolutes, or even summary rules. Different sorts of reasons might be given in support of this. (1) Different cultures have different understandings of human rights and values, and thus social and cultural relativism prohibits the achievement of any significant consensus. (2) Nothing called human nature that has any universality and objectivity to it exists; thus there is no objective basis for designating any norms. (3) When there is agreement by many people on such a statement, as in the United Nations document on human rights, the terms used are so general and vague that it is subject to many diverse interpretations.

b. Certain human rights and values can be designated which are normative for moral reasoning about scientific developments. Granting the difficulties of formulating such a statement, it is nonetheless necessary to attempt it for the sake of human well-being.

Very often the principal issue at stake in these propositions is cast in excessively either/or terms. The sophomoric enthusiasm that many students have when they discover the relativity of the morality they have been taught sometimes leads to the general response that all rights and values are relative (which usually implies "absolutely relative"). Such a response would render any effort to formulate a statement an exercise in futility from the outset. In contrast with this position is the hoary one that has sought to define moral absolutes on the basis of reflection on the nature of man, and has then dogmatized these absolutes and even sought to insist upon their application through various forms of legal coercion and political pressures. Western religious institutions have perpetrated such. For example, the insistence that according to human nature every act of sexual intercourse must be open to the generation of new life has led not only to claims upon Catholics, but to legislation in certain places prohibiting the sale and use of means of birth control.

The complexity of this issue is so great that men easily become discouraged. If such a statement were possible, how would it be authenticated? The efforts that have been made to define moral absolutes either in terms of rights or of values have been based on different ways of knowing. In Judaism and Christianity, for examples, an appeal has been made to revelation. The decalogue is Torah, it is the commandment of God; and even if it were given in a particular set of circumstances, in response to a covenant between God and his people, it is still judged to be of universal applicability because of its source. Where distinctions have been made between what is binding only on those who accept the religion involved and what is binding on all men, various claims have been used. The Noachic commandments, for example, function within Jewish law to indicate what is binding on non-Jews as well as Jews.

The Christian church early absorbed and developed the idea of natural law as a basis for formulating the moral values and principles that were in accord with human nature, and thus binding on all men. This is a second time-honored way of authenticating a universally binding morality. Natural law, in its traditional form, is presumed not to be a "Catholic" position, nor that of any other historically relative community, but to be based upon reason's capacity to apprehend the essential telos or end of human nature, and thus infer from it certain general moral principles and values.[13] Men of the Enlightenment held a similar confidence in the power of reason to apprehend moral absolutes, as every American recognizes when he remembers that the founding fathers of this country said, "We hold these truths to be self-evident."

In addition to revelation and to the apprehension of absolutes through reason, a third way is now being attempted. A process of induction is used from the varieties of human experiences in various cultures that are reported by ethnologists. The authority of various cultural anthropologists is cited to show that, regardless of cultural and social differences, there are certain fundamental requisites for human life which in turn provide norms that are universal in their applicability.[14]

A second important question comes up in following the second alternative. If a list of items about what constitutes "the human" were fashioned and if certain rights and values were inferred from this, would there be a built-in order of priorities? Is it not the case that whenever a set of inviolable human rights, of human values, is defined, these rights or values often conflict with each other in a particular set of circumstances? Thus, the most acute conflicts are not resolved by the establishment of a statement of human rights and values. If the direction of the second proposition were pursued in spite of its difficulties, this question would have to be answered.

One answer is to establish a fixed hierarchy of rights or of values which would effectively settle the cases of conflict. The unsatisfactory character of this proposal becomes patent, however, as soon as an effort is made to fulfill it. While it might provide the satisfaction of consistency, one might find its consequences hard to live with. One can see this in the realm of social policy. To be "human," men need a realm of freedom of thought and action; they seem to rebel against excessive repression. To be "human," men need to be treated justly; they seem to rebel against injustice. Thus, we might infer that persons have a right to liberty and a right to justice; they value liberty and they value justice. In the development of human societies, however, it appears that neither justice nor liberty can be maximally expanded without coming into conflict with each other. In American society it is just to have laws that permit members of minority groups to purchase houses wherever they can afford to do so. But the achievement of this legal justice limits the liberty of persons in a particular neighborhood collectively to determine what sorts of persons they wish to have as neighbors, and it limits the liberty of the individual selling a house to determine on the basis of his own criteria to whom he will sell. No hierarchy of liberty and justice that will be authoritative under all particular historical circumstances is possible. Another example can be taken from the discussions of morally licit abortions. The problem might be stated in this way: the fetus has a right to life (a proposition on which not all men agree), but the parents have a right to determine what size family they wish, or can afford to have, or is proper with reference to the demographic problems of the world. Which right is the overriding one in a case of conflict? Even those who would have a clear answer would have difficulty in persuading opponents that it is the right one. It is difficult, if not impossible, to set up a fixed hierarchy of rights and values of the human that would be applicable under all circumstances and that would be universally agreed to.

The difficulty, however, ought not to keep us from pursuing the basic thrust of the second proposition. Even though there would be a plurality of rights or values that would conflict under certain circumstances, it is nonetheless important to have some clear statement of them in making decisions about research and its uses. Indeed, some rough order of priorities might be established. For example, since the realization of any human values for an individual depends upon the safe and sound development of his physical life, it can well be argued that the value of human physical life is a primary one, or that the right to physical life is primary. If this is granted, at least the benefit of the doubt in any case that would seriously harm or take human life is in favor of the proposed victim. This would not entail that no other values or rights might ever override the right to bodily life, but it would suggest that in questions of this sort not all things are absolutely relative to each other and that at least a summary moral rule can be stated, such as, "Human life ought not to be taken or endangered except where there is a clear and persuasive argument that other claims are ethically prior." Some would want to make a stronger statement; our intention is only to suggest that an ordering which gives some guidance in particular decisions is possible and that it is important to have.

Even in cases in which the conflict is not resolved by the principle stated above, a clarification of what rights and values are at stake gives moral disputes some objectivity and evokes the demand for rational justification of various positions. For example, is it morally justifiable seriously to risk the life of one person in a medical experiment that holds only a modest degree of promise ultimately to bring benefits to many persons? This question sets up a problem that can be responded to dogmatically on the basis of certain emotions which would be evoked either by the potential loss of an individual life or by the potential benefit for many. Or it might be responded to dogmatically by persons who hold consistently to certain moral principles. The person whose principle is that the individual's right to life is inviolable would answer negatively. The person who holds a simple utilitarian position might not even be put off by the promise of only modest prospects of benefits, and answer positively. But the problem set by the question might be developed in a much more complex fashion. Bodily life is to be highly valued. But in this instance is it the bodily life of the potential victim which is to be valued, or the bodily life of those who potentially will benefit from the possible sacrifice of the life of the victim? Or is the issue that of the right of a single individual to bodily life against the benefits that might accrue to others? Are the benefits significant with reference to the preservation of life? Or are they uncertain and relatively trivial (either in terms of the number of persons who might be benefited or in terms of the "quality" of the effects promised)? Further analysis is not necessary for our purposes. The point is that some statement of the rights of persons and of the values that contribute to individual and social well-being provides at least the possibility of more objectivity and rationality in the determination of moral judgments in cases that involve biomedical developments.

8. The previous paragraph leads directly to our eighth issue. Is the principal conflict that between the right of a single individual to bodily life and the benefits that might accrue to others from risking life? In the concrete moral issues of both procedures and uses of research are we forced to make a choice between an ethic whose content is determined by the *rights* of individuals and an ethic whose content is determined by the *benefits* for persons and society? This issue is not only in the center of controversies in ethical theory, but it is also at the heart of many practical matters in the biomedical field. Before stating the contrasting propositions, this issue might be illustrated from the area of the ethics of population control. On the basis of predictions of the harm that uncontrolled population growth will bring, or of the benefits that population control will bring, there are those who would argue that the rights of individuals are of no significant moral importance, such as the right of husband and wife to determine how many children they will have, or the right of the fetus (if such is granted) to come to full term. The benefits anticipated are determinative. Others would obviously disagree with this. Our contrasting propositions follow.[15]

a. The rights of individuals are sacred and primary, and therefore, under no circumstances, are they to be violated in favor of benefits to others that might be gained from their violation.

b. Anticipated consequences judged in terms of the "good" that will be achieved or the "evil" that will be avoided ought to determine policy and action, regardless of the restrictions on individual rights that this might require.

c. Propositions *a* and *b* are both one-sided. Decisions require consideration both of individual rights and of benefits to others. Thus, one of the two can be the base line, and the other can function as the principle which justifies the restrictions on, or the exceptions to, the base line.

With these propositions we return to an issue previously introduced. In a crude sense the issue is that of means and ends, but a statement made in terms of individual rights and benefits to others provides a sharper focus for the ethical issues. It is not difficult to find examples which would give persuasive evidence that either *a* or *b* taken by itself leads to consequences which make most persons morally uneasy. Dr. Henry K. Beecher, of Harvard, for example, has vigilantly exposed instances in which individual rights have been violated in the pursuit of medical experimentation, and many of the instances are indeed disturbing.[16] Instances of experimentation on institutionalized children who have no possibility of giving informed consent readily arouse profound moral resentment, as do the many documented evidences of the infamous activities of physicians in Nazi Germany. Yet the insistence that every fetus has the right to be born, regardless of the consequences for itself (e.g., if it is known to be deformed), for its family, or for the society as a whole, evokes the indignation of many persons whose dedication is to proposition *b*.

It is interesting and important to note that many individuals would morally resent both examples. This suggests that while adherence to either proposition *a* or to proposition *b* would have the effect of providing consistency in action and policy, such consistency seems not to be in and of itself admirable. Most persons would question the admirable character of such consistency because of the consequences to which it leads. (The implications of this latter for ethical theory are matters of importance outside the bounds of our present concerns.) In the face of the prima facie unsatisfactory character of either *a* or *b*, proposition *c* suggests an alternative.

The alternative of *c* is deliberately general. It might well be that under certain circumstances it is morally responsible to make the thrust of individual rights the base line, and under other circumstances the accounting of benefits. Most of the literature with which I am acquainted that deals with experimentation on human beings seems to take the first. The concern to make certain that the subject gives free and informed consent to being used for experimental purposes suggests this. (Perhaps this is because much of this literature has legal questions in mind, or is prepared by lawyers, and it has been a primary function of the law to uphold human rights.) Also, the more specific kinds of questions that are raised in these discussions suggest the same thrust. For example, before experimentation takes place on human beings, has experimentation on animals that might lead to the knowledge sought for been exhausted? The practice of sacrificing animals rather than human beings indicates the widespread acceptance of the intent of the question. Is the knowledge to be gained important enough to risk the violation of individual lives? This question leads to consideration of benefits. If, as in the case of Salk vaccine, the potential benefit is the virtual eradication of polio which reached epidemic proportions over and over again, there would be greater justification than if the benefits would accrue only to the acclaim of the experimenter by his colleagues, or if it would affect only a handful of persons. What are the chances of success in the experimentation? If they are meager, the situation is different from one in which they are great. What is the degree of risk to the human subject? Might it cost his life? Or impair his functions in such a way that he cannot live a "normal" life? Or only slightly impair his functions?

The discussion of the moral issues involved in the transplantation of human hearts is replete with considerations of this sort. In practice, the base line of benefits seems to be primary. Has this surgery been primarily experimental? Or has it been done for the therapeutic benefit of the patients involved? What percentage of successful transplants would qualify as sufficient to warrant the risks that are involved? Indeed, what length of prolongation of life would be judged to count as success? Since procedures used on animals that are of potential benefits to human beings require eventual experiment on human bodies, is it not necessary to risk the violation of individual's right to life to be able to work for the benefit of many? In the cases of heart transplants there has been another qualifying factor. The desperate physical condition of the patients and the prognosis of a relatively brief life span for them in any case, was judged not to involve the same cost as would be the case in the use of subjects with healthy hearts.

There might be other areas in which the counting of potential benefits, rather than individual rights, becomes the base line. As the possibilities of genetic surgery, of "cloning" human beings and the like, emerge, the calculation of benefits appears to be the primary concern, and the secondary question is that of the cost to rights of individuals as we know them now.

The point of proposition c is by now clear. It offers a way to think with some ethical sophistication about complex questions that exist. It is possible that the concerns of a might be accounted for in a sophisticated statement of b, and thus that one might have a consistency of theory. But in the first order of discourse about the ethical problems confronting developments in the biomedical field it is important to keep the polarity between them more clearly in mind for the practical benefit of forcing a sharp awareness of the seriousness and complexity of the issues that are involved. A refined and rigorous development of proposition *c* would have such an effect.

9. When men are confronted with developments that could lead to radical change, they are likely to respond in one of two extreme ways. On the one hand, there is an impulse to guard and preserve the good things that have been achieved, and not allow them to be subject to potential loss in the course of change. On the other hand, there is an impulse to enthusiasm for the novelty that the developments promise to bring, and with it a softening of rigorous concerns for the maintenance of values already achieved. This is evident, for example, in certain reactions to social revolutions that are moving toward a future that is not fully predictable. With these impulses come different basic styles or modes of ethical response. The first is concerned to conserve what exists against the threats that are posed against it; the second moves with freedom and openness toward the future. Something similar occurs when we ponder the issues that emerge from developments in the biomedical field.

a. It is best to restrict the kinds of experimentation that will be permitted through civil legislation and regulation, and through clearly defined general moral rules, in order to preserve human rights and values as we now know them.

b. It is best to ensure the maximum possible freedom for research and for the human capacities for self-development regardless of the risks that are involved.

c. It is best to maintain the maximum possible freedom for research, but at the same time to formulate principles and values that will provide guidelines both for procedures and for uses of research.

These propositions bring us around full circle to those introduced in the first issue, namely, whether there are primarily grounds for confidence and hope, or for anxiety and fear with reference to the future development of man. Those who would opt to support proposition *a* are likely to be those who respond with anxiety and fear, and their support of the use of restrictive regulation would appear to be the proper practical inference to be drawn from the reasons they would give for their anxiety. Those who would opt for proposition *b* are likely to be those who respond with confidence and hope, and this choice would appear to them to be the practical inference from their reasons given for confidence.

Proposition *c* is primarily a qualification of *b*. It shares some of the reasons that would be given in support of *b*, but not all of them. The proponent of *c* might reason in the following way. Man has always been developing new ways to control his own destiny and that of the human race. His history is in part the story of his efforts to intervene in the "natural" course of events to give greater mastery and control over those powers to which he has appeared to be subject. He has not assumed that he is fated by the natural forces that have created pain and suffering, but he has constantly discovered new ways to fulfill many of his aspirations and ends. Indeed, in his development he has seen new dimensions of the meaning of being human; for example, he has found institutions like slavery and capital punishment to be inconsistent with what human fulfillment and life mean. His interventions into nature have led to the irrigation of wastelands, the manufacture of chemicals to increase his food production, and the development of means to control population growth. He has always assumed the right to intervene in nature to be consistent with his capacities for self-determination.

The priority here is on the capacities for exploration, or for intervention, or for what Karl Rahner has called "self-creativity." This is the kind of being man is. He will continue to attempt to do whatever he thinks he has the capacity to do, and his ability to do new things will expand with his knowledge of the fundamental processes of life. Thus far, perhaps the proponents of *b* and *c* share a common outlook.

But man, the active experimenter and intervener, discovers that many things he is capable of doing do not issue in the welfare of the human community. He does this not by reference to some fixed image of what man essentially is and ought to be, as an extrinsic and mechanical test of his deeds, but by responding in moral seriousness to the new possibilities that emerge under new circumstances. It is not that what is known from the past about the values and rights of man is not pertinent to the future, but rather that the ongoing biological development of human life needs a direction toward those values which preserve and enhance the qualities of life that give a sense of fulfillment. His ethical task involves the formulation of those ends and values which give direction to the ways in which he plays the card game of life. It involves seeking out in particular circumstances the limits beyond which he will become destructive of humane qualities of life, and perhaps even enforcing those limits by civil law. But more importantly it involves an ongoing rigorous conversation between those who can best pose the questions of ethics and human values and those who are shaping the most significant developments in the biomedical field.

What c envisages is not so much a restrictive morality that authoritatively addresses each new possibility with an exact determination of what is absolutely right and wrong, good and evil, but an ongoing moral discourse and activity that helps to shape the developments of even biological life toward the end of fulfillment of the valued qualities of human life.

If this approach has merit, the chief task is to develop with both sensitivity and clarity an understanding of the qualities or values of human life and a conception of the basic human rights that will provide the moral guidelines or touchstones for human development. Its chief task is that suggested in the fifth and seventh issues introduced in this essay.[17] The task is obviously not a new one; it has occupied the attention of theologians and philosophers, poets, novelists, and dramatists, scientists, and many others for centuries. But it takes on a qualitatively new importance in the present time, and demands the most of all who can contribute to it. For at stake is the future of humanity.

14

Genetic Engineering
and the Normative View
of the Human

The growing capacities for intervention in the course of development of human life raise in an exacerbated form one of the oldest of philosophical and theological questions, namely, what is the *normatively human*. By normatively human I mean to indicate an evaluative concern. Are there some things we value about man that set limits on what we are morally permitted to do in our biological interventions? Are there some things we value about man that indicate the sorts of qualities of human life that ought to be kept in view in the controlled genetic development of man? The difficulties in coming to a consensus on the normatively human are almost insuperable, yet it is my deepening conviction that some efforts must be made to overcome them.

The development of this thesis requires two distinct stages; namely, making a careful case for the importance of the question and making substantial proposals about how it can be answered. The latter is the most difficult, and to be pursued properly it requires more extensive discussion than is possible in one chapter, or even in one book. Indeed, it requires ongoing discourse between persons representing various points of view and interests,

Reprinted with permission from *Ethical Issues in Biology and Medicine*, ed. Preston N. Williams (Cambridge, Mass.: Schenkman Publishing Co., 1972), pp. 46-58.

scientists, literary artists and other humanists, religious thinkers, and others. Thus, here I shall primarily attend to the first stage, namely, that of marshaling support for the proposal that the question of what constitutes the normatively human is the most important issue that lurks in all the more specific and concrete problems we face when ethical issues are raised about developments in the field of genetics.

As a procedure I shall move from some specific possibilities for intervention to some ways in which arguments can be made about their moral permissibility or nonpermissibility, and attempt to show that at crucial points the decisions one would make depend upon some assumptions about what is valued about human life, that is, what constitutes the normatively human.[1]

I. The Contemporary Emergence of the Question of Normative Humanity

Any number of actual or future possibilities of significant interventions into the biological processes can function as the backdrop for reflection. Genetics is not the only field that raises the question. The attention of the public has been called to such possibilities through various television shows, a number of articles in popular journals, and through such books as Gordon Rattray Taylor's *The Biological Time Bomb*.[2] Dr. Bernard D. Davis' essay in *Ethical Issues in Biology and Medicine* provides a careful assessment of what the major possibilities for genetic engineering or manipulation are. The sort of possibilities that Dr. Davis develops have engendered both anxieties and hopes in many persons. Some of them, as he aptly indicates in his article, raise moral questions of varying degrees of seriousness and difficulty. Perhaps the most dramatic one that has fascinated the reading public is that of cloning human beings. I shall proceed to formulate and discuss four different possible responses to the actual and potential scientific capabilities that Dr. Davis describes and discusses.

1. A scientist has the moral right to do anything he has the technical capacity to do in research, such as the procedures suggested in Dr. Davis' article.

Various reasons might be given in support of this proposition, though they would not all be equally cogent. (a) New knowledge is intrinsically valuable, and therefore it is worth getting regardless of the means that are required. (b) The "right to know" is a basic human liberty, and any restraint upon it is an infringement of the freedom of the scientist. (c) Intellectual curiosity and growth are two of the most distinctive characteristics of the human species, and thus the fulfillment of these capacities is in accord with what it means to be human. (d) It must be assumed that man has the right to know anything he has the capacity to find out; if it is not, fears and suspicions will lead to restrictions of inquiry as they have in the past, and many important and socially useful consequences would not occur. (e) Men will do anything they have the capacity to do anyway; so it might as well be assumed that the right to do something arises from the capacity to do it. (This latter reason probably would lead to negative responses by almost everyone if it were universalized in an unqualified way. The technical capacity to develop the means of germ warfare does not entail the moral right to develop them, and certainly not to use them.)

2. A scientist has no right to intervene in the natural processes of human life, because it is sacred.

This position would not be advanced by any serious intelligent person in the modern world. Obviously, men have intervened in the natural processes from the earliest time of human development in order to make human life more comfortable, healthier, and more rewarding. Thus, once the right to intervene is taken for granted, the lines of discussion can no longer be held to this proposition, but it does provide the antithesis to the first, and therefore is useful to introduce for our purposes in this chapter.

3. A scientist has no right to intervene in the natural processes in such a way that he might alter what men believe to be, and value as, the most distinctively human characteristics.

Various reasons might be given in support of this third proposition. (a) A qualitative difference in the meaning of human life would occur if the effects of research were to radically alter life as we now know and value it. The risk is too great to give up the degree of certitude we have about life's meaning and values for the uncertainty of qualities and meanings that might emerge. (b) A qualitative difference in the powers to control human destiny would occur, and if these powers fall into the hands of those who do not share the same values most men share, they could lead to tyranny and worse. It is, after all, not "man" in general who will be in a position to determine human destiny, but rather, some men who have certain knowledge and power. (c) Man is made in the image of God, and to fundamentally alter the image of man is to "play God," which is not only idolatry in a religious context, but is a movement beyond a healthy recognition of human finitude that keeps various forms of evil in check.

4. A scientist has the right to intervene in the course of human development in such a way that the uses of his knowledge foster growth of those distinctive qualities of life that humans value most highly, and remove those qualities that are deleterious to what is valued.

Various reasons might be given in support of this proposition. (a) The basic motivating reason for any investigation is to achieve some control over the processes to which human life and development have been subject, over the processes to which men have in the past passively consented. This has been the case with the development of surgery, drug therapy, means of birth control, chemical fertilizers, etc. There is an implicit intention in all research to enlarge the human capacities for self-determination. It has been assumed that these capacities are directed toward the goal of the improvement of the conditions of human life, for examples, relief from suffering and prolongation of life. (b) One of the profoundest and most persistent aspirations of human life is to improve its conditions, and improve human life itself so that persons find it to be more "fulfilling," "rewarding," and "pleasant." Thus, any interventions which are in keeping with this profound and persistent aspiration are worthy of moral approval. (c) That which is most distinctively human (in comparison with other forms of created life), and thus that which is in the "image of God," is the capacity for self-determination and "self-creation," and thus the pursuit of interventions which might improve the qualities of human life are themselves in accord with one feature of what is descriptively, and thus in the eyes of some persons normatively, most human.[3]

My judgment is that the second proposition would be universally rejected by scientists, theologians, philosophers, and other humanists. Whatever the "sacredness of life" means, its meaning does not entail a moral prohibition against all forms of intervention into the course of its development, either as a single organism, or as an ongoing developmental system. The first proposition might be more controversial, for there might be some scientists who would distinguish the roles of the pure researcher from those of the technologist who determines how the research is to be applied. They might argue that while the researcher has the right to do anything he has the capacity to do, the same would not hold true for the technologist. Behind this distinction would be an assertion that while the pure researcher creates the necessary conditions for certain technological developments, his causal responsibility for creating these necessary conditions does not entail a moral responsibility for subsequent developments. Even within this distinction which limits the moral accountability of the pure researcher, however, it is possible for him to raise the moral questions about the right to *use* information for any purpose man has the capacity to pursue.

Both the third and the fourth propositions raise the question of what constitutes the distinctively human. It is clear, however, that a simply *descriptive* answer to that question would not be sufficient. The two propositions raise the question of which human characteristics are *valued,* or are to be valued. The third proposition raises this question in terms of the criteria one might set which would limit the sorts of interventions that would be morally permissible or impermissible. The fourth assumes the moral permissibility of interventions, but raises the question of the normatively human with reference to the purposes to which they would be put.

II. Some Efforts to Answer the Question

If the issue were merely what constitutes the *distinctively* human, it might be resolved by empirical comparative research. Distinctively human capacities might be listed and evidence be adduced for their uniqueness to man, such as his advanced capacity for speech and other forms of communication, for abstract reasoning, for intellectual curiosity and exploration, for a different kind of control over his destiny than other animals have, for a sense of moral responsibility, for love, etc. But such a listing, no matter how thorough and well-supported, would not of itself resolve the normative question about what is to be most valued in human life. This becomes clear simply by recalling that it is a distinctive capacity of human beings to develop technologies that deeply upset the ecological balance in nature, and in turn threaten human existence itself. A capacity or capability is not to be highly valued simply because it exists in human beings.

To develop a list of what persons have valued in human existence is also no simple task. Certainly there is the most primitive valuation of physical existence itself; whether one gives theological or other reasons for this makes little difference to the reality that we have a profound respect for life, particularly human life, and most particularly each for his own physical life. All the exceptions to this do not add up to a negation of the generalization.

Sages in various traditions have sought to ascertain what end or goal is most valued on the part of human beings. Aristotle thought through this puzzle by looking for that which human beings sought as an end in itself, and not as a means to any other end, and he came up with eudaemonia, with happiness or a sense of well-being.[4] Hedonistic utilitarians thought through the same puzzle and came up with a complex notion of pleasure.

Some contemporary Christian thinkers use the language of "wholeness" or "completeness" or "maturity" to suggest what it is that makes human life truly (or normatively) human. Paul Lehmann, who discerns the presence of God's action wherever human life is made and kept truly human, at one point defines this normative wholeness or maturity as "the integrity in and through interrelatedness which makes it possible for each individual member of an organic whole to be himself in togetherness, and in togetherness each to be himself."[5] The analogy, though suggested under biblical auspices, appears basically to be drawn from biology.

Not only theologians and philosophers have entered into the efforts to define on one basis or another what is valued or ought to be valued about human beings. Prof. Hermann J. Muller, in one of many places where he makes proposals for positive eugenics, generalizes on the valued qualities of life.

> Among the qualities of man most generally valued are a genuine warmth of fellow feeling and a cooperative disposition, a depth and breadth of intellectual capacity, moral courage and integrity, an appreciation of nature and of art, and an aptness of expression and of communication.

These in turn become "directions" that genetic development ought to take; they become both educational and genetic goals.

> We need a strengthening and extension of the tendencies toward kindliness, affection, and fellow feeling in general, especially toward those personally far removed from us. As regards other affective

traits, there is much room for broadening and deepening our capacity to appreciate both natural and man-made constructions, to interpret with fuller empathy the expressions of others, to create ever richer combinations of our own impressions, and to communicate them more adequately to others.

We also need "advances in those traits of character that lead to independence of judgment and its necessary complement, intellectual honesty," and "also a much greater capacity for analysis, for quantitative procedures, for integrative operations, and for imaginative creation." And Muller does not forget things that imply certain valuations with reference to physical developments of man, "to better the genetic foundations of health, vigor, and longevity; to reduce the need for sleep; to bring the induction of sedation and stimulation under more effective voluntary control; and to develop increasing tolerance and aptitudes in general."[6]

Many other sorts of documents could be brought forth to indicate what people believed to be valuable about human life. America's founding fathers were concerned with "life, liberty, and the pursuit of happiness." The United Nations document on human rights could provide another such list. At this juncture I only wish to indicate that all through the history of man persons have developed statements about what the chief end of life is, about the qualities of life that fulfill it, about the ends and rights that define at least in a loose sense what is normatively human. It is clear that there are significant differences of opinion about the normatively human, and that often the isolation of a single end or value draws so much up into itself that even if one might agree, for example, that happiness is what men seek, the complex question of what constitutes happiness quickly comes to the surface.

In the efforts to flesh out propositions three and four of the first part of this chapter, however, some recourse is taken, implicitly or explicitly, to judgments about what is to be valued about human life. For example, does an intervention in experimentation violate the person's "right to happiness"? Does it eventually contribute to his "pleasure" or to the "pleasure" of a large number of mankind? Does it keep him from achieving "maturity" or does it contribute to his capacity to "be himself in togetherness, and in togetherness . . . to be himself"? Does the research eventually make a contribution to Muller's goals; toward genuine "fellow feeling" and a "cooperative disposition," toward "depth and breadth of intellectual capacity, moral courage and integrity," etc.? Some conception of the normatively human is involved in the development of propositions three and four. The issue that confronts us is what constitutes normative humanity.

III. Epistemological Problems in Answering the Question

The obstacles to the developing consensus on what constitutes the normatively human appear to be insuperable. And certainly the expectation that all men in all cultures could ever agree upon a list is a utopian one. There certainly is no universally acceptable normative concept of what individual rights are inviolable, and what particular values or qualities are sought in personal and social well-being. Different cultures have different conceptions of human rights and values, and thus the fact of cultural relativism prohibits the achievement of a perfect consensus. Also, at different stages of this development men and cultures have different norms, which are related to the particular difficulties that they are currently experiencing. Physical survival, for example, takes priority over the liberty to be self-determining in certain crises, such as our present ecological one.

In spite of these difficulties, men have in the past aspired to provide some basis for common understanding. To do so has required that the epistemological problem be addressed in one way or another. How are these rights and values to be known? How does one come to know what is normatively human? What warrants can be given for any particular conception of it? Certainly any effort to move toward even a modest consensus must face the epistemological issue.

Some of the ways of knowing that have been claimed in the history of Western thought about man are worthy of noting, if only to suggest the markers on the trail and some of the obstacles to be avoided. One of them has been reflection on human experience, and generalization based upon that reflection. This seems to be basically what Aristotle was engaged in in the writing of his *Nicomachean Ethics*. He discerned that many things men valued and desired were means to other ends. One can imagine his observing and wondering about all sorts of human behavior, and thinking about what ends various values seem to serve. Finally, as I noted above, he appears to have asked what end is sought for its own sake, and not for the sake of any other end, and thus he arrived at the concept of eudaemonia. The utilitarians appear to have arrived at the concept of pleasure in a roughly similar way. Hermann Muller seems to have taken the same path; it appears that he observed not only what he valued, but also what was valued by the particular society of which he was a part, and on the basis of that came up with a list of the preferred qualities of life.

Religious thinkers have claimed revelation as a warrant for their understanding of the normatively human. The notion of revelation refers not only to some idea that God in infinite wisdom and power inscribed ideas on stones or in books. If the so-called second table of the ten commandments is taken as an example, it is clear that the ancient Hebrew people gave authorization to certain human rights, obligations, and attitudes on the basis of God's having revealed them to Moses. Murder and bearing false witness are violations of certain God-given rights; the attitude of covetousness is prohibited. In other strands of the development of Jewish religion, justice and mercy are noted as the requirements of God upon man. In Christian theology there developed the notion that the nature of "true manhood" was revealed by God in Jesus Christ. Thus, one looks to the accounts of Jesus' life and teachings for a depiction of what men are meant to be, or at least for certain "prominent lines" of what God wills that human life, both individually and socially, ought to be.

In these religious affirmations of what constitutes normative humanity, other warrants for the particular values and obligations, or for the model of true man, might well be given than a revelation from God. What one has, however, in the religious community, is the affirmation that certain patterns of human life are in accord with what God created man to be, or in accord with the purposes of God for mankind. Walter Rauschenbusch, the social reformer and theologian of the early decades of this century, put it more simply than many other theologians would, but he made a widely affirmed point when he wrote that "the will of God is identical with the good of mankind."[7] In answering what constitutes the "good of mankind" one looks both to the religious tradition and to reflection on human experience.

Christian thinkers did not always seek to define normative humanity exclusively in biblical language; they joined with other philosophers in seeking the telos, the end of man, through the epistemology and the metaphysics that characterized the classic natural law position. The assumption here has been that there is a moral order to the universe, which includes an inherent tendency in individual men and in their togetherness to be inclined toward that which is good. This moral order could be apprehended by rational persons; human reason has the capacity to define the first principles of the natural moral law. And human reason has the capacity to apply these principles through secondary principles to the particular historical occasions of life. Thus, certain moral principles and human values could be stipulated as being grounded in what man is essentially, and therefore what he ought to be normatively. Reasonable men ought to be able to agree, on these assumptions, on what the fundamental goal or end of human existence is, and they ought to be able to deduce from this, or infer from this, what values constitute normative humanity. In turn, they ought to be able to define the fundamental rights of man that cannot be violated, or the fundamental ends of man toward which he and his societies ought to be developing. Though this method of ascertaining the normatively human has been under severe challenge from many quarters for a long time, it remains for some Catholic and secular thinkers the epistemological approach that promises the most fruitful efforts at formulating a public consensus about the values of human life.[8] The fact that it is used to support the official papal position against "artificial" methods of birth control in itself suggests that all rational men do not agree, however, on what either the first or the derivative principles of natural law ought to be.

There are other procedures that have been attempted to give warrant to certain values as being normatively human. The work of certain cultural anthropologists has suggested that there seem to be certain "moral requisites" not only for the survival of persons and societies, but also for their well-being. Prof. David Little has suggested in a recent article that there might well be some basis in the writings of anthropologists Kluckhohn, Linton, Mead, and others for inductively formulating a natural law from cross-cultural studies.[9] The epistemological point is that one would not claim the capacity of reason to apprehend the fundamental moral order of the universe, the inherent telos in all things, but rather, that one could inductively proceed from information about human life in a variety of settings to formulate certain generalizations about what is required for meaningful human life to exist.

This in turn might provide at least certain "conditional absolutes" that would give guidance to the development of man.

Also, there are persons who would appear to rely primarily on the sensitive conscience intuitively to perceive what the truly, or normatively human life is. Among theologians, Paul Lehmann seems to be assuming what the philosopher Maurice Mandelbaum calls a "perceptual intuitionism" as the way in which one discerns under particular circumstances what the normatively human is. Lehmann writes, for example, about the sensitivity of the conscience to perceive what God is doing to make and keep human life human.[10] The most obvious problem with this view is how to settle disputes between persons who perceive the human thing to do to be very different under the same circumstances.

Certainly this enumeration of various epistemological stances that have been used to gain insight into the normatively human suggests that any proposal for clarification of the problem under the pressure of developments in genetics is in serious difficulties. The presence of cultural relativism would appear to provide overwhelming odds against any successful fruition of the enterprise. The high level of generalization that is involved in the formation of normatively human values, no matter what epistemological approach is used, seems to make the application of these values to particular instances of intervention into biological processes a very difficult task. Also, it soon becomes clear that the things that men have determined to be needed for meaningful and fulfilling human life, or all the rights that they have judged to be sacred, do not fall into a neat pattern which removes the abrasiveness and tensions between them.

I would argue, however, that it is imperative at the present time to seek to move toward some rational formulation of certain rights, principles and values to provide at least certain points of reference, or principles of consideration and reconsideration, even though such a formulation would not immediately and absolutely determine what interventions are morally warranted, or what uses of research are held to be morally good.

IV. A Procedural Proposal

How might such a formulation be used with reference to the possibilities of genetic engineering or manipulation? From any formulation of what the complexities of the normatively human are, even from one that states that to be human is ultimately a mystery that defies complete rationalization, two different styles of practical ethics are possible. The first would impose a rigid and static conception of man, what his relations to others ought to be, on to any possibilities for genetic development. This approach would tend to be restrictive in an a priori way about what procedures would be permissible and what ends ought to be sought.

If held to consistently, this mode of practical ethics would restrict many of the interventions into nature which we now accept, not merely as having occurred, but as having resulted in new benefits for mankind. It is characteristic of this mode of practical ethical thinking to have its first disposition to be restrictive; transplantations of organs are questioned because they violate the principle of totality, of the function of an organ in its own total organic complex. Other efforts on the part of science and technology also are brought under restrictive questioning immediately upon proposal. Development, potential progress, experimentation are all stifled in important ways. The meaning of becoming human is not something discovered as man develops in the course of his evolution and changes, but it is something known authoritatively, and thus is imposed upon his actions from without. Institutions with the claimed capacity to know what the human is set themselves as the judges and guides of all processes of human development. Morality is defined by an authoritative voice, and this voice seeks to impose morality on others. Such is one way to deal with ethics and genetic experimentation. One would define the licit and illicit kinds of experiments in the light of an a priori definition of what man is, and everything done both in learning and in doing from what has been learned would have to conform to these determinations.

In contrast to this, let us offer another possibility. It is that man has always been developing new ways to determine his own life and that of the human race. He discovers new procedures for effective education; he finds new modes of relaxation. He has never assumed that he was fated by the natural forces which made him anxious or uncomfortable, but has constantly discovered new ways to fulfill his aspirations and his ends. He has discovered new things about what it is to be human; he has found institutions long accepted by man to be inconsistent with human fulfillment, such as slavery and capital punishment. He has discovered the subtle ways in which he is deprived of certain qualities of life by virtue of social structures and customs; this is the meaning in part of the new black consciousness. He finds thousands of ways to intervene in the natural processes in order to make a better life for the human race. He has improved the qualities of seeds; he has learned to irrigate the barren lands; he has concocted fertilizers and herbicides and pesticides which increase the food production. To be sure, his interventions in natural processes are not unambiguously for the good; he now becomes aware of ways in which the natural balance is adversely affected by his activities, and he discovers that to live he must limit his pollutions of air and streams. But he has assumed and seized the right to intervene in nature, including his own nature.

The priority is on the capacities for intervention, on what Karl Rahner calls "self-creativity." This is the kind of being that man is. He will continue to attempt to do whatever he is able to do, and his ability to do new things will expand with his knowledge of the fundamental processes of life. But he discovers that many things he is capable of doing are not for the well-being of the human community. He discovers this not by imposing upon himself, or having imposed upon himself, some fixed image of what man ought to be in the particularities of his existence as an individual with others. To live in this way would be to live in accordance with ethics which stultify human development. Rather, he discovers the direction in which development ought to go as it is consistent with, or abrasive upon, the moral requisites for human life and community. These requisites, many of which can be delineated and objectified by the human mind, can become the guidemarks and the lights of intention which give direction to the course of future human development.

My basic point, then, is that the procedure for thinking ethically about human experimentation ought not to begin with a fixed image of what was, is, and always ought to be, from which are derived authoritative and unalterable rules which govern experimentation. Rather, the weight is on human initiative, human freedom (if you choose) to explore, develop, expand, alter, initiate, intervene in the course of life in the world, including his own life. But this does not mean there are not guidelines and lights of intention which can give direction to the uses of new knowledge. It does not mean that there is nothing to give warnings against certain possibilities, and to give positive support to others, or to set certain limits beyond which man cannot go.

I would close with a very apt sentence written by a sensitive

French Jesuit that states both the beginning and the end of the moral seriousness of the human situation in which the possibilities of genetic engineering and other technical capacities place the human race. "We have become aware that, in the great game that is being played, we are the players as well as being the cards and the stakes."[11]

Notes

Introduction

1. These distinctions are taken from James M. Gustafson, "Context Versus Principles: A Misplaced Debate in Christian Ethics," *The Harvard Theological Review*, LVIII, No. 2 (Apr. 1965), 171-202. Reprinted in *Christian Ethics and the Community* (Philadelphia: Pilgrim Press, 1971), pp. 101-26.

2. James M. Gustafson, *Treasure in Earthen Vessels: The Church as a Human Community* (New York: Harper & Bros., 1961), pp. ix-x.

3. James M. Gustafson, *Christ and the Moral Life* (New York: Harper & Row, 1968).

4. The following note is perhaps in order about the logical status of the descriptions of human existence with which Gustafson tends to begin moral-theological reflection. It could be argued that Gustafson's descriptions of moral phenomena and his delineations of moral agency are at least indirectly informed by his theological convictions and therefore are not really autonomous from such convictions. This argument is true to the extent that Gustafson has a general perspective or point of view which inclines him to view human experience in categories that are not antithetical to his theological convictions (which, in turn, are also informed by experience). A description of moral agency which left absolutely no room for the exercise of human initiative, for example, would not likely gain Gustafson's full-fledged assent because, at least in part, such a portrait is in conflict with his theological views. Still, the descriptions of human existence that Gustafson gives retain a high degree of autonomy from theological convictions and beliefs. Certainly they are not derived from scripture or revelation; neither, it should be added, are they derived from natural or social scientific perspectives.

5. James M. Gustafson, "A Protestant Ethical Approach," *The Morality of Abortion: Legal and Historical Perspectives*, ed. John T. Noonan, Jr. (Cambridge, Mass.: Harvard University Press, 1970), pp. 101-2. © Copyright 1970 by the President and Fellows of Harvard College. Used by permission.

6. The distinctions in this sentence, of course, are taken from Henry D. Aiken, "Levels of Moral Discourse," *Reason and Conduct* (New York: Alfred A. Knopf, 1962), pp. 65-87.

7. Gustafson, "A Protestant Ethical Approach," pp. 115-16.

8. The heavy stress placed on the role of analysis in theological ethics is far-reaching in its implications for a normative conception of the tasks and functions of the discipline. Gustafson has addressed himself to defining the field of theological ethics on several occasions and in differing contexts, but this introduction is not the appropriate place to attempt a comprehensive or systematic treatment

of this dominant aspect of his thought. It is perhaps worth reiterating, however, that Gustafson does not define the general field of ethics simply in terms of moral analysis and inquiry.

9. The chapter on moral discernment in this book really ought to be read as a companion piece to James M. Gustafson, "Two Approaches to Theological Ethics," *Union Seminary Quarterly Review*, XXIII, No. 4 (Summer 1968), 337-48. Reprinted in *Christian Ethics and the Community* (Philadelphia: Pilgrim Press, 1971), pp. 127-38.

Chapter 3. Education for Moral Responsibility

1. *Meno*, 70A, Jowett translation.

2. F. A. Olafson, *Principles and Persons* (Baltimore: Johns Hopkins University Press, 1967), p. xiv.

3. For an earlier development of the general thrust of this paragraph in relation to Christian ethical literature, see my "Context Versus Principles: A Misplaced Debate in Christian Ethics," *Christian Ethics and the Community* (Philadelphia: Pilgrim Press, 1971), chap. 3.

4. The literature which informs a more elaborate and precise delineation of a theory of action is vast. A sampling might consist of the following:
Hannah Arendt, *The Human Condition* (Chicago: University of Chicago Press, 1958); John MacMurray, *The Self as Agent* (New York: Harper & Bros., 1957), *Persons in Relations* (New York: Harper & Bros., 1961); H. R. Niebuhr, *The Responsible Self* (New York: Harper & Row, 1963); G. E. M. Anscombe, *Intention* (2d. ed., Oxford: B. Blackwell, 1963); S. Hampshire, *Thought and Action* (New York: Viking Press, 1960); E. D'Arcy, *Human Acts* (Oxford: Clarendon Press, 1963); R. Taylor, *Action and Purpose* (Englewood Cliffs, N.J.: Prentice-Hall, 1966); R. S. Peters, *The Concept of Motivation* (London: Routledge & Kegan Paul, 1961); A. Kenny, *Action, Emotion and Will* (London: Routledge & Kegan Paul, 1963); Paul Ricoeur, *Freedom and Nature: The Voluntary and the Involuntary* (Evanston, Ill.: Northwestern University Press, 1966); *Toward a General Theory of Action*, ed. Talcott Parsons and Edward Shils (Cambridge, Mass.: Harvard University Press, 1952). Also there are many articles dealing with the issues by H. L. A. Hart, Roderick Chisholm, J. L. Austin, and others.

5. For a study of the claimed significance of religious beliefs about Jesus Christ for moral life see my *Christ and the Moral Life* (New York: Harper & Row, 1968). The last chapter states a constructive position on the issue.

6. Nicolai Hartmann, *Ethics* Vol. II; *Moral Values* (London: Allen & Unwin, 1932), p. 189.

7. Ibid., p. 226.

8. Luke 10:25-37. See Sallie M. TeSelle, *Literature and the Christian Life* (New Haven: Yale University Press, 1966), for a more extensive study of this point.

Chapter 4. The Theologian as Prophet, Preserver, or Participant

1. See H. Richard Niebuhr, *Christ and Culture* (New York: Harper & Bros., 1951), pp. 45-82. He discusses Tertullian and Tolstoy as illustrations of Christ against culture.

2. Cf. Max Weber's distinction between an "ethic of ultimate ends" and an "ethic of responsibility," in "Politics as a Vocation," *From Max Weber: Essays in Sociology* ed. H. H. Gerth and C. Wright Mills (New York: Oxford University Press. 1946), pp. 120 ff.

3. Ibid., p. 121.

4. See Ernst Troeltsch's discussion of the relations of Christological beliefs, views of the Christian Community, and relations of the community to the world in his famous passage on sects and churches, in *The Social Teaching of the Christian Churches*, Vol. I (Glencoe, Ill.: The Free Press, 1949), pp. 331-43.

5. I would like to call attention to an essay by Karl Mannheim that is not widely known in theological circles, but makes some useful general distinctions pertinent to this chapter. It is "Conservative Thought," *Essays in Sociology and Social Psychology*, ed. Paul Kecskemeti (New York: Oxford University Press,

1953), pp. 74-164. In the course of the essay, Mannheim makes distinctions between "traditionalist," "conservative," and "progressive" forms of thought and behavior. "Traditionalist behavior is almost purely reactive. Conservative behaviour is meaningful (p. 98)." My preserver is meant to be more conservative than traditionalist, but I have allowed for more traditionalist and reactive elements at some points. "Traditionalism is a general psychological attitude which expresses itself in different individuals as a tendency to cling to the past and a fear of innovation. . . . This development of the traditionalist attitude into the nucleus of a definite social trend does not take place spontaneously: it takes place as a response to the fact that 'progressivism' had already constituted itself as a definite trend (p. 99)." In contrasting conservatism and progressivism, Mannheim writes, "One of the most essential characteristics of this conservative way of life and thought seems to be the way in which it clings to the immediate, the actual, the *concrete*. . . . To experience and to think 'concretely' now comes to mean to desire to restrict the range of one's activities to the immediate surroundings in which one is placed, and to abjure strictly all that may smack of speculation and hypothesis. . . . It is concerned with immediate action, with changing concrete details, and therefore does not really trouble itself with the *structure* of the world in which it lives. On the other hand, all progressive activity feeds on its *consciousness of the possible*. It transcends the given immediate present, by seizing on the possibilities for systematic change which it offers. It fights the concrete, *not* because it wants to replace it merely by another *form of the concrete* but because it wants to produce another *systematic starting-point* for further development. . . . *Thus progressive reformism tends to tackle the system as a whole, while conservative reformism tackles particular details* (pp. 103-4)." "Where the progressive uses the future to interpret things, the conservative uses the past: the progressive thinks in terms of *norms*, the conservative in terms of *germs* (p. 111)." These statements about the conservative are fairly apt with reference to the ideal-type of the "preserver," and those about the "progressive" are somewhat apt with reference to the "prophet," and point toward the ideal-type of the "participant" as I shall develop it. Quotations used by permission of the publisher.

6. Karl Rahner, "Experiment: Man," *Theology Digest*, Sesquicentennial Issue, 1968, p. 61. Used by permission.

7. Ibid., pp. 65-66.

8. Daniel Day Williams, *The Spirit and Forms of Love* (New York: Harper & Row, 1968), pp. 106-7.

9. Freeman Sleeper, *Black Power and Christian Responsibility* (Nashville: Abingdon Press, 1969), pp. 57, 73. Part II of the book is an interpretation of the structure of biblical theological ethics.

10. I have sought to elaborate on the significance of Christ for moral theology in *Christ and the Moral Life* (New York: Harper & Row, 1968). This paragraph is a condensation of the last chapter of that book.

11. Rahner, op. cit., p. 61.

12. I have developed this theme extensively in *The Church as Moral Decision-Maker* (Philadelphia: Pilgrim Press, 1970), esp. pp. 83-85, 109-37.

Chapter 5. Moral Discernment in the Christian Life

1. *Christ and the Moral Life* (New York: Harper & Row, 1968), final chap.

2. I have developed this theme in several places, most concisely in "The Church: A Community of Moral Discourse," *The Church As Moral Decision-Maker* (Philadelphia: Pilgrim Press, 1970), pp. 83-95 and "The Voluntary Church: A Moral Appraisal," ibid., pp. 109-37.

3. John T. Noonan, Jr., *Contraception* (Cambridge, Mass.: Harvard University Press, 1966).

Chapter 6. The Place of Scripture in Christian Ethics

1. Edward LeRoy Long, "The Use of the Bible in Christian Ethics," *Interpretation*, XIX (1965), 149-62; David H. Kelsey, "Appeals to Scripture in Theology," *Journal of Religion*, XLVIII (1968), 1-21. For a study of Rauschenbusch's use of scripture see James M. Gustafson, "From Scripture to Social Policy and Social Action," *Andover-Newton Quarterly*, IX (1969), 160-69.

290

2. I have developed a proposal on this point in chap. 7.

3. For elaboration of this see *Christ and the Moral Life* (New York: Harper & Row, 1968), chap. 1, and "Theology and Ethics," *Christian Ethics and the Community* (Philadelphia: Pilgrim Press, 1971), pp. 83-100.

4. "Christian Ethics in America," *Christian Ethics and the Community*, pp. 23-82.

5. See the arguments in support of capital punishment developed by J. J. Vellenga in "Christianity and the Death Penalty," *The Death Penalty in America*, ed. Hugo A. Bedau (Garden City: Doubleday Anchor Books, 1964), pp. 123-30. With reference to Matt. 5:21f, Vellenga writes: "It is evident that Jesus was not condemning the established law of capital punishment, but was actually saying that hate deserved capital punishment (p. 126)." "If one accepts the authority of Scripture, then the issue of capital punishment must be decided on what Scripture actually teaches and not on the popular, naturalistic ideas of sociology and penology that prevail today (p. 129)."

6. The three appeared in *The Christian Century*, LIX (1942), 630-33; 953-55; and LX (1943), 513-15.

7. For a critical analysis of the work that has been called biblical theology see Brevard Childs, *Biblical Theology in Crisis* (Philadelphia: Westminster Press, 1970).

8. James H. Cone, *Black Theology and Black Power* (New York: Seabury Press, 1968), p. 35.

9. See, for example, Shaull's article, "Christian Theology and Social Revolution (I)," *The Perkins School of Theology Journal*, XXI (1967-68), 5-12.

10. I have developed these issues in "Two Approaches to Theological Ethics," *Christian Ethics and the Community*, pp. 127-38.

Chapter 7. The Relation of the Gospels to the Moral Life

1. "As the Father has loved me, so have I loved you; abide in my love. If you keep my commandments, you will abide in my love (John 15:9-10)"; "This is my commandment, that you love one another as I have loved you. Greater love has no man than this, that a man lay down his life for his friends. You are my friends if you do what I command you (15:12-14)."

2. I have examined some of these proposals more fully in *Christ and the Moral Life* (New York: Harper & Row, 1968), chap. 6.

3. Marvin R. Vincent, *A Critical and Exegetical Commentary on Epistles to the Philippians and to Philemon*, International Critical Commentary (New York: Scribners, 1903), pp. 32, 31.

4. Ernst Lohmeyer, *Die Briefe an die Philipper, an die Kolosser und an Philemon*, Meyer Series (Göttingen: Vandenhoeck und Ruprecht, 1954), p. 72.

5. Joachim Gnilka, *Der Philipperbrief* (Freiburg: Horden, 1968), p. 96.

6. Karl Barth, *The Epistle to the Philippians* (London: S.C.M. Press, 1962), pp. 45-46.

7. Vincent, op. cit., p. 57.

8. Lohmeyer, op. cit., p. 90.

9. The issues and the literature pertinent to this point have been explored in a very fruitful way in Stanley M. Hauerwas, "Moral Character as a Problem for Theological Ethics," unpublished Yale Ph.D. dissertation, 1968.

10. Sallie McFague TeSelle, *Literature and the Christian Life* (New Haven: Yale University Press, 1966), p. 114.

11. R. M. Hare, *The Language of Morals* (Oxford: Oxford University Press, 1952), p. 69. See also Paul Taylor, *Normative Discourse* (Englewood Cliffs, N.J.: Prentice-Hall, 1961), pp. 151-58. Antonio S. Cua has written an interesting article, "Morality and Paradigmatic Individuals," *American Philosophical Quarterly*, VI, 324-29, in which he takes a cue from Karl Jaspers and reflects on the significance of individuals in developing a "way of life."

12. Some of the literature that has contributed to my thinking are:

John MacMurray, *The Self as Agent* (New York: Harper & Bros., 1957)
John MacMurray, *Persons in Relations* (New York: Harper & Row, 1961)
H. R. Niebuhr, *The Responsible Self* (New York: Harper & Row, 1963)
G. E. M. Anscombe, *Intention* (2d ed.; Oxford: B. Blackwell, 1963)

S. Hampshire, *Thought and Action* (New York: Viking Press, 1960)

E. D'Arcy, *Human Acts* (Oxford: Clarendon Press, 1963)

R. Taylor, *Action and Purpose* (Englewood Cliffs, N.J.: Prentice-Hall, 1966)

R. S. Peters, *The Concept of Motivation* (London: Routledge & Kegan Paul, 1958)

A. I. Melden, *Human Acts* (London: Routledge & Kegan Paul, 1961)

A. Kenny, *Action, Emotion and Will* (London: Routledge & Kegan Paul, 1963)

P. Ricoeur, *Freedom and Nature: The Voluntary and the Involuntary* (Evanston: Northwestern University Press, 1966)

13. R. M. Hare, op. cit. The term paradigmatic individual was used by Karl Jaspers in *The Great Philosophers: The Foundations* (New York: Harcourt, Brace, 1962) with reference to Socrates, Buddha, Confucius, and Jesus. My development has affinities with, and is no doubt dependent upon, two suggestive discussions by H. Richard Niebuhr: "Toward a Definition of Christ," *Christ and Culture* (New York: Harper & Bros., 1951), pp. 11-29; and "Metaphor and Morals" and "Responsibility and Christ," *The Responsible Self* (New York: Harper & Row, 1963), pp. 149-78. It is also dependent upon Sallie TeSelle, op. cit., pp. 153ff.

14. Cf. the use of the notion as a tool for interpreting developments in scientific thought in Thomas S. Kuhn, *The Structure of Scientific Revolutions* (Chicago: University of Chicago Press, 1962), esp. p. 10. "By choosing [the term paradigms], I mean to suggest that some accepted examples of actual scientific practice—examples which include law, theory, application, and instrumentation together—provide models from which spring particular coherent traditions of scientific research."

15. It might be suggested that Jesus functioned already as a paradigm in the writing of the Gospels. His actions and teachings inform the individual accounts of the writers as his significance flows into and through their several intentions in writing the Gospels. Each writer's compilation and redaction takes place with reference to his context and purposes; the paradigm informs the individuality of the Gospels without creating uniformity among them.

16. Cf. pp. 15-16: "By virtues of Christ we mean the excellences of character which on the one hand he exemplifies in his own life, and which on the other he communicates to his followers. For some Christians they are virtues his example and law demand; for others they are gifts he bestows through regeneration, the dying and rising of the self in him, the first-born of many brothers. But whether Christians emphasize law or grace, whether they look to the Jesus of history or to the pre-existent and risen Lord, the virtues of Jesus Christ are the same." Niebuhr goes on to develop love, hope, obedience, faith, and humility.

Chapter 8. Spiritual Life and Moral Life

1. Max Kadushin, *Worship and Ethics: A Study in Rabbinic Judaism* (Evanston: Northwestern University Press, 1964).

2. Kenneth E. Kirk, *The Vision of God: The Christian Doctrine of the Summum Bonum* (London: Longmans, Green, 1931), pp. ix-x.

3. In a critique of "ultimate concern" and comparable theories of religion, Julian N. Hartt has written that "We ought to say that [man] is not really religious unless he feels that some power is bearing down on him, unless, that is, he believes that he must do something about divine powers who have done something to him." *A Christian Critique of American Culture* (New York: Harper & Row, 1967), p. 52.

4. Given an opportunity for further development, I would extend the discussion to further refinements of the affective, volitional, and intellective consequences. Indeed, the relation of believing in and experiencing God to human actions is central to the enterprise, and requires sophisticated analysis. Julian N. Hartt's Cardinal Bea Lecture provides a suggestive way of proceeding by arguing that belief in God is a "construing belief": "A construing belief is rather more a *believing* than it is a finished product commonly suggested by *belief.* Thus a construing belief is an interpretation of some aspect of experience. But may also be a program, a mandate, as it were, for interpreting all of experience and the world. Such I take *believing in God* to be." "*It means an intention to relate to all things in ways appropriate to their belonging to God.*" "Encounter and Inference in Our

Awareness of God," *The God Experience*, ed. Joseph P. Whelan, S.J. (New York: Paulist/Newman Press, 1971), pp. 30-59 (quotations from pp. 49, 52).
   5. This sentence compacts a whole argument similar to that made by John E. Smith, *Experience and God* (New York: Oxford University Press, 1968), in his discussion of the functions of the traditional proofs for the existence of God, pp. 121-57. "The Absolutely Exalted is grasped by the reflecting self able to understand its own experience; only through understanding and interpreting can the self discover in these signs [awareness of the contingent, awareness of death, awareness of freedom and responsibility] the presence of a reality whose nature it is to be present and directly experienced, but not immediately known (p. 157)."

Chapter 9. The Relevance of Historical Understanding
   1. H. Richard Niebuhr, "Ernst Troeltsch's Philosophy of Religion," (Ph.D. diss., Yale University, 1924); Walter Mueller, "Individual Totalities in Ernst Troeltsch's Philosophy of History," (Ph.D. diss., Boston University, 1933).
   2. The most readily available materials by Troeltsch in English are *The Social Teaching of the Christian Churches*, 2 vols., tr. Olive Wyon (New York: Meridian Books, 1957); and *Protestantism and Progress*, tr. W. Montgomery (Boston: Beacon Press, 1958). *Gesammelte Schriften* was published in four volumes (Tübingen: Verlag von J. C. B. Mohr, 1912-25).
   3. Joseph Fletcher, ed., *Christianity and Property* (Philadelphia: Westminster Press, 1947); Roland Bainton, *Christian Attitudes Toward War and Peace* (New York: Abingdon Press, 1960); id., *The Travail of Religious Liberty* (Philadelphia: Westminster Press, 1951); id., *What Christianity Says About Sex, Love and Marriage* (New York: Association Press, 1957); E. Schillebeeckx, O.P., *Marriage: Secular Reality and Saving Mystery*, 2 vols. (London: Sheed and Ward, 1965); Benjamin Nelson, *The Idea of Usury* (2d ed.; Chicago: University of Chicago Press, 1969); John Noonan, Jr., *The Scholastic Analysis of Usury* (Cambridge: Harvard University Press, 1965); id., *Contraception* (Cambridge: Harvard University Press, 1965); id., ed., *The Morality of Abortion* (Cambridge: Harvard University Press, 1970).
   4. Anders Nygren, *Agape and Eros* (London: S.P.C.K., 1953); R. Newton Flew, *The Idea of Perfection in Christian Theology* (London: Oxford University Press, 1934); K. E. Kirk, *The Vision of God* (London: Longmans, Green, 1931); N. P. Williams, *The Idea of the Fall and Original Sin* (London: Longmans, Green, 1927).
   5. Max Stackhouse properly criticizes my *Christ and the Moral Life* on these grounds in his review in *Interpretation*, XXIII, (July 1969), 333-37.
   6. David M. Feldman, *Birth Control and Jewish Law* (New York: New York University Press, 1968); John T. Noonan, Jr., *Contraception* (Cambridge: Harvard University Press, 1965).
   7. I have chosen briefly to compare Feldman's work with Noonan's because they are recent studies and because Feldman explicitly refers to Noonan. My point could also be made, however, with reference to the issue of war. One could, for example, get the impression that the historical context in which Thomas Aquinas' ideas of just war were developed is of no significance for understanding them precisely. Yet a study of the political struggles, the involvement of Thomas Aquinas' family in them, the specific crusades, the military technology, and other aspects of thirteenth-century history illuminates our understanding of his theory. One sees more clearly how it was applicable in its day and why certain aspects are accented and others (noncombatant immunity, for example) are undeveloped. Further developments in the just-war tradition must be seen against the backgrounds of their times and places. See the excellent dissertation written in the mode of Troeltsch and, more particularly, Noonan, by LeRoy B. Walters, "Five Classic Just-War Theories," Yale University, 1971.
   8. For more extensive discussion of the use of scripture in this way, see chapter 6.
   9. Jürgen Moltmann, *Hope and Planning*, tr. Margaret Clarkson (New York: Harper & Row, 1971), pp. 101-29, passim, esp. pp. 103-4.
   10. Ibid., pp. 107-8.
   11. Ibid., p. 122.

293

12. Ibid., pp. 124-25, 178-99.
13. H. Richard Niebuhr, *Radical Monotheism and Western Culture* (New York: Harper & Row, 1960), esp. pp. 24-89; id., *The Responsible Self* (New York: Harper & Row, 1963), esp. pp. 47-68.
14. This is the basic stance of John Giles Milhaven's essays collected in *Toward a New Catholic Morality* (Garden City, N.Y.: Doubleday, 1970). See, for example, his contrasts between "classical" and "modern" mentalities, pp. 72-82.
15. Bernard Häring, "Dynamism and Continuity in a Personalistic Approach to Natural Law," *Norm and Context in Christian Ethics*, ed. G. H. Outka and Paul Ramsey (New York: Scribner's, 1968), p. 202. Karl Rahner works out a similar intention in a variety of essays, perhaps the most important of which is "On the Question of a Formal Existential Ethics," *Theological Investigations*, 5 vols., tr. Karl-H. Kruger (Baltimore: Helicon Press, 1963), 3:217-34. See the persistent criticism of the "psysicalist" bias in Charles Curran, ed., *Absolutes in Moral Theology?* (Washington: Corpus Books, 1968).
16. Paul Ramsey, *War and the Christian Conscience* (Durham, N.C.: Duke University Press, 1961), chap. 1.
17. Walter G. Muelder, *Moral Law in Christian Social Ethics* (Richmond, Va.: John Knox Press, 1966), pp. 90-94.
18. See Troeltsch's essay, "The Ideas of Natural Law and Humanity in World Politics," app. I, in Otto Gierke, *Natural Law and the Theory of Society* (Boston: Beacon Press, 1957), pp. 201-22.

Chapter 10. Man—In Light of Social Science and Christian Faith
1. Paperback editions are available of Erik Erikson, *Young Man Luther* (New York: W. W. Norton, 1962); and Ernest Jones, *Hamlet and Oedipus* (Garden City, N.Y.: Doubleday Anchor Books, 1954).
2. G. H. Mead, *Mind, Self, and Society* (Chicago: University of Chicago Press, 1934). See also Mead's synoptic essay, "The Genesis of the Self and Social Control," *The Philosophy of the Present* (La Salle, Ill.: Open Court Publishing Co., 1932).
3. Ralph Linton, *Cultural Background of Personality* (New York: Appleton-Century, 1945), p. 139.
4. Gerhard Lenski, *The Religious Factor* (Garden City, N.Y.: Doubleday & Co., 1961), p. 93.
5. Bronislaw Malinowski, *A Scientific Theory of Culture* (Chapel Hill, N.C.: University of North Carolina Press, 1944), especially chap. 10; see also Malinowski, *Magic, Science and Religion* (Garden City, N.Y.: Doubleday Anchor Books, 1954).
6. See Emile Durkheim, *The Elementary Forms of Religious Life* (Glencoe, Ill.: The Free Press, 1947).
7. Guy Swanson, *The Birth of the Gods* (Ann Arbor, Mich.: University of Michigan Press, 1960).
8. Robert Dahl and Charles Lindblom, *Politics, Economics, and Welfare* (New York: Harper & Row, 1953), p. 28.
9. Robert Merton, *Social Theory and Social Structure* (Glencoe, Ill.: The Free Press, 1949), pp. 221-22.
10. Max Millikan, "Inquiry and Policy," *The Human Meaning of the Social Sciences*, ed. Daniel Lerner (New York: Meridian Books, 1959), p. 167.

Chapter 11. The Relationship of Empirical Science to Moral Thought
1. Karl Mannheim, "Conservative Thought," *Essays in Sociology and Social Psychology* (London: Routledge & Kegan Paul, 1953), pp. 74-164.
2. Paul Ramsey, *Fabricated Man* (New Haven: Yale University Press, 1970); Karl Rahner, "Experiment Mensch" *Schriften zur Theologie*, VIII (Einsiedeln: Benziger Verlag, 1967), pp. 260-85; "Zum Problem der Genetischen Manipulation," Ibid., pp. 286-321. The first Rahner article is digested in "Experiment: Man," *Theology Digest*, Sesquicentennial Issue (1968), pp. 57-69.
3. See Gibson Winter, *Elements for a Social Ethic* (New York: Macmillan, 1966), pp. 3-82; Max Stackhouse, "Technical Data and Ethical Norms," *Journal*

for the Scientific Study of Religion, 5, pp. 191-203; and Wilhelm Koyff, "Empirical Social Study and Ethics," *Concilium*, 5 (No. 4), pp. 5-13.

4. John Giles Milhaven, *Toward a New Catholic Morality* (Garden City, N.Y.: Doubleday & Co., 1970), p. 118. In general I am writing a critical but sympathetic response to Milhaven's chapter "The Behavioral Sciences," and to essays of Robert Springer, S.J.

5. Lewis Mumford, *The City in History* (New York: Harcourt, Brace and World, 1961). See also Max Weber's classic study, *The City* (Glencoe, Ill.: The Free Press, 1958).

6. C. Wright Mills, *The Power Elite* (New York: Oxford University Press, 1956); Floyd Hunter, *Community Power Structure* (Chapel Hill, N.C.: University of North Carolina Press, 1953); Robert A. Dahl, *Who Governs* (New Haven: Yale University Press, 1961).

7. Max Weber, *The Methodology of the Social Sciences* (Glencoe, Ill.: The Free Press, 1949). The essays in this volume were first published between 1903 and 1917 during the "method controversies" going on in German scholarship and the natural and "human" sciences. They, together with other literature of that struggle, are still worth serious study today.

8. Max F. Millikan, "Inquiry and Policy: The Relation of Knowledge to Action," *The Human Meaning of the Social Sciences*, ed. Daniel Lerner (New York: Meridian Books, 1959), p. 167.

9. The choice of both the previous example from economics and this one from medicine is intended to respond to John Giles Milhaven's statements in his "Exit for Ethicists," *Commonweal*, 91 (Oct. 31, 1969), p. 139. "Thus the ethical question can be purely a question of economics and an economics course appropriately replace the encyclicals." "Good medicine was good morality, and vice versa."

Chapter 12. What Is the Normatively Human?

1. Paul Lehmann, *Ethics in a Christian Context* (New York: Harper & Row. 1963), *passim, et passim*; William Van der Marck, *Toward a Christian Ethic* (Westminster, Md.: Newman Press, 1967), p. 14; "Apart from [Christ] there is no humanity, and all humanity there can possibly be exists in him. In other words, there is nothing human that does not show forth the face of God, and it is the face of God himself that becomes visible to us in all that is human." Virtue, for Van der Marck, is "authentic humanity" and vice is "lack of humanity."

2. Robert Johann, *On Building the Human* (New York: Herder and Herder, 1968).

3. See José M. R. Delgado, *Physical Control of the Mind: Toward a Psychocivilized Society* (New York: Harper & Row, Colophon Books, 1969).

4. J. G. Milhaven, *Toward a New Catholic Morality* (Garden City, N.Y.: Doubleday & Co., 1970), p. 53.

5. Gene Outka and Paul Ramsey, *Norm and Context in Christian Ethics* (New York: Scribners, 1968), pp. 175-97.

6. Ibid., pp. 188-89.

7. "Christian Humanism and the Human Mind," *Christian Ethics and the Community* (Philadelphia: Pilgrim Press, 1971).

8. *American Philosophical Quarterly*, 6, pp. 324-29.

9. Van der Marck, op. cit., pp. 25, 35.

Chapter 13. Basic Ethical Issues in the Biomedical Fields

1. Pierre Teilhard de Chardin, *The Phenomenon of Man* (New York: Harper & Row, 1959), pp. 231, 229.

2. Karl Rahner, "Experiment: Man," *Theology Digest*, Sesquicentennial Issue (Feb. 1968), p. 58. Used by permission.

3. A sampling of literature that has appeared in recent months: "Reflections on the New Biology" (eleven essays), *UCLA Law Review*, XV (Feb. 1968), 267-550.
"Ethical Aspects of Experimentation with Human Subjects" (sixteen essays), *Daedalus* (Spring 1969).

Gordon R. Taylor, *The Biological Time Bomb* (New York: World Publishing Co., 1968).

M. H. Pappworth, *Human Guinea Pigs* (Boston: Beacon Press, 1968).

Leroy Augenstein, *Come, Let Us Play God* (New York: Harper & Row, 1969).

Daniel Labby, ed., *Life or Death: Ethics and Options* (Seattle: University of Washington Press, 1968).

John Roslansky, ed., *Genetics and the Future of Man* (Amsterdam: North-Holland Publishing Co., 1966).

John Roslansky, ed., *The Control of Environment* (Amsterdam: North-Holland Publishing Co., 1967).

John Roslansky, ed., *The Human Mind* (Amsterdam: North-Holland Publishing Co., 1967).

John Roslansky, ed., *The Uniqueness of Man* (Amsterdam: North-Holland Publishing Co., 1969).

Frederick Osborn, *The Future of Human Heredity* (New York: Weybright & Talley, Inc., 1968).

4. Rahner, op. cit., p. 65.

5. Taylor, op. cit., p. 183.

6. Rahner, op. cit., p. 60.

7. James D. Watson, *The Double Helix* (New York: Atheneum Press, 1968).

8. The vast literature was provoked most of all by G. E. Moore's *Principia Ethica* (Cambridge, 1903), and the statement of the "naturalistic fallacy."

9. The issues of moral responsibility are very complex, and could be refined a great deal more than is done here. There are many essays in moral philosophy and theology that deal with these matters. For a critical interpretation in a theological framework, see Albert R. Jonsen, S.J., *Responsibility in Modern Religious Ethics* (Washington, D.C.: Corpus Publications, 1968). Two of many recent philosophical essays that refine the use of the term are H. L. A. Hart, "Responsibility and Retribution," *Punishment and Responsibility* (New York: Oxford University Press, 1968), pp. 210-30, and Kurt Baier, "Responsibility and Freedom," *Ethics and Society,* ed. Richard T. De George (Garden City, N.Y.: Doubleday, 1966), pp. 49-84.

10. Martin P. Golding, "Ethical Issues in Biological Engineering," *UCLA Law Review,* XV, 443-79; see especially his section, "Obligations to the Future," pp. 451-57.

11. The literature on justice is vast. A very influential recent analysis is that made by Chaim Perelman, *The Idea of Justice and the Problem of Argument* (London: 1963).

12. The disputes on these matters exist not only among philosophers, but also among moral theologians. Among philosophers, English intuitionists such as Prichard and W. D. Ross evoked a strong critical response from the subsequent generation of moral philosophers such as R. M. Hare, Nowell-Smith, and many others. In Protestant Christian ethics something like "perceptual intuition" (the phrase is used by Maurice Mandelbaum, *The Phenomenology of Moral Experience* [Glencoe, Ill.: Free Press, 1955], chap. 2) is involved both in H. R. Niebuhr's concept of the "fitting response" and Paul Lehmann's view of discerning "what God is doing to make and keep human life human." See Niebuhr, *The Responsible Self* (New York: Harper & Row, 1963), chap. 1, and Lehmann, *Ethics in a Christian Context* (New York: Harper & Row, 1963), especially chap. 14.

13. See, for example, the statement by John Courtney Murray, S.J., in *We Hold These Truths* (New York: Sheed & Ward, 1960), pp. 109ff, also pp. 295-336.

14. Both David Little and I have made proposals of this sort. See my "Christian Humanism and the Human Mind," in John Roslansky, ed., *The Human Mind,* op. cit., especially pp. 101-5. Little draws on more anthropological data and theory in his "Calvin and the Prospects for a Christian Theory of Natural Law," in Gene H. Outka and Paul Ramsey, eds., *Norm and Context in Christian Ethics* (New York: Scribner's, 1968), pp. 175-97.

15. An older, but still useful discussion of this issue is W. D. Ross, *The Right and the Good* (London, 1930), especially Ch. II, "What Makes Right Acts Right?"

16. Among his many articles, the one in Daniel Labby, ed., *Life or Death* (see n. 3), pp. 114-51, provides an excellent summary of both Beecher's evidences and his ethical position.

17. I have attempted to do this with reference to brain research in my paper, "Christian Humanism and the Human Mind," cited in n. 14.

Chapter 14. Genetic Engineering and the Normative View of the Human

1. I am, of course, building upon the previous chapter which is more comprehensive in scope. In this chapter I have deliberately not opened the question of the locus of moral accountability, whether it is in the researcher or in the technologist who applies the research.

2. Gordon Rattray Taylor, *The Biological Time Bomb* (New York: World Publishing Co., 1968).

3. Karl Rahner, S.J., comes close to this position in his paper, "Experiment: Man," *Theology Digest,* Sesquicentennial Issue (Feb. 1968), pp. 57-69.

4. Aristotle, *Nicomachean Ethics.* Book II.

5. Paul Lehmann, *Ethics in a Christian Context* (New York: Harper & Row, 1963), p. 55.

6. Hermann J. Muller, "Should We Weaken or Strengthen Our Genetic Heritage?" Reprinted by permission of *Daedalus,* Journal of the American Academy of Arts and Sciences, Boston, Mass. Summer 1961, *Evolution and Man's Progress.*

7. Walter Rauschenbusch, *The Social Principles of Jesus* (New York: Association Press, 1916), p. 128.

8. For example, see the statements by John Courtney Murray, S.J., *We Hold These Truths* (New York: Sheed and Ward, 1960), pp. 109ff., 295-336.

9. David Little, "Calvin and the Prospects for a Christian Theory of Natural Law," *Norm and Context in Christian Ethics,* ed. Gene Outka and Paul Ramsey (New York: Scribner's, 1969), pp. 186ff.

10. Lehmann, op. cit., see pp. 116-17, 358-59. Mandelbaum's argument for intuitionism is built from the work of several Oxford philosophers of a previous generation, and is found in his *Phenomenology of Moral Experience* (Glencoe, Ill.: The Free Press, 1955), chap. 2.

11. Pierre Teilhard de Chardin, S.J., *The Phenomenon of Man* (New York: Harper Torchbooks, 1961), p. 229.

Bibliography of the Writings of James M. Gustafson, 1951-73

Books

The Advancement of Theological Education by James M. Gustafson, H. Richard Niebuhr, and Daniel Day Williams. New York: Harper & Bros., 1957. JMG is author of chapters 7 and 8, and the Appendix.

Treasure in Earthen Vessels: The Church as a Human Community. New York: Harper & Row, 1961.

Christ and the Moral Life. New York: Harper & Row, 1968.

On Being Responsible: Issues in Personal Ethics, ed. James M. Gustafson and James T. Laney. New York: Harper & Row, 1968. JMG is author of introductions, pp. 3-18, 111-19, 175-83. English edition, London: SCM Press, 1969.

The Church as Moral Decision-Maker. Philadelphia: Pilgrim Press, 1970.

Christian Ethics and the Community. Philadelphia: Pilgrim Press, 1971.

Articles in Books

"Christian Ethics and Social Policy," *Faith and Ethics: The Theology of H. Richard Niebuhr*, ed. Paul Ramsey. New York: Harper & Bros., 1957, pp. 119-39.

"Justice," *Handbook of Christian Theology.* New York: Meridian Books, 1958, pp. 191-93. Reprinted in *The Chaplain*, XV (Oct. 1958), 43-45.

"Society," *Handbook of Christian Theology*, pp. 351-54.

Introduction to H. Richard Niebuhr, *The Responsible Self.* New York: Harper & Row, 1963, pp. 6-41.

"The United Church of Christ in America: Actualizing a Church Union," *Institutionalism and Church Unity*, ed. Nils Ehrenstrom and Walter Muelder. New York: Association Press, 1963, pp. 325-51.

"Christian Ethics," *Religion*, ed. Paul Ramsey. The Princeton Studies of Humanistic Scholarship in America. Englewood Cliffs, N.J.: Prentice-Hall, 1965, pp. 285-354.

"The Clergy in the United States," *The Professions in America*, ed. Kenneth Lynn. Boston: Houghton-Mifflin, 1965, pp. 170-90 (reprint of *Daedalus* article).

"The Ethics of Promotion," *Stewardship in Contemporary Life,* ed. T. K. Thompson. New York: Association Press, 1965, pp. 147-73.

"Theology and Ethics," *The Scope of Theology*, ed. Daniel T. Jenkins. Cleveland: World Publishing Co., 1965, pp. 111-32.

"Context Versus Principles: A Misplaced Debate in Christian Ethics," *New Theology #3*, ed. Martin E. Marty and Dean Peerman. New York: Macmillan, 1966, pp. 69-102. Reprinted from *Harvard Theological Review* (Apr. 1965).

"A Look at the Secular City," *The Secular City Debate,* ed. Daniel Callahan. New York: Macmillan, 1966, pp. 12-16. Review of Harvey Cox, *The Secular City,* published in *Wind and Chaff* (Oct. 1965).

"Man—In the Light of Social Science and Christian Faith," *Conflicting Images of Man,* ed. William Nicholls. New York: Seabury Press, 1966, pp. 51-70.

"A Theology of Christian Community?" *Man in Community,* ed. Egbert De Vries, New York: Association Press, 1966, pp. 175-93; also "Eine Theologie der Christlichen Gemeinschaft?" *Die Kirche als Faktor einer Kommenden Welt-gemeinschaft.* Berlin: Kreuz Verlag, 1966, pp. 118-32.

"The Voluntary Church: A Moral Appraisal," *Voluntary Associations: A Study of Groups in Free Societies,* ed. D. B. Robertson. Richmond: John Knox Press, 1966, pp. 299-322.

"Christian Faith and Moral Action," *Frontier Theology,* ed. Dean Peerman. Richmond: John Knox Press, 1967, pp. 134-40. Reprinted from *Christian Century,* LXXXII, No. 44 (Nov. 3, 1965), 1345-47.

"Christian Humanism and the Human Mind," *The Human Mind,* ed. J. Roslansky. Amsterdam: North-Holland Publishing Co., 1967, pp. 85-109.

"Dialogue on the Moral Life," *Readings in Biblical Morality,* ed. C. Luke Salm, E.S.C. Englewood Cliffs, N.J.: Prentice-Hall, 1967, pp. 142-48. Reprinted from *Ecumenist,* III, No. 5 (July-Aug. 1965), 75-78.

"Love Monism," *Storm over Ethics.* Philadelphia: United Church Press, 1967, pp. 26-37. Adapted from review article of Joseph Fletcher, *Situation Ethics* and Paul Ramsey, *Deeds and Rules in Christian Ethics,* published in *The Christian Century,* LXXXIII, No. 20 (May 18, 1966).

Translation of Introduction to H. Richard Niebuhr, *The Responsible Self;* also a brief foreword to Japanese edition, tr. Shin Ohara. Tokyo: Shinky Shuppansa Publishing Co., 1967.

"Moral Discernment in the Christian Life," *Norm and Context in Christian Ethics,* ed. Gene Outka and Paul Ramsey. New York: Scribner's 1968, pp. 17-36.

Reprint of part of review of Joseph Fletcher, *Situation Ethics* and Paul Ramsey, *Deeds and Rules in Christian Ethics,* in *The Situation Ethics Debate,* ed. Harvey Cox. Philadelphia: Westminster Press, 1968, pp. 79-82. Reprinted from *The Christian Century,* LXXXIII, No. 20 (May 18, 1966).

Translation: "Christlicher Glaube und Moralisches Handeln," *Theologie im Umbruch.* Munich: Chr. Kaiser Verlag, 1968, pp. 138-44. First published as "Christian Faith and Moral Action," *The Christian Century,* LXXXII, No. 44 (Nov. 3, 1965), 1345-47.

"Two Requisites for the American Church: Moral Discourse and Institutional Power," *The Future of the American Church,* ed. Philip J. Hefner. Philadelphia: Fortress Press, 1968, pp. 30-45.

Commentary on Daniel Callahan, "The Sanctity of Life," *The Religious Situation 1969.* Boston: Beacon Press, 1969, pp. 346-52; also in *Updating Life and Death,* ed. Donald R. Cutler. Boston: Beacon Press, 1969, pp. 230-36.

"Faith, Unbelief and Moral Life," *The Presence and Absence of God* (Bea Lectures), ed. Christopher Mooney, S.J. New York: Fordham University Press, 1969, pp. 19-30.

Foreword to Albert R. Jonsen, S.J., *Responsibility in Modern Religious Ethics.* Washington, D.C.: Corpus Books, 1968, pp. v-x.

"Political Images of the Ministry," *The Church, the University and Social Policy,* ed. Kenneth W. Underwood. Middletown, Conn.: Wesleyan University Press, 1969, II, 249-62.

"A Theology of Christian Community?" *New Testament Themes for Contemporary Man,* ed. Rosalie M. Ryan. Englewood Cliffs, N.J.: Prentice-Hall, 1969, pp. 77-93. Reprinted from *Man in Community,* ed. De Vries, 1966.

"All Relative Things Are Not Equally Relative," *Sexuality on the Island Earth.* New York: Paulist Press, 1970, pp. 28-35. Reprinted from *The Ecumenist,* VII, No. 6 (Sept.-Oct. 1969), 87-89.

"Education for Moral Responsibility," *Moral Education: Five Lectures,* ed. Nancy F. and Theodore R. Sizer. Cambridge, Mass.: Harvard University Press, 1970, pp. 11-27.

"Ethik der Revolution," in James M. Gustafson, Johan Marie de Jong, and Richard Shaull, *Zur Ethik der Revolution.* Stuttgart: Kreug-Verlag, 1970, pp. 9-24.

Foreword to Libertus A. Hoedemaker, *The Theology of H. Richard Niebuhr.* Philadelphia: Pilgrim Press, 1970, pp. vii-xi.

"On the Threshold of a New Age," *The Continuing Quest,* ed. James B. Hofrenning. Minneapolis, Minn.: Augsburg Publishing House, 1970, pp. 13-22.

"A Protestant Ethical Approach," *The Morality of Abortion,* ed. John T. Noonan, Jr. Cambridge, Mass.: Harvard University Press, 1970, pp. 101-22. Revised version of essay "A Christian Approach to the Ethics of Abortion," *Dublin Review,* No. 514 (Winter 1967-68).

"The Study of Religion in Colleges and Universities: A Practical Commentary," *The Study of Religion in Colleges and Universities,* ed. Paul Ramsey and John F. Wilson. Princeton, N.J.: Princeton University Press, 1970, pp. 330-46.

"The Theologian as Prophet, Preserver, or Participant," *Christian Action and Openness to the World,* The Villanova University Symposia, Vols. II-III, ed. Joseph Papin. Villanova, Pa.: Villanova University Press, 1970, pp. 97-117.

"What Is the Contemporary Problematic of Ethics in Christianity?" *Judaism and Ethics,* ed. Daniel J. Silver. New York: KTAV Publishing House, 1970, pp. 49-67. Reprinted from Central Conference of American Rabbis *Journal* (Jan. 1968).

Foreword to Knud Loegstrup, *The Ethical Demand.* Philadelphia: Fortress Press, 1971, pp. ix-xi.

"Patterns of Christian Social Action," *Moral Issues and Christian Response,* ed. Jersild and Johnson. New York: Holt, Rinehart & Winston, 1971, pp. 13-21. Reprinted from *Theology Today,* XVIII (1961).

"The Relation of the Gospels to the Moral Life," *Jesus and Man's Hope,* ed. Donald Miller and D. Y. Hadidian, Pittsburgh, Pa.: Pittsburgh Theological Seminary, 1971, II, 103-17.

"The Relevance of Historical Understanding," *Toward a Discipline of Social Ethics: Essays in Honor of Walter George Muelder,* ed. Paul Deats. Boston: Boston University Press, 1972, pp. 49-70.

"Toward Ecumenical Christian Ethics: Some Brief Suggestions," *Transcendence and Immanence: Festschrift in Honour of Joseph Papin,* ed. Joseph Armenti. St. Meinrad, Ind.: Abbey Press, 1972, pp. 33-37.

"Genetic Counseling and the Uses of Genetic Knowledge—An Ethical Overview," *Ethical Issues in Human Genetics,* ed. Hilton, Callahan, Harris, Condliffe, and Berkley. New York: Plenum Press, 1973, pp. 101-13.

"Genetic Engineering and the Normative View of the Human," *Ethical Issues in Biology and Medicine,* ed. Preston N. Williams. Cambridge, Mass.: Schenkman Press, 1973, pp. 46-58.

"Religion and Morality from the Perspective of Theology," *Religion and Morality,* ed. Gene Outka and John P. Reeder. Anchor Book; Garden City, N.J.: Doubleday, 1973, pp. 125-54.

"A Theology of Christian Community" and "Man in the Light of Social Science and Christian Faith," *Contemporary Religion and Social Responsibility,* ed. Norbert Brockman and Nicholas Piediscalzi. New York: Alba House, 1973, pp. 53-65, 153-63. Reprinted from earlier publications.

Articles in Periodicals

"Our Covenant," *Chicago Theological Seminary Register,* XLI, No. 4 (Nov. 1951), 8-10. Address.

"An Analysis of the Problem of the Role of the Minister," *Journal of Religion,* XXXIV (1954), 187-91.

Co-author with H. Richard Niebuhr and Daniel Day Williams, "Main Issues in Theological Education," *Theology Today,* XI (1955), 187-91.

"New Insight for the Minister from Recent Sociological Studies," *Yale Divinity News* (Jan. 1956), pp. 5-7.

"What Our Seminaries Are and Ought to Be Doing," *Advance,* CIIL, No. 2 (Jan. 25, 1956), 16ff.

"When Is Self-indulgence a Virtue?" *Advance*, CIL, No. 4 (Feb. 27, 1957), 13ff.
"Protestant Sociology of the Family," *Religious Education*, LII, No. 2 (Mar-Apr. 1957), 89-93.
"Decision-Making," *The YWCA Magazine* (Apr. 1957), pp. 15ff. A summary of an address and comments.
"This New Word 'Automation,'" *Crossroads*, VII, No. 4 (July 1957), 12-14.
"The Church and Business Culture," *Christianity and Crisis*, XVII, No. 22 (Dec. 23, 1957), 171-74.
"Facing Our Fear of Social Change," *Crossroads*, VIII, No. 3 (Apr. 1958), 9-11.
"Religion and Prosperity," *Challenge*, Institute of Economic Affairs, New York University, VI, Nos. 11-12 (Aug.-Sept. 1958), 35-39.
"Conformity to What?" *United Church Herald*, II, No. 3 (Jan. 29, 1959), 12ff.
"Education After Sputnik," *Crossroads*, IX, No. 2 (Apr. 1959), 8-11.
"Christian Attitudes Toward a Technological Society," *Theology Today*, XVI (July 1959), 173-87.
"Sociology of Religion in Sweden," *Review of Religious Research*, I (Winter 1960), 101-9.
"Patterns of Christian Social Action," *Theology Today*, XVIII, No. 2 (1961), 159-71.
"Bigger Churches, But Only If Better Churches," *United Church Herald*, IV, No. 4 (Feb. 23, 1961), 8-9ff.
"Religiosity: An Irritating Necessity," *Christianity and Crisis*, XXI, No. 12 (July 10, 1961), 123-27.
"The Living Past," *Proceedings of the Ninth International Congregational Council*. London: Independent Press, 1962, pp. 33-42. Address.
"Bases of Church Union Noted from Congregational Christian History," *Midstream* (Council on Christian Unity, Indianapolis, Ind.), II, No. 1 (Sept. 1962), 18-32.
"Types of Moral Life," *Religious Education*, LVII, No. 6 (Nov.-Dec. 1962), 403-10.
"Authority in Pluralistic Society," *The Lutheran World*, X, No. 1 (1963), 24-33; "Autorität in einer pluralistischen Gesellschaft," *Lutherische Rundschau* (13 Jahrgang, 1963), pp. 35-49.
"The Clergy in the United States," *Daedalus* (Proceedings of the American Academy of Arts and Sciences), VIIIC, No. 4 (1963), 724-44.
"Chief Justice Warren and His Startling Proposal," *United Church Herald*, VI, No. 3 (Feb. 7, 1963), 12-13ff.
"Teologi, Samfund, och Samhälle i U.S.A.," *Vår Lösen*, LIV, No. 6 (June 1963), 253-59.
"The Church: A Community of Moral Discourse," *The Crane Review*, VII, No. 2 (1964), 75-85.
"Goldwater: Yes or No," *The Christian Century*, LXXXI (July 8, 1964), 879.
"Churchman as God's Deputies," *Presbyterian Outlook*, CXLVI, No. 32 (Sept. 14, 1964), 5-6. Excerpts from an address.
"The Clergy in the United States," *Social Compass* (International Review of Socio-Religious Studies), XII, Nos. 1-2 (1965), 35-52. Reprint from *Daedalus*.
"Comments" to a paper by Thomas O'Dea on "Sociology of Religion" in "A Report on an Invitational Conference on the Study of Religion in the State Universities." New Haven: The Society for Religion in Higher Education, 1965, pp. 15-20ff.
"Christian Conviction and Christian Action," *Presbyterian Action*, XV, Nos. 1-2 (Jan.-Feb. 1965); also excerpted as "Churchmen as God's Deputies," *Presbyterian Outlook*, CXLVI, No. 32 (Sept. 14, 1964), 5-6.
"The Eclipse of Sin," *Motive*, XXV, No. 6 (Mar. 1965), 4-8.
"Context Versus Principles: A Misplaced Debate in Christian Ethics," *Harvard Theological Review*, LVIII, No. 3 (Apr. 1965), 171-202.
"Wondering About Death," *Yale Divinity News*, LXII, No. 4 (May 1965), 10-12.
"Dialogue on the Moral Life," *The Ecumenist*, III, No. 5 (July-Aug. 1965), 75-78. Reprinted in *The Catholic Mind*, LXIII, No. 1197 (Nov. 1965), 37-41; also in

The Ecumenical Digest, I, No. 2 (Apr. 1966), 14-19.

"The Study of Religion at Yale" (with Robert C. Johnson), *Reflection*, LXIII, No. 1 (Nov. 1965), 1-3.

"Christian Faith and Moral Action," *The Christian Century*, LXXXII, No. 44 (Nov. 3, 1965) 1345-47 (in a series: "How I Am Making up My Mind").

"Situation versus Principles," *Theology Digest*, XIV, No. 3 (1966), 188-94.

"The Shouting of Slogans," *Commonweal*, LXXXIII, No. 19 (Feb. 18, 1966), 582-83. A response to articles on the "new morality."

"Foundations of Ministry," *Minister's Quarterly*, XXII (Spring 1966), 3-9.

"Christian Style of Life: Problematics of a Good Idea," *Una Sancta*, XXIV, No. 1 (1967), 6-14.

"A Community of Reflection," *Focus: A Theological Journal* (Student publication of the S.J. Canadian students, Regis College, Willowdale, Ontario), IV (Summer 1967), 7-15.

"A Christian Approach to the Ethics of Abortion," *Dublin Review*, No. 514 (Winter 1967-68), pp. 346-64.

"Christian Humanism and the Human Mind," *Reflection*, LXII, No. 2 (Jan. 1968), 1-5. Excerpts from article by same title in *The Human Mind*, ed. J. Roslansky (Amsterdam: North-Holland Publishing Co., 1967), pp. 85-109.

"What Is the Contemporary Problematic of Ethics in Christianity?" Central Conference of American Rabbis *Journal*, XV, No. 1 (Jan. 1968), 14-26.

"New Directions in Moral Theology," *Commonweal*, LXXXVII, No. 20 (Feb. 23, 1968), 617-23. Review article, primarily of Van der Marck's *Toward a Christian Ethic*; correction of printing error in Mar. 15, 1968 issue, p. 727.

"Two Foci of Moral Development," *The Acquisition and Development of Values*, Report of a Conference. Bethesda, Md.: National Institute of Child Health and Human Development, May 1968, pp. 24-25. Report of a paper.

"Two Approaches to Theological Ethics," *Union Seminary Quarterly Review*, XXII, No. 4 (Summer 1968), 337-48.

"Toward Maturity in Decision Making," *The Christian Century*, LXXXV, No. 28 (July 10, 1968), 894-98.

"Kenneth W. Underwood, 1918-68," *Journal for the Scientific Study of Religion*, VII (1969), 286.

"The Transcendence of God and the Value of Human Life," *Proceedings* of the 23d Annual Convention of the Catholic Theological Society of America, XXIII (1969), 96-108.

"What Ought I to Do?" *Proceedings* of the American Catholic Philosophical Association, XLIII (1969), 56-70.

"From Scripture to Social Policy and Social Action," *Andover Newton Quarterly*, IX, No. 3 (Jan. 1969), 160-69. A Greene Lecture on Walter Rauschenbusch.

"The Relevance Gap," *Catholic High School Quarterly Bulletin*, XXVI, No. 4 (Jan. 1969), 20-25. An address given at a conference.

"Situation contra Prinzipien," *Zeitschrift für Evangelische Ethik*, XIII, No. 1 (Jan. 1969), 14-40. First published as "Context Versus Principles," *Harvard Theological Review*, LVIII, No. 3 (Apr. 1965), 171-202.

"Law and Morality," *This Is TCU*, XI, No. 3 (Spring 1969), 4-16. Record of JMG's participation in a public discussion.

"Theological Education as Professional Education," *Theological Education*, V, No. 3 (Spring 1969), 243-61.

"Why Read Barth's Ethics?" *Reflection*, LXVI, No. 4 (May 1969), 10-12; also appeared in *Karl Barth and the Future of Theology*. New Haven, Conn.: Yale Divinity School Association, 1969, pp. 15-20.

"A Protestant Response" to "Sexuality on the Island Earth" by David Darst and Joseph Forgue, *The Ecumenist*, VII, No. 6 (Sept.-Oct. 1969), 87-89.

"Responsibility and Utilitarianism," *Commonweal*, XCI, No. 5 (Oct. 31, 1969), 140-41. A response to John Milhaven, "Exit for Ethicists."

"Ethical Theory and Moral Practice," *The Christian Century*, LXXXVI, No. 51 (Dec. 17, 1969), 1613-17.

Special Editor: *The Annals*, CCCLXXXVII (Jan. 1970) "The Sixties: Radical Change in American Religion."

"Fragen zur Ethik der Revolution," *Lutherische Monatshefte*, IX (May 1970), 237-41.

"Basic Ethical Issues in the Bio-Medical Fields," *Soundings*, LIII, No. 2 (Summer 1970), 151-80.

"The Place of Scripture in Christian Ethics: A Methodological Study," *Interpretation*, XXIV (Oct. 1970), 430-55.

"Spring, 1970 and Theological Education," *Reflection*, LXVIII, No. 1 (Nov. 1970), 3-7.

"The Burden of the Ethical: Reflections on Disinterestedness and Involvement," *The Foundation* (Gammon Theological Seminary), LXVI, No. 4 (Winter 1970), 8-15. Presidential address, American Society of Christian Ethics, Atlanta, Ga., Jan. 23, 1970.

"The Conditions of Hope: Reflections on Human Experience," *Continuum*, VII, No. 4 (Winter 1970), 535-45.

"The Relationship of Empirical Science to Moral Thought," *Proceedings of the 26th Annual Convention of the Catholic Theological Society*, XXVI (1971), 122-37.

"Moral Authority of the Church," *The Chicago Theological Seminary Register*, LXI, No. 4 (May 1971), 1-14.

"What Is the Normatively Human?" *The American Ecclesiastical Review*, CLXV, No. 3 (Nov. 1971), 192-207.

"What Does It Mean to Be a Moral Person?" (by Don Saliers), *Face to Face*, IV, No. 4 (Nov. 1971), 19-21: Interview.

"Spiritual Life and Moral Life," *Theology Digest*, XIX, No. 4 (Winter 1971), 296-307.

"Mongolism och rättan att leva," *Vår Lösen*, LXIII, No. 4 (1972), 247-59. Excerpts from Kennedy Foundation paper.

"Ethics and Faith in the Life of the Church," *Perkins Journal*, XXVI, No. 1 (Fall 1972), 6-13.

"Will God Indeed Dwell with Man on Earth?" *The Iliff Review*, XXIX, No. 1 (Winter 1972), 3-9.

"Mongolism, Parental Desires, and the Right to Life," *Perspectives in Biology and Medicine*, XVI, No. 4 (Summer 1973), 529-57.

"On Seeing the Kingdom," *Criterion*, XIII, No. 1 (Autumn 1973), 7-9. Sermon.

"The University as a Community of Moral Discourse," *Journal of Religion*, LIII, No. 4 (Oct. 1973), 397-409.

Reviews

Howard R. Bowen, *Social Responsibilities of the Businessman*, in *Christianity and Society*, XIX, No. 1 (Winter 1953-54), 21-23.

Daniel T. Jenkins, *Congregationalism: A Restatement*, in *Church History*, XXIV, No. 1 (Mar. 1955), 79-80.

George F. Thomas, *Christian Ethics and Moral Philosophy*, in *The Chaplain*, XVIII, No. 2 (Apr. 1956), 43-44.

Dietrich Bonhoeffer, *Ethics*, in *Advance* (Apr. 4, 1956), p. 21.

Marion J. Bradshaw, *Baleful Legacy*, in *The Christian Century* (May 2, 1956), pp. 555-56.

George Forell, *Faith Active in Love*, in *Journal of Religious Thought*, XIII (Spring-Summer 1956), 148-49.

Pitirim A. Sorokin, *Fads and Foibles in Modern Sociology and Related Sciences*, in *The Christian Century* (Oct. 31, 1956), pp. 1264-65.

Albert T. Rasmussen, *Christian Social Ethics*, in *Advance* (Nov. 2, 1956), pp. 23-24.

Margaret Mead, *New Lives for Old*, in *The Christian Century* (Jan. 16, 1957), pp. 79-80.

H. Richard Niebuhr, *Social Sources of Denominationalism*, in *The Meridian*, I, No. 1 (Spring 1957), 3.

Wilfrid Fleisher, *Sweden: The Welfare State*, in *The Christian Century* (Apr. 3, 1957), p. 426.

Zevedei Barbu, *Democracy and Dictatorship*, in *The Christian Century* (Apr. 17, 1957), p. 492.

Joseph Schiffmann, ed., *Edward Bellamy—Selected Writings on Religion and Society*, in *The Christian Century* (Apr. 24, 1957), p. 534.

Wayne Cowan, ed., *What the Christian Hopes for in Society*, in *Union Seminary Quarterly Review*, XIII, No. 1 (Nov. 1957), 57-59.

Georgia Harkness, *Christian Ethics*, in *Advance* (Jan. 17, 1958), p. 23.

Barbara Miller Solomon, *Ancestors and Immigrants*, in *The Christian Century* (Jan. 22, 1958), p. 105.

Wilson Smith, *Professors and Public Ethics*, in *Church History*, XXVII, No. 1 (Mar. 1958), 85-86.

David Riesman, *Constraint and Variety in American Education*, in *The Christian Century*, LXXV, No. 17 (Apr. 23, 1958), 512-13.

John A. Hutchinson, *The Two Cities*, in *Union Seminary Quarterly Review*, XIII, No. 4 (May 1958), 68-69.

Pitirim A. Sorokin, *Social and Cultural Dynamics*, in *The Christian Century* (Oct. 15, 1958), p. 1182.

Joachim Wach, *Sociology of Religion*, in *The Christian Century* (Nov. 5, 1958), pp. 1275-76.

Judith N. Shklar, *After Utopia—The Decline of Political Faith*, in *The Christian Century* (Nov. 12, 1958), pp. 1305-6.

Charles Péguy, *Temporal and Eternal*, in *The Westminster Bookman*, XVII, No. 4 (Dec. 1958), 16-17.

Joseph Sittler, *The Structure of Christian Ethics*, in *The Chicago Theological Seminary Register*, XLIX, No. 1 (Jan. 1959), 10-11.

Daniel Jenkins, *The Protestant Ministry*, in *Religion in Life*, XXVIII (Spring 1959), 317-18.

Hannah Arendt, *The Human Condition*, in *The Christian Century* (Apr. 1, 1959), p. 391.

Reinhold Niebuhr, *Love and Justice*, ed. D. B. Robertson, and *Pious and Secular America*, in *Union Seminary Quarterly Review*, XIV, No. 4 (May 1959), 59-60.

Charles West, *Communism and the Theologians*, in *Interpretation*, XIII (July 1959), 345-48.

Joachim Wach, *The Comparative Study of Religion*, in *Religious Education*, LIV (July-Aug. 1959), 394-95.

Walter Leibrecht, ed., *Religion and Culture*, in *Theology Today*, XVI (Oct. 1959), 400-01.

K. M. Olsson, *Kontakt med Kyrkan*, in *Svensk Kyrkotidning* (Swedish Church Times), LVI (Mar. 17, 1960), 167-69.

John Godsey, *The Theology of Dietrich Bonhoeffer*, in *The Westminster Bookman*, XIX, No. 2 (June 1960), 12-13.

Paul Ramsey, *War and the Christian Conscience*, in *Religion and Life*, XXXI (1961), 133-34.

Guy Swanson, *The Birth of the Gods*, in *Review of Religious Research*, II (1961), 176-77.

"Nutida Amerikansk Teologi" (a review of Paul Tillich, *Theology of Culture*: H. R. Niebuhr, *Radical Monotheism*; and G. Kaufman, *Relativism, Knowledge, and Faith*), in *Tro och Liv* (*Faith and Life*, a theological journal of the Swedish free churches), No. 2 (1961), pp. 66-70.

Clinton Gardner, *Biblical Faith and Social Ethics*, in *Religion and Life*, XXX, No. 2 (Spring 1961), 305-6.

Carl Michaelson, *Japanese Contributions to Christian Theology*, in *Faculty Forum* (Board of Higher Education, The Methodist Church), No. 17 (May 1961).

Donald B. Meyer, *The Protestant Search for Political Realism 1919-1941* in *United Church Herald*, IV, No. 17 (Sept. 21, 1961), 30.

Paul Abrecht, *The Churches and Rapid Social Change* and E. De Vries, *Man in Rapid Social Change*, in *Theology Today*, XIX (1962), No. 2, 302-4.

D. C. McClelland, *The Achieving Society*, in *Religious Education*, LVII (1962), 472.

D. O. Moberg, *The Church as a Social Institution*, ibid., p. 471.

W. L. Warner, *The Living and the Dead* and *The Family of God*, in *Religious Education*, LVII, No. 2 (1962), 151-52.

Kenneth Boulding et al., *What Is the Nature of Man? Images of Man in Our American Culture*, in *United Church Herald*, V, No. 14 (July 19, 1962), 27.

J. W. Smith and A. L. Jamison, eds., *Religion in American Life*, Vols. I, II, and IV, "Religion in America," *The Virginia Quarterly Review*, XXXIX, No. 4 (Autumn 1963), 645-51.

Robert Paul, ed., *An Apologeticall Narration*, in *Bulletin of the Congregational Library*, XV, No. 2 (Jan. 1964), 5-6.

Paul Lehmann, *Ethics in a Christian Context*, in *Union Seminary Quarterly Review*, XIX, No. 3 (Mar. 1964), 261-65.

John R. Fry, *The Immobilized Christian: A Study of His Pre-Ethical Situation*, in *United Church Herald*, VII, No. 6 (Mar. 15, 1964), 32.

Edmund Morgan, *Visible Saints: The History of a Puritan Idea*, in the *Journal of Presbyterian History*, XLII, No. 3 (Sept. 1964), 216-17.

Dietrich Bonhoeffer, *The Communion of Saints*, in *Theology Today*, XXI, No. 4 (Jan. 1965), 527-29.

J. F. Porter and W. J. Wolf, eds., *Toward the Recovery of Unity: The Thought of F. D. Maurice*, in *Religious Education*, LX, No. 2 (Mar.-Apr.1965),158-59.

George D. Kelsey, *Racism and the Christian Understanding of Man*, in *Drew Gateway*, XXXVI (Autumn-Winter 1965-66), 50-52.

Harvey Cox, *The Secular City*, in *Wind and Chaff* (National Student Christian Federation), III, No. 1 (Oct. 1965), 3.

Joseph Fletcher, *Situation Ethics* and Paul Ramsey, *Deeds and Rules in Christian Ethics*, "How Does Love Reign?" *The Christian Century*, LXXXIII, No. 20 (May 18, 1966), 654-55.

O. R. Whitley, *Religious Behavior*, in *Religious Education*, LXI (1966), 466-68.

Thomas O'Dea, *The Sociology of Religion*, in *Religious Education*, LXI (Nov.-Dec. 1966), 468-70.

Franz Böckle, *Law and Conscience*, in *Commonweal*, LXXXV (Dec. 16, 1966), 328-29.

John T. Noonan, Jr., *Contraception*, in *Una Sancta*, XXIII, No. 4, 111-12.

John Hick, *Evil and the God of Love*, in *Union Seminary Quarterly Review*, XXII, No. 2 (Jan. 1967), 182-84.

James Sellers, *Theological Ethics*, in *Religious Education*, LXII (Jan.-Feb. 1967), 77-78.

Gibson Winter, *Elements for a Social Ethic*, in *Journal for the Scientific Study of Religion*, VI, No. 2 (Fall 1967), 283-84.

Ian Ramsey, ed., *Christian Ethics and Contemporary Philosophy*, in *Journal of the American Academy of Religion*, XXXV, No. 3 (Sept. 1967), 285-89.

Walter D. Wagoner, *The Seminary: Protestant and Catholic*, in *Religious Education*, LXII, No. 5 (Sept.-Oct. 1967), 460.

Donald L. Metz, *New Congregations: Security and Mission in Conflict*, in *American Sociological Review*, XXXII, No. 6 (1967), 1015-16.

Paul Ramsey, *Who Speaks for the Church?* in *Ecumenical Review*, XX, No. 1 (Jan. 1968), 98-100.

Peter Berger and Thomas Luckmann, *The Social Construction of Reality* and Thomas Luckmann, *The Invisible Religion*, in *Journal for the Scientific Study of Religion*, VII, No. 1 (Spring 1968), 122-25.

Theodore R. Sizer, ed., *Religion and Public Education*, in *Harvard Educational Review*, XXXVIII, No. 2 (Spring 1968), 391-96.

Charles Curran, ed., *Absolutes in Moral Theology* and Charles Curran, *A New Look at Christian Morality*, in *National Catholic Reporter*, Fall Book Report (Oct. 2, 1968), pp. 5, 13.

D. H. Labby, ed., *Life or Death: Ethics and Options*, in *Commonweal*, LXXXIX, No. 1 (Oct. 4, 1968), 27-30.

Robert Johann, *Building the Human*, in *Thought*, XLIV No. 173 (Summer 1969), 309-12.

David M. Feldman, *Birth Control and Jewish Law*, in *The Christian Century*, LXXXVII, No. 20 (May 20, 1970), 632-33.

Daniel Callahan, *Abortion: Law, Choice, and Morality*, in *National Catholic Reporter*, VI, No. 37 (Aug. 7, 1970), 9-10.

Peter Berger, *A Rumor of Angels*, in the *Journal for the Scientific Study of Religion*, IX, No. 3 (Fall 1970), 255-56.

Arthur M. Brazier, *Black Self-Determinism*, in *Encounter*, XXXII (Spring 1971), 181-82.

Bernard Gert, *The Moral Rules*, in *Commonweal*, XCIV, No. 18 (Aug. 20, 1971), 434-35.

John Giles Milhaven, *Toward a New Catholic Morality*, in *Theological Studies*, XXXII, No. 3 (Sept. 1971), 523-25.

Paul Ramsey, *Fabricated Man: The Ethics of Genetic Control*, ibid., 521-23.

W. Widick Schroeder, *Cognitive Structures and Religious Research*, in *The Chicago Theological Seminary Register*, LXI, No. 5 (Sept. 1971), 39-42.

Max Stackhouse, *The Ethics of Necropolis*, in *Andover Newton Quarterly*, XII, No. 2 (Nov. 1971), 118-20.

Edmund Fuller, *Prudence Crandell*, in *Review of Books and Religion*, I, No. 4 (Dec. 15, 1971), 5.

Charles West, *The Power to Be Human*, in *Theology Today*, XXVIII, No. 4 (Jan. 1972), 504-6.

Roger Mehl, *Catholic Ethics and Protestant Ethics*, in *Religious Education*, LXVII, No. 2 (Mar.-Apr. 1972), 154-55.

Arnold Toynbee, *Surviving the Future*, in *Worldview*, XV, No. 4 (Apr. 1972), 49-50.

William Barclay, *Ethics in a Permissive Society*, in *National Catholic Reporter*, VIII, No. 26 (Apr. 28, 1972).

John Rawls, *A Theory of Justice*, in *Theology Today*, XXX, No. 3 (Oct. 1973), 306-12.

N. H. G. Robinson, *The Groundwork of Christian Ethics*, in *Theological Studies*, XXXIV, No. 4 (Dec. 1973), 745-47.

Index

God (*continued*)
    as enabling and requiring, 42-43, 46, 71, 76, 110-19, 139, 141,
        145; cf., 171
    cf., as engendering, 151, 166
    purposes of, 88, 91, 140, 190, 281
    who acts, activity, 129f., 135ff., 184
Golding, Martin P., 245, 255, 295
Good Samaritan, the, 67

H

Halachah, halachic, 130, 162, 180
Hampshire, Stuart, 288, 291
Hare, R. M., 151, 290-91, 295
Häring, Bernard, 50, 191, 195, 293
Hart, H. L. A., 288, 295
Hartmann, Nicolai, 64, 66, 288
Hartt, Julian N., 245, 291
Hartzell, Karl, 245
Hauerwas, Stanley M., 290
History, 76, 81, 89
    meaning of, 123, 126f., 142
    theory of, 184
    historical understanding, 177-95
Human, the
    normatively, 225, 229-44, 259ff., 273-86
    ontological approaches to, 86, 152, 190, 239, 241
    paradigms of, 154ff., 239f.
Human situation, limits and possibilities of, 39, 139; cf., 167f.,
        269f.
Hunter, Floyd, 220, 294

I

Ideals, moral, 131f.
Intention(s), 62, 65, 123, 127f., 141, 143, 153-59
Isaiah 11:6f., 131
Is-ought problem (fact-value, descriptive-evaluative/normative),
        137, 222, 226, 232, 235-43, 277
    descriptive (only), 217, 230, 235, 241

315

TeSelle, Sallie, 151, 288, 290-91
Theresa of Calcutta, 176
Thomas Aquinas, 153, 191, 292
Torah, 130, 148, 263
Toulmin, Stephen E., 123
Troeltsch, Ernst, 178-95 passim, 288, 292

U

Unconscious, the, 63
Utilitarian, 128f., 278

V

Values, human and/or moral, 44, 92, 113, 142, 239, 261ff., 283
  valuing, 277
Van der Marck, William, 229, 241f., 294
Vellenga, J. J., 290
Vincent, Marvin R., 149f., 290

W

Walters, LeRoy B., 292
Watson, James D., 250, 252, 295
Weber, Max, 77, 221, 288, 294
Wesley, Charles, 174
Williams, Daniel Day, 86-87, 289
Williams, Norman Powell, 179, 292
Winter, Gibson, 293